HAMATSA

HAMATSA

THE ENIGMA
OF CANNIBALISM
on the
PACIFIC NORTHWEST COAST

JIM MCDOWELL

RONSDALE PRESS
1997

HAMATSA
Copyright © 1997 Jim McDowell

RONSDALE PRESS
3350 West 21st Avenue
Vancouver, B.C., Canada
V6S 1G7

Set in New Baskerville, 11 pt on 14
Typesetting: Julie Cochrane
Printing: Hignell Printing, Winnipeg, Manitoba
Cover Design: Ken White
Cover Art: *Hamatsa's multi-headed mask,* carved in 1953 by Mungo Martin.
    (Courtesy: Royal British Columbia Museum, CPN 9201)

The publisher wishes to thank the Canada Council, the Department of Heritage and the British Columbia Cultural Services Branch for their financial assistance.

CANADIAN CATALOGUING IN PUBLICATION DATA
McDowell, Jim, 1934–
    Hamatsa

Includes bibliographical references and index.
ISBN 0-921870-47-7

    1. Hamatsa (Indian rite)   2. Indians of North America — British Columbia — Pacific Coast — Rites and ceremonies.   3. Cannibalism.   I. Title.
E78.B9M32 1997   971.1'00497   C97-910009-7

To my mother,
with affection and appreciation

ACKNOWLEDGEMENTS

I GRATEFULLY ACKNOWLEDGE the advice and generous assistance provided by the publisher, Dr. Ronald Hatch. His sustained commitment, patient support, and helpful suggestions were invaluable. I also thank those who read and critiqued different versions of the manuscript, especially Noel Elizabeth Currie, Rose Esparza and Dr. Christon I. Archer. Finally, I appreciate the assistance of personnel at the following libraries and museums: Bancroft Library, Berkeley; Simon Fraser University Library, Burnaby; University of British Columbia Library, Vancouver; University of Washington Library, Seattle; Vancouver Public Library, Special Collections; American Museum of Natural History, New York City; American Philosophical Society, Philadelphia; Museo Naval, Madrid; Museo de América, Madrid; Peabody Museum of Archaeology and Ethnology, Harvard University; Royal British Columbia Museum, Victoria; Umista Cultural Centre, Alert Bay, British Columbia; University of British Columbia Anthropology Museum, Vancouver; Vancouver Maritime History Museum.

CONTENTS

Illustrations   *viii*
Author's Note   *xi*
Introduction   *xv*

PART ONE: RED SMOKE

CHAPTER 1: From Suspicion to Allegation   31
CHAPTER 2: Meares, Martinez and Maquinna   55
CHAPTER 3: Eliza and Malaspina Fuel the Debate   75
CHAPTER 4: Murder and Unfriendly Feasts   93
CHAPTER 5: Assessing the Record   117
CHAPTER 6: The House that Billowed Red Smoke   129

PART TWO: WHITE FLAMES

CHAPTER 7: Cannibalism: The Prime Taboo   157
CHAPTER 8: Clash of Cosmologies   173
CHAPTER 9: Fallacy of the "Savage"   183
CHAPTER 10: The Myth of Man-Eating   197
CHAPTER 11. The Hamatsa Reality   209
CHAPTER 12: The Natives' World View   225
CHAPTER 13: Conjuring a New Morality   237
CHAPTER 14: Seeking a New Journey of Purpose   251

Afterword   263
Notes   265
Bibliography   273
Index   289
About the Author   299

ILLUSTRATIONS & MAPS

Hamatsa's multi-headed mask	Cover
Map of Northwest Coast Indian tribal boundaries	xxvii
Mowachaht man at Yuquot	35
Mowachaht woman at Nootka	38
Mowachaht man at Nootka Sound	45
Mowachaht bow hunter at Nootka Sound	51
Maquinna and Callicum, Mowachaht chiefs	58
Chief Natsapa	61
Chief Maquinna and his wife	71
Nootka Chief Tlupananul	79
Southern Kwakiutl chief	81
Nootak Chief Tetaku	89
Men's dance on the beach at Yuquot	97
Chief Maquinna entertains Bodega y Quadra and George Vancouver at Tahsis in 1792	102
George Hunt and family with Franz Boas at Fort Rupert in 1894	131
Painting on the front of a *mawil*	136
Southern Kwakiutl guests at a feast hosted by anthropologist Franz Boas in 1894	138
Taming of an *hamatsa* initiate reenacted	145
Earliest known portrayal of New World inhabitants	164
Hamatsa's multi-headed mask from Fort Rupert	177
An incident in Vespucci's voyage of 1501	186
La femme et l'homme sauvage	190

The replete cannibal   194
Hamatsa dancer   203
Hamatsa dancer   213
Hamatsa head ring   214
Typical cannibal pole   216
Winter ceremony at Gilford Island in 1946   218
Koskimo *hamatsa* emerging from the woods   228
Two masked performers in the Kwakiutl winter
      dance represent Cannibal Raven and *Hoxhok*   231
Three *hamatsa* masks   236
Haida transformation (or double) mask   247
Bella Coola *tsonoqua* mask   262
Haida painting of a shark   264

AUTHOR'S NOTE

If man is a wonder, then what is wonderful
must lie in the mass of his contradictions.
ROBERT ARDREY (1976, 9)

THIS BOOK EXAMINES the concept of cannibalism from more than one cultural perspective. Throughout, my research has been tempered by the conviction that it is in the interaction of cultures that we are most likely to find new insights, broaden our views, and gain the inspiration needed to reshape our vision of human potential. To this end I found myself continually challenged to recognize my bias, to question conventional conclusions, and to remain focused on the dynamics of the cultural encounters that I was probing.

In writing about the centuries-old, persistent ideological differences between Euroamerican and Native American cultures, I ran into problems with terminology. Whatever terms I chose conveyed both a point of view and its limitations. The ambiguities and contradictions embedded in the selected words, which flowed from an inescapable ethnocentric view of the world, reminded me that a cross-cultural probe must be tentative, cautious, and respectful.

To maintain that perspective, I found it helpful to recall that the name *America* did not appear on a map until the beginning of the sixteenth century. In 1496, the Basque navigator Juan de la Cosa Vizcaino, who owned Christopher Columbus' flagship *Santa María* and served as his pilot, drew a crude world map on a sheepskin. For the first time, it showed the continent that Columbus mistook for India. Ten years later, the Venetian cartographer Gasparo Contarini used Ptolemy's astronomical projections to draw the first printed world map. He named the new continent *America,* after the Italian explorer Amerigo Vespucci (1451-1512), whom Vizcaino had also served as pilot and mapmaker. The realization that America and Asia were separate continents did not hit home in Europe until 1522, when survivors of Ferdinand Magellan's voyage around the world returned to Portugal.[1]

The word *Indian* memorializes Columbus' error, and it was the first term that caused me to hesitate and reflect. During the period of explosive cultural contact — Eurocentrically dubbed the "golden age of discovery" — most Europeans described themselves by their nationality, ethnic group, or religion. Since we refer collectively to Spanish, French, and English explorers as Europeans, it might seem appropriate to call the aboriginal people they encountered and their descendants either Americans or First Americans.

But the former term conflicts both with the "Americans" who conquered and occupied the entire so-called New World and with those who settled what is now its dominant nation. The latter term may be politically correct, but, like "first people," it is too general. Some native Americans call themselves Indians; others object to it as a white man's label. Both the euphemistic "first Americans" and the often derogatory "Indians" obscure the actual diversity and distinctiveness of remarkable aboriginal cultures. The term "first nations" — now widely employed — provides the necessary singularity and equivalence, if agreement exists as to the definition of nationhood. Here I take nation to mean each of the numerous large congregations of people that claim a similar ethnic background, often share the same language, and occupy a distinct territory which is ruled by one government.

In this book, I have used tribal or national names as much as possible in discussing the lives of specific groups of aborigines. But one needs general terms to juxtapose with "Europeans," "Euroamericans," "whites," "invaders," and "intruders." So I use "Indians," "Amerindians," "natives," "Native Americans," "first nations," and the adjectives "native," "aboriginal," and "indigenous."

The verb *discover* is another word fraught with contradiction. It is patently impossible to discover land that is already inhabited. Thousands of years before Columbus' landfall, America had been discovered by people either trekking across the Bering Strait land bridge from East Asia or sailing along the Pacific Northwest Coast. But the urge to explore new lands, meet strange people, and investigate unfamiliar lifestyles has also been a driving force throughout Euroamerican history. "What animated Columbus more than anything else, more than God or glory or gold," wrote American historian Arthur Schlesinger Jr., "must surely have been those primal passions of curiosity and wonder, the response to the challenge of the unknown, the need to go where [no Europeans] had gone before" (Schlesinger 1992, 27).

The everlasting quest for new frontiers and genuine acts of discovery warrant recognition. More important, cultural self-discovery deserves continual celebration. One way for persons with European roots to do that is to rediscover their past by revisiting earlier cross-cultural encounters. Reliving these first contacts between alien cultures can serve as a significant act of cultural renewal. But it demands intellectual discipline and emotional honesty.

In the eighteenth and nineteenth centuries, few Western historians hesitated to describe these first contacts as one-way acts of discovery. Today, most interpreters of the past recognize that the encounters were always two-way meetings. Accurate portrayals of those events require efforts to interpret them from more than one point of view. That involves finding ways to move outside a Eurocentric outlook. At the same time, it means accepting the impossibility of divorcing ourselves completely from a largely European consciousness, of adopting a neutral international outlook, or of pretending to remember the past from the native perspective. Our views are strongly influenced by a particular historical tradition that resonates with Western civilization's deepest values and aspirations. One of its motifs is the idea of discovery. But today, relationships between the "discoverers" and those who were "discovered" are of equal importance.

An intense, dramatic two-way discovery occurred on the Pacific Northwest Coast. Europeans met previously unknown lands and inhabitants. The natives encountered white people and their technology. But many of those who were overpowered by Western civilization found that its interest in discovery soon turned into avarice, arrogance, ruthlessness, and brutality. Many acts that today's Euroamericans celebrate as pioneering achievements of progress and enlightenment are viewed as devastating crimes against humanity by the people their predecessors vanquished and subjugated. The reality of that legacy is starting to sink in. Revisionists are forcing all of us to re-examine the impact that Western civilization has had on the rest of humanity. There is a constant, growing need for balanced cross-cultural investigations.

INTRODUCTION

Like the feud, the idea that others at some
distance eat human flesh knows no
beginning and probably will know no end.
WILLIAM ARENS (1979, 10)

HISTORIANS HAVE A PREDILECTION for footnotes. These additions to an author's text provide verification, supportive information, interesting asides, and promising leads for further investigation. In a way, it was a footnote that prompted me to begin this inquiry.

In reading about Pacific Northwest Coast history over the years, I continually ran across vague, often contradictory references to alleged practices of cannibalism among Northwest Coast Indians. About 20 years ago, I first read Warren Cook's *Flood Tide of Empire* — the classic overview of early Spanish explorations in this part of the world. Commenting on cannibalism, Cook noted that "the topic is the touchiest in northwest coast ethnography" (Warren Cook 1973, 190). In a long footnote, the historian listed more than 20 sources that warranted reexamination. The subject sounded fascinating and appeared to need thorough study, but at the time I was preoccupied with other projects. I filed the intriguing footnote for future reference.

In 1990, I started research for a book about a late eighteenth-century Spanish-Mexican mariner, who participated in many of

Spain's key expeditions to the Pacific Northwest Coast. Once again I found myself revisiting the old commentaries about cannibalism by Captain James Cook and his men, by English and American fur traders, and by Spanish mariners and priests. The more I probed these references, the more confusing this part of the historical record became. I also found many more sources than those listed by Warren Cook in his provocative footnote. I decided it was time for me to gather all the accounts, analyze them, and render a well-balanced judgment about the central question: Did the early Northwest Coast natives practise cannibalism, and if so, what was the dominant motivation behind it — survival, dietary enhancement, or religious ritual?

As I collected the historical documentation, I realized it would be impossible to understand or appreciate the significance of the cannibalistic customs that allegedly occurred among these aboriginal people unless I first looked at the findings of ethnologists and anthropologists who had studied these groups. That reading led me to two additional realizations. First, the historical record was so ethnocentric as to be highly suspect. Second, to probe its true meaning for contemporary society, I would have to examine other complex issues: Where did the cannibal concept come from? What has it meant to different cultures? In cannibalism's ritualistic form, what is its underlying religious significance? If Northwest Coast natives practised *ritual* cannibalism, do the moral and ethical principles behind those ancient ceremonies have any application to today's world?

What began as a straightforward historical study had turned into a complex, interdisciplinary, cross-cultural investigation of a controversy that is at least 200 years old. The cultural clash between Europeans and native people that occurred on America's northwest coast in the eighteenth and nineteenth centuries sparked numerous ideological conflicts, which continue to reverberate today. One of the most contentious is the fascinating, perplexing issue of cannibalism — anthropophagy, or literally *man-eating*.

This ancient concept has been misinterpreted and only partially understood by Westerners who have been inclined to forget that, especially with cannibalism, motive means everything. When most of us encounter the word cannibalism, we tend to assume that the only practice being addressed is the one implied by the term's literal meaning: human use of human beings as tasteful, nourishing food. But this is just one of the forms man-eating appears to have assumed in the distant past. Known as *gustatory* or *dietary cannibalism,* it seems to have occurred rarely, if at all, in certain isolated, widely separated, mainly prehistoric cultures.

As we will see, early European travellers claimed that they found cannibalistic practices almost everywhere they ventured in the so-called New World. They applied the term cannibalism to a wide variety of acts that ranged from trophy-taking to human sacrifice, all of which, they believed, indicated human beings were probably being eaten as food. What they repeatedly failed to recognize were more common, but also more private, practices of *ritual cannibalism* — deeply religious ceremonies, rooted in certain ancient cultures, which included simulated or actual eating of human flesh. All involved the belief that eating certain parts of another individual's body could enable the feaster to acquire the other person's essence, increase spiritual power, and even ensure supernatural protection for the group.

Nowhere in the world were these cannibalistic rites so elaborately developed as they were among the Northwest Coast Indians. But the significance of these rituals was missed entirely by eighteenth-century European invaders, most of whom were blinded by ignorance, preconceptions, prejudice, and fears. Preoccupied by acquisitive motives, they made extremely superficial observations about the strange, new societies they encountered. Nothing reflected this bias more starkly than their perception of what appeared to be gustatory cannibalism among indigenous people and their failure to examine, let alone appreciate, ritual cannibalism.

This tunnel vision reflected a "cannibal complex" among our European ancestors. The same disorder continues to cloud our outlook today. We still tend to equate cannibalism only with isolated, culturally restricted acts of eating human flesh. But, in its ritualistic forms, such behaviour — both simulated and actual — conveyed profound metaphors for timeless metaphysical messages about spiritual renewal. Only a few scholars have probed that aspect.

During most of this century, historians and anthropologists have tended to skirt the issue of cannibalism among Northwest Coast natives and gloss over its implications. The probable cause is clear. The documented accounts were clouded by so much ethnocentrism that scholars almost uniformly discounted gustatory cannibalism on the Pacific Northwest Coast. But in their haste to avoid ethnic bias, researchers neglected to give sufficient attention to the presence and importance of ritual cannibalism. From 1900 to 1980, cannibalism had almost become a forbidden topic to scholars writing about Northwest Coast Indians. Since then, the few historians who have addressed the subject stick to the party line: it never happened. Anthropologists tend to say, if it happened, it occurred so far in the past that it can't be studied.

But the historical record about those who lived at the place mistakenly called Nootka by the famous English Captain James Cook forces us to address some crucial questions. Did the Mowachaht ("the people of the deer") who lived at Yuquot eat human flesh? Was the Mowachaht's legendary Chief Maquinna — the most powerful of all Nootka leaders — a cannibal? Did other Northwest Coast natives engage in the practice? In any of these cases, what type of cannibalism was involved? Were the European explorers duped by natives into making gross exaggerations? Or were they simply biased in their views of all native peoples? Was the moral outrage exhibited by some Europeans actually an attempt to justify their exploitation of native people and cover up their abuse of aboriginal women and children? Did the suspicion that others were "man-eaters" only reinforce European convictions of moral and cultural superiority and blind these observers to the true significance of imagined atrocities? These are only some of the questions that remain unresolved.

* * *

Since the time when Europeans invented the cannibal epithet, it has been used to depict almost every human group. Throughout history, members of Western civilization have branded other cultures — especially those belonging to dark-skinned people — as cannibalistic. Has this controversial label been pinned unfairly or inaccurately on early Northwest Coast Indians?

The orthodox answer to that question among contemporary historians either minimizes such behaviour, portrays it as an ancient but merely simulated ritual, disputes the evidence, or accepts the natives' claims that they never practised man-eating. This book challenges that superficial position.

Among historians, Frederick W. Howay staked out the conventional view in 1941 when he edited *Voyages of the Columbia*. "The established opinion today is that the Indians of the Northwest Coast were not cannibals," said Howay. "Anything that appeared to be cannibalism was in reality merely formal and a part of some ceremonial. [Numerous English and Spanish explorers] entertained the view that these people were cannibals, but not one well authenticated instance of cannibalism has been produced. . . . Anything of that nature was purely ceremonial and symbolic. . . . None of [the European explorers] ever saw any cannibalism. All their evidence fits equally with mere ceremonial or religious rites" (Howay 1941, n66, n289).

By minimizing the significance of religious ceremonies, Howay disregarded an important reality. He failed to point out that it was precisely these rituals that revealed the most profound aspects of native culture. To understand the Northwest Coast natives, one has to probe the intellectual, ideological, and religious significance of ritual cannibalism. To dismiss it as "purely ceremonial and symbolic" evades that challenge and misleads those who might address it.

Howay based his conclusions on some of the opinions advanced by the revered anthropologist Franz Boas, but the historian was too selective. In the late 1890s, Boas had found no gustatory cannibalism being practised on the Pacific Northwest Coast. But, among numerous bands, he observed ceremonies that featured masked initiates engaged in highly refined ceremonial cannibal dances, which involved numerous symbolic acts of man-eating. As we will see, Boas also presented additional information about these performances' antecedents, which went beyond simulation. Howay either overlooked or ignored this crucial research.

As Northwest Coast natives were still following ritual cannibalism in the late nineteenth century, Boas concluded that, at an earlier time, they had probably incorporated some forms of "man-eating" in their ceremonies. Most likely it was not practised by all members of a band, but elite, secret warrior societies were common. For example, to kill a slave captured in war, would have been an impressive way to reenact the victory for admirers. To go a step further and eat the dead captive's flesh, would have been a dramatic way to commune with the most powerful of all spirits. At the very least, it would have been an awesome way for a chief to establish and maintain his authority.

But most scholars would have us believe ceremonial "man-eating" had always been nothing more than an elaborate, symbolic, simulated performance. This interpretation was also promoted by some anthropologists who followed Boas. One of the most influential and oft-quoted is Philip Drucker, who studied the Nootka in the 1930s. "The situation as to ceremonial cannibalism is not clear," said Drucker. "It may have been practised after successful raids, although modern informants deny it unanimously. If it ever was customary, as so many of the early explorers maintain, it went out of use early in the historic period" (Drucker 1951, 342). That assertion is contradicted by both the historical and anthropological record.

In 1979, the maverick anthropologist William Arens shook up the academic community by declaring that cannibalism never existed anywhere in the world. His provocative but suspect argument (see chapter 10) stirred up anthropologists and historians alike. It gave the latter a convenient premise for discrediting all early European accounts of cannibalism on the Pacific Northwest Coast.

In 1980, the historian Donald C. Cutter, an expert on the scientific voyage of Captain Alejandro Malaspina to the Pacific

Northwest Coast in 1791, stated unequivocally: "It was never proved conclusively that Maquinna practised ceremonial or dietary cannibalism, though he was charged with both and such charges were investigated [by Malaspina]" (Cutter 1980, n83). With respect to the evidence against Maquinna, Cutter's conclusion was accurate, but it did not address the issue of more widespread cannibalistic practices. Cutter also gave more weight to Malaspina's probe than it deserved. Malaspina, a reputable natural scientist, attempted an extensive investigation, but it was brief, somewhat biased, superficial, and inconclusive. Furthermore, Malaspina did not speak the native language.

Another respected historian expanded on Cutter's position in 1980. In the most complete study of the historical record to date, University of Calgary professor Christon I. Archer rejected the notion that Northwest Coast Indians practised any kind of cannibalism. He correctly stated that alleged practices of gustatory cannibalism "were figments of the European imagination." But he also asserted that "there is no solid evidence to support the ritual [cannibalism]" alluded to by several eighteenth-century European adventurers. Only in passing did Archer concede that "the ethnographical literature points out that some tribes had their own dark myths and cannibal dances" (Archer 1980, 473, 478-9). He did not explain how those ceremonies conveyed the important ideological and religious content of the ancient myths.

As we will see, the historical evidence of ritual cannibalism among the Mowachaht is limited. But it does exist and it deserves to be re-examined in the context of the ethnographic record that was developed later. As an historian, Archer stopped short of doing this. He simply made the point that early European observers were preoccupied with gustatory cannibalism and almost totally unaware of its ritual aspects. Archer left that for others to examine.

In 1982, Robin Fisher, Professor of History at Simon Fraser University in Burnaby, British Columbia, gave another indication of why allegations of cannibalism among the Northwest Coast natives need more study. Citing Arens' categorical comments,

Fisher urged historians to exercise skepticism about the presence of cannibalism among the Mowachaht. Noting that "a major problem is the fact that the evidence, both then and now, seems very pliable," Fisher concluded that "commentators are divided on the question of whether anthropophagy was practised among the Nootka" (Fisher and Bumsted 1982, 17-18). This difference of opinion points up the importance of reopening constructive debate about ritual cannibalism among the Northwest Coast Indians.

The need for a renewed examination is reinforced by the fact that, with one notable exception, other ethnographers and historians who touched on the subject during the 1980s failed to plow new ground or address the unanswered questions sharply. For example, in a provincial government publication produced in 1983 about the Indians of Vancouver Island, ethnographer Eugene Arima conceded that these people were fierce warriors, but he stopped short of probing the significance of headhunting — often considered an indicator of cannibalistic practices. "All the slain were beheaded," said Arima "but scalps were not taken nor does there seem to have been cannibalism" (Arima 1983, 107).

One scholar who did recognize the need for a reassessment was Joyce Wike, an anthropologist at Nebraska Wesleyan University. In 1984, she contributed a chapter to *The Tsimshian and their Neighbours* (Wike 1984, 239-54), in which she attempted to "reconcile the impressions" of European mariners and traders of "actual cannibalism" on the Pacific Northwest Coast in the late eighteenth century with the ceremonies studied by ethnographers one hundred years later. Wike's re-evaluation provided a succinct summary of the views that emerged from the historical sources. But her short article did not present the full citations or their context, so readers could make their own appraisal. Filling in the gap left by Archer's earlier reassessment of similar sources (1980), Wike proceeded to summarize the ethnographic record. She made four claims: "belief in real cannibals and cannibalism on the Northwest Coast . . . was a cultural fact"; gustatory cannibalism was *not* in vogue at Nootka in the late eighteenth century; a distinctive kind of ceremonial cannibalism was probably present at the time; "ritual cannibalism had existed as early as the sixteenth century."

Wike's assertions and the sources used to support them deserve scrutiny and more extensive discussion; especially because she ends up saying "cannibalism is not a valid cultural category" and the term, in its usual — overgeneralized — connotation, "should follow 'totemism' into the analytical scrap heap." On the contrary, the term begs for even more penetrating analysis — especially on the Pacific Northwest Coast, and Wike's excellent article broadens the platform for such a study. Yet contemporary historians seem to have overlooked her contribution.

In 1986, historian John S. Kendrick wrote a best-selling book about the Spanish explorations of the Pacific Northwest Coast. In his frankly partisan account, Kendrick not only shied away from dealing with the issue of cannibalism, he swept it under the rug with a distortion. "Other than [Moziño's account], at no place does any writer of the time whose works I have read mention the sacrifice of other people or animals," wrote Kendrick. "Sacrifice was self-inflicted and was confined to the chiefs" (Kendrick 1986, 89).

Kendrick's assertion seems puzzling when one looks at the bibliography to his book. He cites *Flood Tide of Empire,* in which Warren Cook first exposed the twentieth-century attempt to rewrite the history of cannibalism among Northwest Coast natives. As noted earlier, Cook identified at least 19 writers of the time who had commented on the practice in sharp detail. None of these observers actually saw natives spontaneously eating human flesh. But they piled up an impressive amount of circumstantial evidence during an 18-year period. The credibility of their conclusions is enhanced by the consistency of their reports and the fact that the authors came from several different ethnic backgrounds. Such reports could be chalked up to Maquinna's enemies, exaggeration by ignorant adventurers, rumour-mongering among the Spaniards, or competitiveness and distrust of the Spanish by English and American mariners. But the stories came

from several sources and went into great detail about rituals that
were generally not practised by other American tribes. Most of the
reports stemmed from European contact with natives at Nootka
Sound — the centre of fur trading activity on the coast. The impor-
tance of this circumstantial evidence needs to be reassessed thor-
oughly.

Yet the standard version persists. Tomas Bartroli, a former
member of the Department of Hispanic and Italian Studies at
the University of British Columbia, has written a number of
monographs about Spanish involvement on the Pacific Northwest
Coast. In 1991, he presented a paper at the Bicentennial of the
Malaspina Expedition in Vancouver, British Columbia, which was
published the following year. "No document has provided first-
hand and conclusive evidence that, at this time in their history,
cannibalism was practised by the Nootkans or by any other com-
munity on the American coast," wrote Bartroli. He endorsed
Cutter's analysis (Inglis 1992, 96), which was published in a new
form at that time (Cutter 1992, 100-103; also see chapter 3).

For decades, most anthropologists, archaeologists, and histo-
rians have tended to ignore the significance of the evidence about
cannibalistic practices on the Pacific Northwest Coast. They have
been inclined to interpret history to suit a modern, romanticized
view of natives as either nature's children or as oppressed victims
— the "Hiawatha syndrome." Idealizing Indians in this saccharine
way has dehumanized them no less than the inclination of earlier
observers to demonize them. Both fail to respect the self-expres-
sion of aboriginal people.

In an effort to be politically correct, some scholars have con-
tinued to downplay the historical record, minimize the massive
amount of documentary material collected by Boas, and ignore
the prehistoric function of cannibalism among Northwest Coast
Indians. Most recently, art historian Aldona Jonaitis edited a
splendid collection of Kwakiutl art used in cannibal dances and
ceremonies. In her preface, Jonaitis salutes the cult of political
correctness. "The larger society has today generally abandoned
sensationalism in dealing with Native Peoples," she says. "Anthro-

pology has played a major role in the development of more accurate accounts and humane interpretations" (Jonaitis 1991, 11).

Striving for accuracy and fairness is a worthy effort as long as a culture's apparently vexatious aspects are not ignored, played down, or treated superficially. But in Jonaitis' book, anthropologist Wayne Suttles limits his analysis of ceremonial cannibalism to the obvious motivations of claiming status or outshining a rival. Only by footnote (105, n284) does he mention "possible unconscious motives, latent functions, useful consequences of which the potlatcher is unaware, etc." Yet these are the precise factors that help us begin to gain some insight into how another group of people thinks and feels.

Suttles gives us a revealing example of how those who are bent on correcting the ethnographic record to fit contemporary views often only succeed in making things more obscure. Suttles mentions that two linguists have tried to sanitize Boas' translation of *Baxbakwalanuxsiwae* — the most powerful supernatural figure in Kwakiutl mythology. Boas' literal translation was "Cannibal-at-the-North-End-of-the-World." But his new-age followers (Hilton and Rath 1982) would change the name to something like "ever more perfect manifestation of the essence of humanity." It is not surprising that most native speakers find Boas' less euphemistic version more accurate (Jonaitis, n184). It has the ring of linguistic and intellectual clarity.

This summary of scholarly opinions about cannibalism among the early Northwest Coast natives gives us at least four reasons for laying out the full record for reexamination. First, there are many important, unanswered questions. Second, the early explorers found numerous indications of what they believed was cannibalism but historians have either ignored the evidence, treated it superficially, or misinterpreted its meaning. Third, relationships between oft-alleged gustatory cannibalism and largely overlooked ritual cannibalism beg for a thorough cross-disciplinary investigation of the historical and ethnographic records. Fourth, there is enough disagreement among scholars to justify reopening a debate about ritual cannibalism. Did it exist? To what extent was it practised? What was its significance? These are the key questions.

It is time to take a fresh look at the evidence — not to denigrate first people by sensationalizing a startling religious practice, but to remove the misunderstandings that, for centuries, have masked the significance of ritual cannibalism among Northwest Coast Indians. That is our first objective. Then we will ask what that ancient practice means in today's world. The purpose is not to reproduce the past but to link it with the present, and to acknowledge its import for a society that appears to be losing its moral and ethical bearings.

This book divides such an examination into two parts. Part one *(Red Smoke)* analyzes in chronological order, all the documented references to alleged gustatory cannibalism that were recorded by English, Spanish, American, and French traders, adventurers and explorers who visited Nootka Sound between 1744 and 1884. This part also evaluates similar extracts from the studies of ethnographers, anthropologists, and other scholars who subsequently addressed the issue of cannibalism on the Pacific Northwest Coast.

Part two *(White Flames)* places alleged "man-eating" practices on the Pacific Northwest Coast in perspective by summarizing the history of cannibalism around the world and examining the clash of world views that led to misunderstandings. It goes on to explain how a "cannibal complex" developed world-wide in the minds of eighteenth-century European explorers, priests, and scientists and how twentieth-century anthropologists perpetuated the controversial notion of "man-eating." It ends by revealing the religious significance of ritual cannibalism as it was practised by Northwest Coast natives, and by showing how the wisdom contained in this ancient stabilizing mythology can serve as a framework for developing a coherent world view in an era confronted by spiritual uncertainty and confusion.

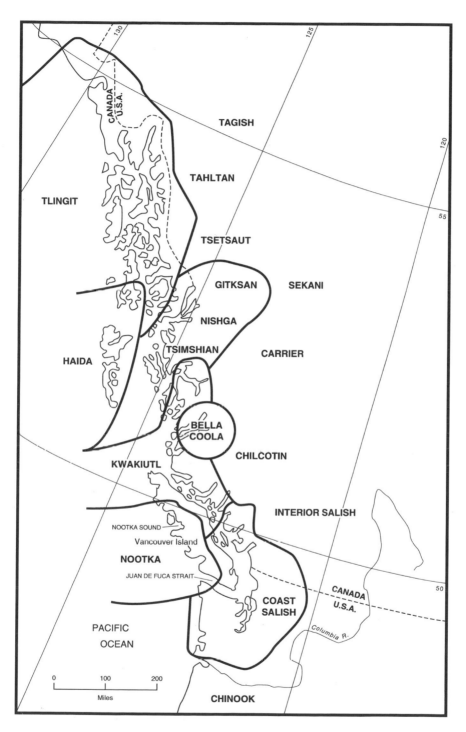

Map of Northwest Coast Indian tribal boundaries.
Drawn by Teresa McDowell at the author's direction.

PART ONE

■

RED SMOKE

Some circumstantial evidence is very strong,
as when you find a trout in the milk.

HENRY DAVID THOREAU,
Journal, November 11, 1850

1

From Suspicion to Allegation

*We had no reason to judge
unfavourably of their disposition.*
CAPTAIN JAMES COOK (attrib.)

*We have reason to suppose that it is
only their enemies they eat.*
W. HUNTER

UNTIL THE MID-1960s, the general public and most scholars believed that the English explorer Captain James Cook was the first person to describe in writing the cannibalistic practices of indigenous people living on the Pacific Northwest Coast in the eighteenth century. Now it is known that Cook's original records of his voyage to that part of the world contained no direct reference to cannibalism among the aboriginals. We also know that Cook's account was not the first journal of the expedition which was published. But the heavily edited official version of Cook's report was the one that set the tone for centuries. Its impact on the perceptions of explorers who followed Cook and on our reading of his records today will require careful scrutiny.

Between 1768 and 1779, Cook made three historic voyages. Until he was killed on February 14, 1779, he kept a log and a journal of his experiences. In 1784, the official edition of Cook's journals was published posthumously as *A Voyage to the Pacific Ocean*. Ordered by King George III, the publication was heavily edited by Dr. John Douglas, Bishop of Salisbury, who had been commissioned by the Lords of the Admiralty. For nearly 200 years, this version remained the uncontested authority. Few people realized that some of the most sensational statements contained in the journal of Cook's third voyage — especially those that ascribed gustatory cannibalism to natives on America's northwest coast — were not written by Cook, but added by Bishop Douglas to fit information provided by some of the Captain's officers (Currie 1994; Currie 1995; MacLaren 1994, 8-9), to boost enthusiasm for "spreading . . . the blessings of civilization (James Cook and King 1784, 1:lxxvii)," and apparently to "sell books" (Fisher and Bumsted 1982, n18).

A *Voyage* garnered widespread interest and inspired many of Cook's subordinates, as well as merchant and naval mariners who followed in their wake, to write their own accounts. (It may also have influenced key overland explorers.)[1] Echoing what were thought to be Cook's suggestive remarks, many of these ambitious journal-writers saw what they believed were definite indications of alleged "man-eating." But most of them misunderstood what they considered certain signs of gustatory cannibalism and they over-looked other aspects of native culture that were much more important. To complicate matters further, the seafarers who questioned or disputed their mates' popular conclusions failed to have their opinions published for hundreds of years. As the European "age of discovery" reached its zenith, only one version of events prevailed. It caused mere suspicion to spawn colorful rumours, questionable allegations, and gross distortions. This misinformation influenced native-white relations on the Pacific Northwest Coast for two centuries.

* * *

Captain Cook's three voyages of exploration in the Pacific Ocean rank among the great scientific adventures of all time. Between 1768 and 1775, he spent most of his first two expeditions exploring the South Pacific before circumnavigating the globe. In July 1776, the intrepid Cook set out from Plymouth, England on his third voyage with the warships *Resolution* and *Discovery*. He aimed to explore the North Pacific and America's northwest coast. Along with many other European explorers, he was searching for a Pacific entrance to the fabled Northwest Passage. The nation that found the shortest route to the Orient could control lucrative East-West trade for decades.

After finding the Sandwich (Hawaiian) Islands in early 1778, Cook reached the Pacific's northwest coast in the spring of that year, and anchored near the Indian village of Yuquot ("village exposed to the winds") on March 30.[2]

The Mowachaht had occupied this storm-lashed site for at least 4,000 years but they probably had lived on the coast for about 10,000 years (Carlson 1992, 19). One writer has called them "Peoples of the Sea Wind" (Brown 1977). Another says the name came from the word *mowatca,* meaning "place where the deer come to drink" (Jones 1991, 16).

Most archaeologists believe humans probably came to North America from Siberia across a land bridge that was intermittently exposed during the ice ages, when water was locked up in massive ice sheets and sea levels dropped. The link was last uncovered during the latter stages of the Pleistocene epoch, displacing much of the Bering and Chukchi seas. The early people who took this route established hunting camps in what is now Alaska and the Yukon.

About 11,000 years ago, rising ocean waters cut off the land bridge.[3] Formerly impassable glaciers, up to two kilometres thick, began to melt, allowing the hunters to travel south, probably along the coast. The flooding peaked about 9,500 years ago, inundating much of the land along the coast.

Recent underwater research by a Parks Canada crew supervised by archaeologist Daryl Fedje has uncovered human artifacts in the waters off the Queen Charlotte Islands that date back more than 9,000 years (Munro 1993). The archaeological record tells us that the Northwest Coast Indians started trading obsidian and shells about 9,000 years ago. Salmon became their most important food staple about 7,000 years ago. By 5,000 years ago, they had formed an intense interest in status, rank, and powerful spirits. Between 4,000 and 3,500 years ago, these people developed highly sophisticated, stylized artistic traditions and spiritual ceremonies. Both gave expression to strong beliefs in spirit power and shamanism. The art and rituals also revealed a complex social structure. These natives expressed their world view most vividly through the potlatch ceremony, which validated changes of status, reinforced property rights, redistributed wealth, and maintained fundamental relationships with the spirit world. The spoon, which was used for feeding dead ancestors, symbolized the funerary potlatch. Evidence suggests that about 2,500 years ago, Northwest Coast natives shifted from actually feeding the dead to burning food for ancestors (Carlson 1992, 11-12, 19-20).

In 1778, about 2,000 people lived at Yuquot, the Mowachaht's summer village (James Cook and King 1784, 2:313). In the winter, they moved to another camp — originally located at the northeast entrance to Tahsis Inlet — and later moved to the head of the inlet. Another 2,500 Mowachahts lived elsewhere. The Tlupana Arm group had its winter village at the mouth of Hoiss Creek. There were about 22 other native villages around Nootka Sound. Some camps contained huge lodges that were up to 75 feet long, each housing a few hundred people. The entire Mowachaht confederation, one of the most powerful confederacies on the coast, totalled between 7,000 (Duff 1964, 39) and 20,000 (Curtis [1915-16] 1978, 11:177)[4] people. It consisted of six Mowachaht tribes and eight smaller bands. By the time the Europeans arrived, these groups had been coming together each summer at Yuquot. Down through the centuries, they had developed a rich, integrated culture and a strong civilization.

Because Cook was warmly received at Yuquot, he named the bay Friendly Harbor and, distorting the native language, misnamed the village "Nootka."[5] The name caught on among other Europeans, who also misapplied it to Indians of the surrounding area. (It would take 200 years to correct the mistake. In 1980, the Vancouver Island Tribal Council adopted Nuu-chah-nulth — "All along the mountains" — as the name for all the West Coast people who occupied a territory that stretched about 2,300 kilometres

Mowachaht man at Yuquot: *engraving of a watercolour by John Webber in 1778. (Courtesy: British Columbia Provincial Museum, PN 5075)*

along most of the Pacific side of what is now called Vancouver Island.)

From Nootka, Cook went on to penetrate the Bering Straits and make contact with Russian fur traders. Then he returned to Hawaii, where he was killed by disillusioned, angry natives in February 1779. His comrades made another fruitless effort to find the Northwest Passage before sailing homeward via Macao and the Cape of Good Hope. After four years at sea, the voyagers reached England in the fall of 1780.

The expedition had stayed at Nootka for less than a month and the British were unable to converse with the natives. Thus, Cook and his officers could not hope to probe the complexities of the unknown and elaborate native culture. But that did not keep them from perceiving what they believed were alarming signs of cannibalism. In their travels, Cook and his men had seen many examples of what they believed was "man-eating," so they were on the lookout for the telltale signs. Another reason these sailors were alert for indications of anthropophagy was the fact that European seamen often resorted to survival cannibalism throughout the sailing era (Simpson 1984, 145). According to *A Voyage*, Cook and some of his crew became convinced that they found the evidence they were looking for at Nootka.

On March 30, 1778, Cook reported that the natives surrounded his ships all day, trading furs, clothing, and various implements. He said they also carried

> . . . human skulls and hands *not yet quite stripped of the flesh, which they made our people plainly understand they had eaten, and, indeed, some of them had evident marks that they had been upon the fire. We had but too much reason to suspect, from this circumstance, that the horrid practice of feeding on their enemies is as prevalent here as we found it to be at New Zealand and other South-Sea islands.* (James Cook and King 1784, 2:4:270-71)

But the italicized comments above were not written by Cook. Bishop Douglas had usurped the authority of the dead explorer's voice and put his officers' words in Cook's mouth. These observations and opinions do not appear in the authoritative edition of Cook's journals (Beaglehole 1967, 3:1:296-97), published in 1967 to correct such misrepresentations: *The Journals of Captain James Cook on His Voyages of Discovery*, by J.C. Beaglehole. This standard scholarly source was the result of a 20-year editing project. It made available for the first time the journals actually written by Cook. It also revealed that, during his third voyage, Cook may have hinted that the Northwest Coast Indians engaged in cannibalism, but he stopped short of actually ascribing the practice to them.

The dismemberment that Cook described made some of his men suspect gustatory cannibalism was being practised. But it did not mean human flesh was definitely eaten. No member of the crew saw it happen. While the burn marks were suggestive, bite marks would have been more convincing. (In chapter three, we will learn that bite marks also may have been present.) The body parts that the natives bartered probably stemmed from trophy-taking. But the Indians also had other kinds of trade in mind.

According to *The Journals*, on April 1, Cook recorded in his log that "one man offered to barter a child about five or six years of age for a spike-nail." He said, "I am satisfied we did not mistake his intention" (Beaglehole 1967, 3:1:n297). Was Cook simply amazed at the inequity of the exchange, or did he suspect this apparent disdain for a child's life signified cannibalistic tendencies? The perceived "intention" remains unclear. It did not seem to occur to him that the native trader might have mistaken the Europeans' interest in human body parts as a sign of their cannibalism. Yet we will see that some of Cook's men would find themselves in similarly ambiguous situations.

Throughout his month-long visit at Nootka, Cook remained completely non-committal in *The Journals* on the issue of cannibalism. But in *A Voyage*, Bishop Douglas inserted his own views about cannibalism, creating the false impression that all of the following words flowed from Cook's pen just before the captain left Nootka on April 26th:

Mowachaht woman at Nootka Sound: *pencil and wash drawing
by John Webber in April 1778. (Courtesy: Peabody Museum,
Harvard University, #41-72-10/498; N27994 by Hillel Burger;
Copyright, President & Fellows of Harvard College, 1997)*

Though these people cannot be viewed without a kind of horror, when equipped in such extravagant dress, yet, when divested of them, and beheld in the common habit and actions, they have not the least appearance of ferocity in their countenances. . . . Though there be but too much reason, from their bringing to sale human skulls and bones, to infer that they treat their enemies with a degree of brutal cruelty; this circumstance rather marks a general agreement of character with that of almost every tribe of uncivilized man, in every age, and in every part of the globe, than that they are to be reproached with any charge of peculiar inhumanity. We had no reason to judge unfavourably of their disposition in this respect. They seem to be a docile, courteous, good-natured people. (James Cook and King 1784, 2:4:308-9)

Although only the last five words were actually written by Cook, the philosophical observations composed by Douglas reinforced a distorted profile of the Mowachahts in the minds of Europeans for hundreds of years.

Famous as an experienced navigator, successful explorer, and responsible captain, Cook attracted a large number of intelligent, skilful, and enterprising men who were eager to join his expeditions. One of those who won a place on Cook's third voyage was the wayfaring American, John Ledyard. Serving as a corporal of marines in the British army, Ledyard ranked fourth in the *Resolution's* marine detachment. During the winter of 1783 — more than two years after the voyage ended, and one year before Cook's journal was published — Ledyard wrote a journal about his experiences. It eventually inspired him to undertake his own fur-trading venture in the northwest Pacific.

Writing from memory, Ledyard was the first English-speaking mariner on the Pacific Northwest Coast to mention cannibalism specifically in print. The young Connecticut Yankee described in detail the behaviour of the natives he met at Nootka:

Like all uncivilized men, they are hospitable. The first boat that visited us in [Ship's] Cove brought us what no doubt they thought the greatest possible regalia, and offered it to us to eat: a human arm roasted.

>I have heard it remarked that human flesh is the most deli-
>cious. Therefore I tasted a bit. So did many others without swal-
>lowing the meat or the juices. But either my conscience or my
>taste rendered it very odious to me.
>
>We intimated to our hosts that what we had tasted was bad,
>and expressed as well as we could our disapprobation of eating it
>on account of its being part of a man like ourselves. They seemed
>to be sensible by the contortions of our faces that our feelings
>were disgusted, and apparently paddled off with equal dissatis-
>faction and disappointment themselves. (Munford 1963, 73)

Ledyard explained (inaccurately) that the Sandwich Island natives had offered similar gifts at their first encounter with the English expedition.[6] Then he launched into a long-winded, gratuitous, Biblically-based essay about the worldwide custom of sacrificing human flesh.

In 1781, Heinrich Zimmerman, another of Cook's sailors, published his notes in German. He noted that the Mowachaht had "dried human flesh which they ate with relish and which they wished us to try." Zimmerman said the crew "traded with them for several dried human hands which we took back with us to England." He also said the natives were "skilful in the use of their crossbows and in general are a very warlike and stout-hearted people, and as far as we could discover, in a constant state of warfare amongst themselves, the slain being devoured" (Howay 1930, 71-72).[7]

The journals of other officers on the expedition, which remained unpublished until recently, elaborated on the trade in human body parts. On March 30, 1778, astronomer William Bayly wrote: "We bought 3 or 4 human hands which they brought to sell, they appeared to have been lately cut off as the flesh was not reduced to an horny substance but raw — they made signs that they were good eating, & seemed to sell them to us for that purpose or at least all of us understood them in that light. They likewise brought on board two or three human skuls and offered them to sale — our surgeon bought one of them" (Beaglehole 1967, 3:1:n297).

The natives' eagerness to sell human body parts actually gave no clear indication that personal experience had convinced them that the items were "good eating." As avid traders, they could not have failed to notice how interested the European mariners were in these things. Trophies, which probably had nothing to do with gustatory cannibalism, were simply popular items of trade.

These possibilities left some of Cook's men ambivalent about the existence of cannibalism at Nootka. One of them was David Samwell, the surgeon aboard *Discovery*, who purchased a human skull from the natives. As he took an active sexual interest in native women, he knew the aborigines better than some of his colleagues. On April 3, he noted: "The Indians trading with us as usual. Among other things they offered some human skulls for sale and also 2 or 3 hands with the flesh dried on; we enquired as well as we could by signs whether they eat human flesh & by the answers they made us we were led to think that these people are cannibals, however of this we had no certain proof" (Beaglehole 1967, 3:2:1092).

Samwell's reservations were echoed by other officers. One of them was Lieutenant Charles Clerke:

> Our people have a strong notion they are canibals, which idea took its rise from the following circumstance: they brought on board frequently, among other articles of traffick, some human sculls and dried hands, and one day a little girl in perfect health, which they wanted much to sell, and to enhance her price, gave us to understand she was very good to eat; the child I believe was 3 or 4 years old, the price demanded for her a small hatchet. They do make motions seemingly of having eat the parts from the heads and hands; but we are so perfectly unintelligible to each other that matters between us are very easily confused and misunderstood; however, this is the argument for their being canibals, whether they are or no, the Lord knows; I think here seems some ground for suspicion, but in my opinion by no means a sufficient foundation to pronounce them such. (Beaglehole 1967, 3:2:1329)

The significant language gap that kept the two groups from understanding each other satisfactorily is clear. So is the tension between suspicion and doubt that affected the skeptics.

That skepticism was made even more explicit on April 21, 1781 by Lieutenant James King, who commented on the confusion involved when a native boy was offered for sale:

> The man who brought the boy made motions of knocking the child on the head, which being observd by some of our gentlemen, they conceiv'd the fellow brought the boy to sell for food, & made motions to the man if they should eat the boy, which he nodded his assent to; but I was present & rather conceiv'd that the mans motions signified only that he wantd iron to cut, & it is certain he only want'd a hatchet, therefore it would be cruel to bring this as any proof of so horrid a charge as that of devouring their own species. (Beaglehole 1967, 3:2:1414)

Not only was King's reasoning sound, but his pithy example also forces us to ask: Who thought who ate people? — the buyer or the seller? Looked at from the aborigines' perspective, one might conclude that their visitors' preoccupation with human body parts made the natives suspect that it was the English who were cannibals.

Ship's master (i.e. navigator) Thomas Edgar, who reported directly to King, recorded his reservations on April 25th. He noted that the natives' behaviour initially gave the English "all the reason in the world" to assume they were cannibals. "But it was evident we did not understand them or that they did not understand us," he wrote, "for I had this morning a most convincing proff of the falsity of our notions." He explained how he bought a severed hand from a native "and then desir'd him to eat it, which he would not do." Raising the ante, Edgar "then offered him more iron & brass than wou'd have purchas'd one of their most elegant dresses, if he would eat part of it." Edgar said the Indian contemptuously rejected the invitation and left the ship in anger. "Yet there are several gentleman in the two ships, who still continue prepossessed in their former opinion," he concluded (Beaglehole 1967, 3:1:n297).

As the journals of these skeptical subordinate officers would remain unpublished for almost two centuries, Cook's supposed observations and those of Ledyard stood unquestioned by most adventurers who followed them to the Pacific Northwest Coast during the next few decades.

In 1784, news of Cook's voyages alerted Britain, the rest of Europe, and the rebellious American colonies to the potential riches that could be derived from the North Pacific coast, especially from seal and sea otter pelts. For the next decade, the maritime fur trade would become a powerful instrument of social, political, and cultural change in this remote part of the world, which was still relatively unexplored by Europeans and Americans. Rumour and gossip between the fur traders began to feed a colourful fable about widespread gustatory cannibalism among Northwest Coast natives.

Like all native North Americans, the Northwest Coast Indians hunted to survive. But the Russians, English, French, and "Boston men" (Americans) who first explored the northwest Pacific were driven by "fur fever" and visions of enormous profits. Some aboriginal leaders quickly learned how to capitalize on the fur traders' craving for pelts. Chief Maquinna would grow wealthy by trading furs to the Europeans. (During the years in which Maquinna cornered the market, he boosted the price of furs tenfold.) The clash of values and customs that stemmed from this interchange would transform native culture forever.

By 1787, two years after the maritime fur trade had started, commerce along Vancouver Island's west coast was controlled by three large trading blocks dominated by a trio of powerful chiefs (Meares 1967, 228-31). Each governed a separate territory, but all three, along with their closest subordinates, were related by marriage.

In the south was Chief Tatooch, whose main village was located on an island at the entrance to Juan de Fuca Strait. To the north was the exceptionally wealthy Chief Wickaninish, whose oligarchy ruled the central coast from his villages in Clayoquot Sound. Farther north was Maquinna, a young man in his thirties who lived in the Nootka Sound area. These three leading chiefs formed a loose alliance, which allowed them to call on each other for assistance.

In the northernmost territory, Maquinna was the highest ranking chief of a loose confederacy of at least seven groups, each of which had its own influential chief. Unlike Wickaninish and Tatooch, Maquinna did not enjoy relatively unchallenged power. He held nominal political control of the confederation, but strong, competitive subchiefs were ready to take over if he faltered. As sea otter were scarce in the immediate vicinity of Nootka, Maquinna collected furs from several tribes living along the coast and from the Nimpkish on the eastern side of Vancouver Island. The latter were reached by a long overland trail. In his trade with Europeans, Maquinna was assisted by Chief Callicum, a man in his fifties who was the confederacy's second ranking chief. In their absence, Chief Hannape would take charge.

Although Maquinna was not as powerful as either Wickaninish or Tatooch, he was an adroit leader of considerable social status who maintained his prominence through diplomacy, persuasion, guile, and intermarriage. Maquinna held no official position of overall authority, but as an informal "umbrella" chief he took the lead role in the fur trade (Marshall 1992, 2-5).

In their dealings with the Europeans, all these chiefs would convey different, sometimes conflicting information about various practices that the whites viewed as active cannibalism. But none of the native informants would gain more attention, nor remain more puzzling than Maquinna.

* * *

Many fur traders became adept at writing intriguing, entertaining narratives about their adventures among the Pacific Northwest Coast "savages." Intent on telling a good story, they did not worry about expressing their ignorance through distortion or exaggeration. They blended fact and fiction in their accounts of doing business with the natives. Accurate ethnology was the least of their interests. Since many of them were preoccupied with being eaten by Indians, it is not surprising that cannibalism was one of the

Mowachaht man at Nootka Sound: *watercolour by John Webber in April 1778. (Courtesy: Peabody Museum, Harvard University, #41-72-10/497; N27999 by Hillel Burger; Copyright, President & Fellows of Harvard College, 1997)*

topics they discussed. The theme may also have been used to discourage competitors from invading prime hunting grounds or to keep mutineers from deserting to live with the natives (Archer 1980, 465).

The English merchant-captain James Strange was fascinated by the published account of Captain Cook's celebrated voyage around the world. It inspired him to lead a commercial expedition from Bombay, India to America's northwest coast in 1785. Capt. Strange aimed to establish a new branch of trade between the Pacific Northwest and China. During his two-year voyage, he became the second English captain after Cook to visit Nootka,[8] arriving there June 27, 1786. Wanting to be close to his customers, Strange anchored at Friendly Cove for more than a month and kept an extensive journal. Despite obvious prejudices and a verbose, stilted writing style, he recorded his firsthand experiences with candour and a twist of morbid humour.

Like most white fur traders, Strange remained preoccupied with commerce and self-justification. He viewed the natives at Nootka with disdain and disgust. He found them depraved, dirty and dishonest. Worst of all, he concluded they were addicted to devouring human flesh. On July 6, 1786, he made the following entry:

> The practice of bringing hands and heads for sale, obtained [occurred] now, in like manner as when Captain Cook was here. In my second visit to the shore I had the pleasure, or more properly the dissatisfaction, to ascertain for a fact (and which, when Captain Cook visited Nootka remained a matter of doubt in his mind) that the savage and barbarous practice of devouring human flesh exists here as well as in the Sandwich Islands.
>
> In the course of this day's excursion, I was accosted by one of the most celebrated warriors in the sound, named Clamata [Callicum], who had been previously introduced to me by Maquilla [Maquinna, who was Callicum's father-in-law], as a man famous for his bravery and address in war, having personally slain eight and twenty of the enemy within the last ten moons. Having beckoned me aside to the most retired part of

the walk, he took from under his garment a basket, from whence he drew three hands and a head, which he desired me to buy.

I conceived this to be a very favourable occasion to learn with certainty, what were the purposes for which these people thus preserved the hands and heads they so frequently presented to us for sale. At the same time, I had no doubt in my own mind but that they were applied to the very purposes which I shall now relate. To this end I represented to [Callicum] that I was ignorant what use I should make of them if I purchased them. He informed me *they were good to eat.*

I seemed to discredit the assertion with a view to urge him to the commission of that act, which on any other occasion than the present I should have shunned the sight of with abhorrence.

My 'hero' now gave me ocular demonstration and very composedly put one of the hands in his mouth and, stripping it through his teeth, tore off a considerable piece of the flesh, which he immediately devoured with much apparent relish.

However prepared I was for this exhibition, I could not help expressing horror and detestation at the act. He immediately comprehended my meaning and endeavoured to reconcile me to the deed by assuring me that if I died, or if my friend or his friend died, he would not eat us. [He said] the hand he had then eaten was the hand of his enemy, whom he had killed in war and that the eating of it was a deed acceptable in the eyes of heaven, to which he at the same time pointed.

[Then] he pressed me to buy them, which I positively refused doing and, indeed on every occasion, I strongly discountenanced the purchase of them, lest it might become an inducement to these savages to go purposely to war in hopes of being able to dispose to advantage of the miserable remains of their conquered foe.

This kind of traffic was always carried on with seeming secrecy and an apparent fear of being detected by their own countrymen. They therefore watched the occasion of parting with their goods at a time when their companions were otherwise busied. From hence I should infer that the practice either was considered among themselves as dishonourable or that this secrecy was only assum'd with a view thereby to enhance in our

eyes the value of the goods. For they were never purchased but
at a most exorbitant rate. (Ayyar 1928, 27)

The obviously biased Capt. Strange was intent on proving that
Cook's suspicions were true. He supposedly came away from this
incident with both eyewitness evidence of gustatory cannibalism
and Callicum's confession that human flesh is "good to eat." But
this incident tells us much more about intercultural trade than it
does about the alleged cannibalism. Rather than revealing his
inclination to eat human flesh, Callicum seems to have been
doing whatever he could to advertise the value of his trophies,
jack up the price, and corner the market in body parts. Having
killed so many men, he apparently had a large supply. Callicum
may have been trying to build up his reputation as a trader so he
could compete with Maquinna in the far more lucrative fur mar-
ket. Or perhaps he was demonstrating to a European, some of
whom the natives may have suspected indulged in cannibalism,
that this dried human flesh was edible. As most of Strange's com-
munication with Callicum was based on sign language, one also
wonders how many aspects of this transaction were missed or mis-
construed.

Strange's observations were echoed by W. Hunter, a member
of the fur trader's crew. He recorded his remarks in a letter, which
indicated the expedition's two ships were anchored in Friendly
Cove until July 27th:

> We found the people answer Captain Cook's description of
> them so accurately that I shall say nothing of them except to
> clear the doubt that they are cannibals. We have reason to sup-
> pose that it is only their enemies they eat, for we found some
> bodies deposited in a basket lying on the ground covered with
> leaves. They are excellent curers, for some of our Gentlemen
> carried some heads with them which keep perfectly dried. One
> day they brought the head and arms of a man they had just
> killed and offered them for sale. (Hunter 1940, 3)

Despite Hunter's unequivocal assertion that "they are cannibals,"
he provided no solid evidence. He substantiated Strange's allu-

sions to preserved heads and hands, which were probably taken in war as trophies. But he provided no new information.

What could have become the most reliable eyewitness account of suspected cannibalism at Nootka was provided by Alexander Walker, the 21-year-old ensign who assisted Strange as commander of 15 East India Company soldiers. But his report would go through many transformations before it was finished, and his opinions would waffle accordingly. Nevertheless, his second-hand account of another mariner's direct experience would suggest the need for an entirely new line of inquiry.

Spurred by scientific curiosity, Walker made a detailed description of the first people at Nootka Sound in 1785. The only earlier ethnographic observations were recorded by Cook. But Walker's original journal was lost. Working from notes, he reconstructed his account between 1813 and 1831. Remarkably, the entire journal remained unpublished until 1982 (Fisher and Bumsted). While he was at Nootka, Walker became convinced the Mowachaht were cannibals. "Most of us took a great dislike to them," he reported. "This was chiefly occasioned by our discovery about this time (July 14-19) that they eat human flesh" (Fisher and Bumsted 1982, 57). He went on to explain what he saw and heard:

> We had reasons for believing these people to be cannibals, but not in the extensive sense of eating human beings for the sake of food and to gratify hunger. This disgusting practice was apparently confined to devouring their enemies and probably some choice bits only were selected. The part that we chiefly saw were hands, and on comparing those that came into our possession, they turned out all to be right hands. They were preserved with care, and by a preparation which made them keep like hams. They were kept in boxes and reserved as a delicacy. They appeared at first to be kept out of our view, and it fell to my lot to make the discovery of this revolting and barbarous practice.
>
> A considerable time after our arrival, being in an obscure hut, a woman offered to sell me two human hands. Having purchased them, I enquired if they were for eating; she readily

answered in the affirmative, but observing me to be in doubt, she put one of the hands into her mouth and tore part of the palm to pieces with her teeth. Some time elapsed before we saw any more hands, but as we continued to enquire after them and offered a great price, they were at last brought in considerable numbers. All those who wished to indulge their curiosity had now repeated opportunities of ascertaining these people to be cannibals. I have been more than once invited by them to partake of this disgusting food and have, as often as I thought necessary, seen them tearing human flesh. They would testify their pleasure by stroking their bellies and licking their lips, exclaiming 'klookh, klookh,' 'good, good.' When we expressed our abhorrence, they were at great pains to convince us that it was their enemies only which they treated in this manner. Our dissuasions against this habit were to no purpose. I have seen Mokquilla [Maquinna], after we had been expressing our detestation in the strongest manner, appear for a few minutes to agree with us, saying, as we told him, that it was bad food, a wicked custom and the like, but having in this way repeated all our arguments, he would laugh aloud and thrust the hand into his mouth.

We saw many bare skulls in the possession of these people and one [with] the flesh and hair upon it, and which was still bloody. They ate part of this raw before us, and as usual expressed the highest relish for the food. Upon another occasion they produced an arm half roasted, feeding on it in the same manner. . . . Although at first the natives shewed no inclination to expose these things, yet as soon as they perceived us willing to buy them, they brought such numbers as became disgusting, and forced us to drive them away from the vessels. (Fisher and Bumsted 1982, 81-83)

In this account, we finally have extensive, direct observation by one of the more open-minded early European mariners. If this much of Walker's eye-witness testimony is taken at face value, it confirms that the Mowachaht engaged in trophy-taking as well as the preservation and the sale of body parts. He also saw the natives eat raw and cooked human flesh. On the surface, this

Mowachaht bow hunter at Nootka Sound: *sketch by John Webber in April 1778. (Courtesy: Peabody Museum, Harvard University, #41-72-10/496; N27992 by Hillel Burger; Copyright, President & Fellows of Harvard College, 1997)*

appeared to be convincing evidence of the gustatory cannibalism that the Europeans had suspected for so many years. But gradually, Walker apparently became less certain that the Mowachaht ate human flesh. Eventually, he would decide they probably did not. In the process, he unintentionally left researchers a hint that something more elusive might have been involved.

In Walker's final draft, he added some remarkable, but highly dubious, information that he obtained from "Doctor" John Mackay — the surgeon's assistant whom Captain Strange left at Nootka during the winter of 1786 after the expedition returned to Asia. Strange wanted to make sure the Mowachaht did not sell the furs he had gathered to someone else.

The ship's "doctor" had cured Maquinna's only daughter, Apenas, of a scabby disease. If the Mowachaht chief practised cannibalism, Mackay would have had a unique opportunity to observe it first hand. He was the first European to see how the natives lived during the winter, when they held their most important ceremonies. Although Mackay apparently kept no written account of his experiences, his reported observations subsequently became part of an investigation of cannibalism by the Spanish scientist-mariner Alejandro Malaspina (see chapter 3).

Walker interviewed Mackay later in India, and obtained the only account of the young man's harrowing experience with the Mowachaht (see chapter 3 for a brief summary). Unfortunately, it had left him physically sick and emotionally broken. Mackay suffered from memory loss, he had become a heavy drinker, and he could only respond to a list of prepared questions. The tedious interviews caused Walker to conclude that "the fact . . . of their being absolutely cannibals has been qualified by McKoy [Mackay]. . . . He was of the opinion that they did not actually devour their captives and slain enemies. They only washed their hands in their blood and tasted it. The dried hands he insisted were preserved as trophies and charms" (Fisher and Bumsted 1982, 83).

In recounting Mackay's adventures among the Mowachaht, Walker provided the following description of human sacrifice, which the ship's "doctor" observed:

The inhabitants of the village . . . debated vehemently concern-
ing the disposal of their captives. . . . The assembly, in the vio-
lence of their debate had been drawn closer to the sea, tram-
pling under foot their unhappy prisoners, when some of those
who were for instant execution, began to carry the sentence
into effect by beating out the brains of their captives with large
stones. When this work was begun, the opposite party . . . lent
all their assistance to complete the infernal sacrifice. The whole
community was now in motion: men, women and children;
aged and young. Those who could not approach the bodies
while they were alive, satisfied their thirst for blood, by man-
gling and tearing to pieces the dead carcase. In this horrid
scene, the women bore the most distinguished part. After the
first ebulitions of rage, the men left the remaining orgies to
them. It was the women who chiefly cut and disfigured the bod-
ies. Both sexes besmeared themselves with the blood of the vic-
tims. While it was warm and streaming from the wounds, each
person tasted it. (Fisher and Bumsted 1982, 185)

Walker went on to report that Mackay did not know what hap-
pened to the bodies afterwards, "but he did not think they were
eaten by the savages." He said Mackay insisted that the preserved
hands were simply trophies or charms, "which were brought forth
in the case of sickness and applied to the part in pain or produced
at their feasts as memorials of courage and achievement" (185).
Earlier in the interview, Mackay said he had not heard of any
human flesh being eaten that winter (see chapter 5), even though
the Mowachahts suffered a severe food shortage (180-81).

The bogus "doctor" Mackay subsequently drank himself to
death. Yet, inexplicably, Walker overlooked Mackay's degenerat-
ing state of mind, questioned his own earlier direct experience,
and surprisingly reached a new conclusion. "The testimony of
McKoy [MacKay], must be admitted of superior weight to our cur-
sory observations," he said "and it at least leaves the fact in doubt
whether these people are really cannibals" (185).

We will assess the significance of Walker's change of mind in
chapter five. For now, it is sufficient to note that he rejected only
one conclusion: the probability that the Mowachaht practised

what had been suspected for so long — gustatory cannibalism. It is important to remember that the fur traders knew nothing about the subtleties of ritual cannibalism, the superficial aspects of which MacKay probably had observed without realizing their full meaning.

2

Meares, Martinez and Maquinna

We were very much disposed to believe that
Maquinna himself was a cannibal.
> CAPTAIN JOHN MEARES

Maquinna ate the little boys among his enemies
who had the misfortune to fall prisoner.
> ANONYMOUS FRANCISCAN

DURING 1788 AND 1789, Nootka became a focal point for political, economic, and social conflict on the Pacific Northwest Coast. England and Spain competed for sovereignty. English merchant mariners contended for control of the lucrative fur trade with an increasingly influential breed of American entrepreneurs. European and native lifestyles clashed repeatedly. At the centre of this discord were three men: the English fur trader John Meares, the Spanish explorer Esteban José Martínez, and the Mowachaht leader Chief Maquinna. Two American captains — Robert Gray and John Kendrick — watched from the sidelines. One factor that fueled the disputes was escalating allegations of cannibalism.

Meares, a former lieutenant in the Royal Navy who had become an enterprising and conniving merchant-captain, played a prominent role in increasing tension over this controversy. His accounts would transform reports of widespread trophy-taking into far more gruesome types of man-eating ceremonies. His grisly tales would also brand Chief Maquinna a cannibal in the eyes of almost all European visitors.

In 1786, Meares set out from Calcutta, India on a trading voyage between China and America's northwest coast. He commanded a ship acquired by the East India Company. Meares encountered numerous problems, which prevented him from reaching his destination and forced his backers to revise their mode of operation. Before returning to India, Meares landed in Hawaii on August 1, 1787. Departing a month later, he was joined by Kaiana, a chief of Kauai and brother of King Kamehameha, monarch of Oahu. Referred to as Tianna by Meares, the chief proved to be a hardy sailor and worthy explorer in his own right. In his early thirties, the muscular chief stood nearly six-feet five-inches tall.

In January 1788, the East India Company gave Meares two ships — the *Iphigenia Nubiana* and the *Felice Adventurer* — and sent him off again on a two-fold mission: to trade for sea otter furs, and to return Kaiana and several other natives to their homelands. Among them was Maquinna's younger brother, Comekela. In 1787, the young boy had travelled secretly but voluntarily to China aboard a vessel commanded by Captain James Hanna, an associate of Meares. Hanna had made his second visit to Nootka in 1786 to obtain furs. Comekela stayed in good health and was extremely observant. In his two years at sea, he would learn enough sailing skills to help scuttle a fur trading ship in 1803, after Maquinna's raiding party killed the captain and slaughtered all but two of the crew.

Meares Indicts Maquinna — Meares arrived at Nootka for the first time in May 1788. No one aboard his ship was more excited than Maquinna's brother. "Comekela, who for several days had been in a state of most anxious impatience, now enjoyed the inexpressible delight of once more beholding his native land," wrote Meares (Meares 1967, 109). The youngster donned his most colourful outfit for the occasion. He wore a copper breastplate under a scarlet regimental coat decorated with brass buttons. A military hat set off by a rakish cockade perched atop his head. Copper ornaments hung from his ears and "he had so many copper saucepans hanging from his hair that his head was kept back by the weight of them," said Meares (110).

Members of the expedition traded with the Mowachahts and built a small hut. On June 8, Meares recorded his first suspicions of cannibalism:

A strange canoe with several people in it entered the cove, and, coming alongside the ship, sold us a small number of sea otter skins. They also offered for sale an human hand, dried and shrivelled up; the fingers of which were compleat, and the nails long; but our horror may be better conceived than expressed, when we saw a [metal] seal hanging from the ear of one of the men in the canoe, which was known to have belonged to the unfortunate Mr. Millar, of the *Imperial Eagle*, whose melancholy history was perfectly well known to every one on board. The sailors scarcely hesitated a moment in expressing their opinion that it must have been the hand of Mr. Millar, and that the people before them were the murderers of that officer. . . .

They proved, however, to be innocent of the crime of which they had been suspected. We were assured, the next day, by Maquinna himself, on his own knowledge, that they had received the articles which had occasioned so much disgust to us, in the way of trade, from the natives of Queenhythe [the Makah on Washington state's Olympic Peninsula], which was the very place where [in 1787] Mr. Millar and his associates had been murdered.

But the chief did not attempt to deny that the hand had belonged to one of our unhappy countrymen. From his manifest *confusion* in conversing on this subject, and various other concurring circumstances which will be related hereafter, we were very much disposed to believe that Maquinna himself was a cannibal. There is, indeed, too much reason to apprehend that the horrible traffic for human flesh extends, more or less, along this part of the continent of America. Even our friend Callicum reposed his head at night upon a large bag filled with human skulls, which he showed as the trophies of his superior courage. It is more than probable that the bodies of the victims to which they belonged had furnished a banquet of victory for him and the warriors that shared his savage glory. (Meares 1967, 124-25)

Maquinna and Callicum, Mowachaht Chiefs: *by unknown artist on Meares expedition, published in 1790. (Courtesy: Vancouver Maritime Museum)*

As we have seen, the preserved human hand was probably a trophy taken in battle. So was the earring, which the English were intent on using as evidence of murder. Despite Meares' admission that Callicum's sack of skulls was another example of trophy-taking, he suspected a much more sinister motivation. Given the level of Meares' suspicion, it is little wonder that Maquinna appeared confused, if not defensive.

Meanwhile, Captain William Douglas aboard the *Iphigenia Nubiana* was making his way south toward Nootka along the Alaskan coast. He was accompanied by Chief Kaiana. Instead of waiting for Douglas to arrive, Meares led a trading expedition south along what is now the Oregon coast, then returned to Nootka. On August 27, 1788, both ships met at Friendly Cove. Meares reported that Chief Kaiana was overjoyed to see his old friends. Meares recorded the Hawaiian chief's reaction to the alleged signs of cannibalism among the Nootkans:

> While we were visiting the village, Maquinna and Callicum re-
> turned from their war expedition. On entering the sound, the
> little army gave a shout of victory. They certainly had obtained
> some advantages, as they brought home in their canoes several
> baskets, which they would not open in our presence, and were
> suspected by us, as it afterwards proved by the confession of
> Callicum, to contain the heads of enemies whom they had slain
> in battle, to the amount of thirty. . . .
>
> Chief Kaiana did not, as we first expected, discover any
> surprise at the sight of Maquinna and his army. The frequent
> communication of the *Iphigenia* with the natives along the
> coast, from Cook's River [Cook's Inlet] to King George's Sound
> [Nootka Sound], had rendered them and their manners no
> longer an object of novelty, as they had never been an object of
> consideration in the eyes of Kaiana.
>
> When he, with his colossal figure, stood by Maquinna, who
> was rather of a low stature [compared to the Hawaiian but not
> to his own people], the difference [struck] every beholder. . . .
> Kaiana and Comekela were old acquaintances, but by no means
> intimate friends, as the former held the latter in a very low

degree of estimation. . . . As Comekela had been at the Sandwich Islands on his first leaving America, the ship having stopped there for refreshments, he was qualified to give Maquinna an account not only of Kaiana, but the country from whence he came.

Kaiana held the customs of the Nootka in detestation and could not bear the idea of their cannibal appetites without expressing the most violent sensations of disgust and abhorrence. . . . The [Mowachaht] are nasty to a degree that rivals the most filthy brutes. . . .

Callicum and Hanapa [Natsapa] both declared their aversion to eating human flesh. But they acknowledged it existed among them and that Maquinna was so attached to this detestable banquet as to kill a slave every *moon* to gratify his unnatural appetite. The chiefs gave us the following account of this bloody ceremony.

When the fatal day arrived which was to be celebrated by the feast of a human victim, a certain number of [Maquinna's] slaves were assembled in [his] house. [He] selected the object to be eaten by him and his guests in the following curious manner. The inferior chiefs, who were invited to partake of the approaching banquet, performed the ceremonies which were appointed to precede it. These consisted of singing the war song, dancing around the fire and fomenting the flames by throwing oil into them. A bandage was tied over Maquinna's eyes, who tried to seize a slave in this blindfolded state. His activity in the pursuit, with the alarms and struggles of the unhappy wretches to avoid it, formed another part of this inhuman business. When some of the slaves were caught, death followed instantly. The carcass was immediately cut in pieces and its reeking portions were distributed to the guests. Those who escaped shouted as one to declare their joy at deliverance.

A circumstance [soon] took place which induced Maquinna to confirm the truth of this cruel history and to name even the very time when the last scene of his tragic gluttony occurred. (Meares 1967, 208-10; 255-56)

This colourful tale of alleged human sacrifice was taken seriously by the early mariners, who repeatedly referred to it when accusing

Maquinna of practising gustatory cannibalism. But it was all hear-
say, supposedly obtained from Callicum and Natsapa. If any of
their information were true, the most intriguing portions were
their references to the periodic ceremonial aspects of Maquinna's
alleged cannibalistic practices. This was the first reference by
European mariners to anything resembling a remnant of ritual
cannibalism. The gruesome story would soon be echoed by Span-
ish naval officers and priests.

Chief Natsapa, *Maquinna's brother-in-law and rival as leader of the
Nimpkish tribe of the Kwakiutl. Drawn by Tomás de Suría in 1791.
(Courtesy: Museo de America)*

Meares went on to recount how Maquinna cut his leg boarding the fur trader's vessel and refused to let the ship's doctor treat his wound. Instead the chief sucked the flowing blood. Meares implied that this was more "evidence" that the chief habitually ate human flesh.

> When we expressed our astonishment and disgust, he licked his lips, patted his belly and exclaimed: 'Cloosh, cloosh (Good, good.)' He then confessed that he ate human flesh and told us how much he enjoyed banqueting on his fellow creatures. He not only avowed the practice of which he had been accused, but he informed us that only a short time earlier the ceremony of killing and eating a slave had taken place in Friendly Cove. We terrified him into promising that no such barbarity would be practised again by him or anyone else in his territories and we gave him to understand that he would not survive another repetition. (Meares 1967, 257)

Meares certainly knew how to build an indictment: collect some circumstantial evidence, surround it with enough hearsay to create suspicion, and drive it home with a confession. Given Meares' reputation for self-serving exaggeration, one wonders how much Maquinna actually "confessed" and how much was invented by Meares. Later, the Spanish explorer-scientist Alejandro Malaspina would have similar reservations.

Meares reported that the American sloop *Lady Washington* out of Boston arrived at Nootka Sound September 17, 1788, under the command of Robert Gray. He was the first American captain to reach Friendly Cove. Meares left Nootka on the 24th aboard the *Felice Adventurer,* returning to Canton for the winter. He transferred Kaiana to the *Iphigenia Nubiana,* which he sent to Hawaii under Captain Douglas' command. The two merchant-captains agreed to meet at Nootka in the spring of 1789.

Before winter set in, another Boston ship, the *Columbia,* sailed into Nootka under the command of John Kendrick. The only record of the first voyage of these two American ships is a log written by Robert Haswell, second mate aboard the *Lady Washington.*

He claimed to have witnessed cannibalism at Nootka but left little proof. On March 15, 1789, he wrote: "Thes people are canables and eat the flesh of their vanqu[i]shed enemies and frequently of their slaves who they kill in cool blud. They make but little serimoney in owning the fact and I have seen them eat human flesh myself" (Howay 1941, 66).

All we know about Maquinna and his people is what European eyes saw and what their pens recorded. Aside from what is suggested in the natives' rich and important oral tradition, this is also all that the Mowachaht descendants know. How accurate were those European eyes? How exact were their pens, especially those of the fur traders? They were largely acquisitive, greedy "get-rich-quick" entrepreneurs and adventurers. They were also world travelers who had seen and heard enough to suspect that gustatory cannibalism was prevalent throughout the New World. Most of them did not understand the native language. Finally, they were almost completely ignorant of the religious aspects of ritual cannibalism.

Spain Makes Its Bid — To understand how Spanish influence modified the broader picture of international political and economic developments at Nootka Sound, we must step back almost five decades, to 1741 — 37 years before Captain Cook arrived. A brief backward glance will also place the Spaniards' post-fur trade perceptions of cannibalism in perspective.

Although Cook was the first European who actually went ashore in Nootka Sound, he was not the first white explorer to reach the Pacific Northwest Coast and make contact with the natives. That distinction belonged to the Danish navigator Vitus Bering and the Russian captain Aleksei Chirikov. In 1741, their Russian expedition explored the Aleutian Islands and the Alaskan coast, opening the north Pacific coast to the lucrative fur trade.

Thirty-three years later, Spain would begin its exploration of the northwest Pacific Ocean. In part, it was a delayed response to the Bering-Chirikov expedition. But unlike the Russians, English and French, the Spanish never emerged as successful fur traders on the Pacific coast. Initially, they were preoccupied with finding gold and silver. Later, their empire-building concentrated on conversion and settlement. By 1769, the Spaniards had started setting up a string of coastal missions northward from Mexico. This system of colonization would last 50 years.

A Spaniard also preceded Cook to the Northwest Coast. In 1774, Captain Juan Pérez had anchored near the mouth of Nootka Sound[1] but he did not enter or take formal possession. He bartered there with natives, who paddled their canoes alongside the Spanish ships. Pérez and his companions made no mention of cannibalism. In fact, their reports led Spanish officials to credit the Northwest Coast Indians with having attained a much higher level of civilization than the California Indians (Archer 1980, 456, 458).

For both the Spaniards and the Mowachaht, this first contact involved strange and unfamiliar experiences. The Europeans' impressions were recorded by two Roman Catholic priests who accompanied Pérez and kept daily accounts (Griffin 1891). Fray Juan Crespi recorded hearing a "mournful crying out" as the Indians approached the Spanish ship. According to native stories about that first meeting, passed down to the present day through oral tradition, the Mowachaht perceived a spiritual significance in the arrival of the mysterious looking sailing vessel. In 1792, when José Moziño visited Nootka, the natives told him their predecessors thought Pérez' ship carried *Qua-utz*, a supernatural being of great powers who was making a second visit, possibly to punish misdeeds (Wilson 1970, 66).

During the next 15 years, Spain sent two other expeditions northward into Alaskan waters but neither of them entered Nootka Sound. In 1775, Bruno de Hezeta and Juan Francisco de la Bodega y Quadra stopped on the northern coast of what is now Washington State, where natives massacred a well-armed party of sailors and carried off dismembered limbs. But again, Spanish reports said nothing about cannibalism. Lieutenant Hezeta attributed the dismemberment to trophy-taking, not to the consumption of human flesh (Wilson 1970, 458-59).

In 1779, Ignacio de Arteaga and Bodega made a second voyage into Alaskan waters and contacted the Tlingit people, who were determined to employ armed force to preserve their own way of life. The Spaniards began an ominous form of trade, exchanging pieces of iron and cloth for five young native children. The ships' chaplains, alarmed by the scuttlebut that asserted these fiercely resistant natives were cannibals, encouraged the transactions to save the youngsters from what they feared would be unhappy fates. As later experience would confirm, the children offered for sale by the natives were either prisoners of war or expendable outcasts. Unfortunately, two of the youths perished on the return voyage and two others died of disease in San Blas (Archer 1980, 14-15). Each of the officers and chaplains kept a detailed journal of observations about the natives, but none reported any suspected acts of cannibalism beyond their generalized fears that led to purchasing children (Archer 1980, 459-61). Once again, the written record tells us more about European preconceptions than it does about native behaviour.

For nearly a decade, Spain neglected its interests on the northwest coast of America. But by 1788, the Viceroy of New Spain, Manuel Flóres, had grown concerned about fending off Russian, English, and American challenges to Madrid's claims along the coast. He became convinced that an outpost at Nootka was essential to defending Spanish imperialism. By reviving the base, Spain re-entered the competition. In the process, the issue of cannibalism would become one of the most aggravating factors in Spanish-Indian relations at Nootka.

Meanwhile, the mission system begun in 1769 had degenerated into a form of systematic exploitation. In the name of saving souls, the Franciscan friars of the Colegio de San Fernando in Mexico City converted natives to Christianity and obtained a workforce that was made docile and kept inexpensive. But this system of domination could not have existed without soldiers to keep the natives in subjection. Because of tight military control, in 1787, only 22 Franciscans were needed to run 10 California missions. By 1789, the mission system reached from San Diego to Nootka Sound, but the isolated northern outpost would never prove practicable (Archer 1992 [1993], 2-4). Before the Spanish occupation ended, 75 percent of the native people taken into the missions would die, mostly from European diseases.

On February 17, 1789, Esteban José Martínez — a zealous but imprudent second-rate explorer — set sail from San Blas, Mexico aboard the *Princesa* in command of Spain's second expedition to Nootka. He had been a junior pilot with Pérez in 1774. Martínez carried instructions from Viceroy Flóres, ordering him to build "a large hut" at Nootka and "pretend that you are engaged in settling yourself in a formal establishment."

Martínez would remain preoccupied with protecting territory which Spanish mariners believed had belonged unequivocally to Spain for at least 275 years because the Spaniard, Vasco Nunez Balboa, had discovered the Pacific Ocean in 1513.[2] But Martínez also would be one of the few Spaniards to toy with the idea of getting rich by exploiting the fur trade as a sideline.

As the first Europeans to attempt to occupy the Pacific Northwest Coast, the new wave of Spanish explorers would be forced to examine the issue of cannibalism far more closely than those mariners who had previously made only temporary visits. Because the Spaniards were experienced at collecting detailed ethnological information about newly contacted frontier cultures, they stood a somewhat better chance of remaining open-minded about the consumption of human flesh by native people. But they also harboured fears and prejudices, and these would be fed by the fur traders' inflammatory tales.

Martínez Meets Maquinna — Martínez arrived at Nootka on May 5, 1789 to find the harbour occupied by the *Iphigenia Nubiana,* commanded by Captain Douglas, who was waiting for Meares to arrive. Two American ships were anchored in a bay seven miles away. Captain John Kendrick of the *Columbia* and Captain Robert Gray aboard the *Lady Washington* had wintered there for repairs.

While Martínez pondered what to do about the *Iphigenia Nubiana,* he visited Kendrick and Gray. During their chats, Kendrick talked about feasting with the natives. He mentioned that they had offered him a human hand and a chunk of meat from a four-year-old child. Kendrick told Pilot José Tobar y Tamiriz that the natives kept young male and female prisoners of war whom they butchered and sold in pieces (Archer 1992, 30; Fisher 1993, 144-45). Joseph Ingraham, Gray's young first mate, informed Martínez the Americans suspected that the natives were cannibals because of Captain Cook's account and the fact that the natives had "owned without hesitation they not only eat their enemies but bought men for the purpose of eating" (Ingraham, 1789).[3] Martínez had heard that the Mowachaht had attacked one vessel and eaten two crewmen (Archer 1980, 468). But he had assumed that the practice of cannibalism had ceased. The Yankee reports convinced him to purchase several slave children to save them from a similar fate.

By this time, Cook's A Voyage had become the authoritative handbook regarding native customs on the Pacific Northwest Coast. Prior to reading the English captain's official journal, learning about Meares' stories, and hearing the mariners' reports above, the Spaniards had made no mention of cannibalism in the area. But that would soon change.

The natives' main leader at Nootka, Chief Maquinna, was aware that Europeans of every nationality abhorred cannibalism. The dignified, muscular chief firmly denied the practice. The Mowachahts said it had never existed among them. But the Spanish kept receiving reports that it was still going on. Many of them came from the Catholic priests who accompanied every voyage. Because of their long, brown robes and jet-black hair, the natives called them the Raven Men.

One of the accounts of eating human flesh that the Spaniards found most disturbing came from an anonymous Franciscan,[4] one of four who sailed with Martínez:

> Maquinna ate the little boys among his enemies who had the misfortune to fall prisoner. For this purpose he tried to fatten them up first, and then when they were ready, got them all together in a circle (he did this some eight days before our people left that waterway), put himself in the middle with an instrument in hand and, looking at all the miserables with furious vis-

age, decided which one was to serve as dish for his inhumane meal. Then, advancing upon the unhappy victim of his voracious appetite, he opened its abdomen at one blow, cut off the arms, and commenced devouring that innocent's raw flesh, bloodying himself as he satiated his barbarous appetite. (Cook 1973, 190)

This appears to be an abbreviated version of Meares' vivid tale, which we examined earlier. Portions of the anonymous priest's gory account were confirmed by two other friars, but none of the three had actually seen what they described. Padre Francisco Miguel Sanchez wrote: "These brutes eat boys and girls captured in wars," especially in winter during shortages of fish (Archer 1992, 30; Fisher 1993, 145). Fray Lorenzo Socies described the details of Maquinna's alleged bloodthirsty slaughter (Archer 1980, 472; Archer 1992, 30; Fisher 1993, 145). The fourth priest, Father Severo Patero, who was the chief Franciscan at Nootka, noted that several fur traders had alleged that the "fatal, inhuman, thievish" natives "ate each other" but he concluded that they were actually well behaved and friendly (Archer 1980, 472).

Neither the friars nor the Spanish naval officers had much opportunity to learn for themselves personal information about the native culture. Lacking complete control of the fur trade, the Spaniards had no way to familiarize themselves with Indian cultures, let alone exert much influence. They were also not strong enough to protect the natives from abuses by the fur traders. Accustomed to the much easier missionizing that they had known in California, discouraged by the inhospitable climate, and frightened by fur traders' tales about cannibalism and other cruelties, the Franciscans never launched a serious missionary assault on the native religion. Instead, they seldom strayed from their encampment, where they were protected by soldiers. Relying heavily upon the English and American fur traders for most of their ethnological information, the priests continued to spread horrifying rumours about cannibalism (Archer 1992, 27-30; Fisher 1993, 143-45). This also helped to justify an improvisational way of obtaining converts — they began to promote the purchase of native children.

With his fears confirmed, Martínez acquired a five- or six-year-old boy in June 1789 and placed him in the care of missionaries for instruction and baptism. The child was christened Esteban, after the commander (Barreiro-Meiro 1964, 81-82, 111, 113). Several months would pass before Martínez could barter for more children.

On June 24, Martínez claimed ceremonial possession of Nootka, after setting up the customary cross and firing salutes as numerous English merchant sailors watched.

In his zeal to declare Spain's sovereignty, Martínez captured two English vessels and took the captains and crews prisoners of war. Martínez was on board one of these ships July 13, when Chief Callicum, Chief Maquinna's son-in-law, came alongside in a canoe and appeared to shout accusations about Martínez being a thief. Infuriated by what he assumed were insults, Martínez grabbed a musket and pulled the trigger, but the gun evidently misfired. A Spanish sailor fired another gun. Hit by one of the shots, Callicum fell dead.[5] During the furor that followed, it remained unclear whether the chief was accusing Martínez of stealing the ships or of misappropriating lumber from the Mowachaht. But the natives would remember the incident with bitterness for years and blame Martínez.

* * *

In July 1789, Kendrick and Gray switched ships and left Nootka on their second voyage of discovery. Under Gray's command, the *Columbia* left Friendly Cove July 30 and sailed for Canton with her first load of furs. The ship returned to Boston the following year — the first American vessel to sail around the world. Joseph Ingraham, who served as an officer on America's first circumnavigation and returned in 1791 aboard his own ship, would conclude that the consumption of human flesh occurred among some natives on the Queen Charlotte Islands. When the *Columbia* and the *Lady Washington* revisited the Pacific Northwest Coast in 1792, two crew members would record specific first-hand accounts of cannibalism among the Mowachaht.

* * *

Despite the enmity that Martínez had stirred up among the natives, Maquinna came back to visit the Spanish commander on August 25, 1789 and again on September 1st. Two days later, Chief Natsapa, Maquinna's brother-in-law and rival as leader of the Nimpkish tribe of Kwakiutl[6] at Alert Bay, traded an eight-year-old girl to Martínez for a pot and a frying pan. She was christened María de los Dolores (Barreiro-Meiro 1964, 81, 111, 113). On September 30, Martínez recorded the following in his diary:

> When the natives have war among themselves, the warriors that take captives invite the chiefs to eat them when there is a shortage of fish. They are also accustomed to selling them among each other. Maquinna, principal chief of this place, and Callicum are the ones who have made most use of human meat. But they seem to have stopped the practice because of the many protests by foreigners. I have tried to buy some of the boys and they have always asked me if it was to eat them. (Barreiro-Meiro 1964, 124; Sanchez 1789)

Martínez seems to have confused two phenomena and misinterpreted both of them. We have already seen that trophy-taking was common, and that it probably did not point to cannibalism. We have also seen how the natives might have been convinced that the Europeans were cannibals. Perhaps the chiefs' slave children were as frightened of being eaten by their professed benefactors as they were of suffering the same fate at the hands of their captors.

On October 31, Martínez completely evacuated Nootka and set sail for San Blas with his captured ships and prisoners. His departure placed Spain's claim to the surrounding area in serious jeopardy. But the Mowachaht and their deeply offended leader were relieved to see him leave.

* * *

Chief Maquinna and his wife, *drawn by Tomás de Suría in 1791.*
(Courtesy: Museo Naval)

Reflecting on Maquinna's performance as a leader during these two years of intense crisis, one begins to understand why the legendary chief left such an indelible mark on the history of the Pacific Northwest Coast. Remarkable for his appearance and character, he was a powerful political leader and shrewd trader. Nearly six feet tall, the dignified chief stood straight as a tree, towering above most of his subjects. A prominent arched nose distinguished him from other Mowachaht.

Warfare was as important among the Nootka as it was in any other Northwest Coast Indian society. Maquinna repeatedly proved that he was a bold warrior and skilful hunter. Clever, proud, and sensitive, Maquinna ruled his people with a firm hand and a sympathetic, understanding attitude. His great capacity for friendship enabled him to form working alliances with other chiefs, build a potentially powerful confederation, and establish positive relations with European emissaries.

The politically astute chief won the respect of a variety of white mariners and struck shrewd deals with the tough, tricky, and brave fur traders who courted his favour. He knew how to play along with any white person who sailed into Friendly Cove. He usually managed to side with those who had the upper hand. Maquinna recognized the dual advantages of forming proprietary business relations with the traders: both his wealth and prestige increased. By cornering the fur market for a decade, he drove prices to remarkable heights.

Maquinna could also be moody and sullen. He was quick tempered and easily offended. Through his exploitation of the early fur trade, Maquinna heightened his stature and influence. But it would not last. As the traders gradually shifted their activities to Clayoquot Sound, they paid him less respect. Insulted by an American captain in 1803, the bitter chief would wreak terrible revenge, butchering the skipper and all but two of his crew. From then on, white mariners viewed the proud chief as a treacherous monster. But his people revered their ruler to the end.

Renowned for his whale-hunting skills, Maquinna had faithfully executed his religious obligation to maintain the hereditary ritual secrets that ensured abundance of this food source. The Mowachaht believed the dead had a mysterious power over whales: elaborate whaling rites could cause dead whales to drift ashore in the group's territory. Chiefs and their helpers stole corpses and skulls from burial places and constructed shrines deep in the woods. The corpses and skull-topped posts encircled a whale's image. It would be rumoured, but never substantiated, that some chiefs, including Maquinna, killed slave children (Drucker 1965, 155-56), infants (Boas 1930, 267), or boys (Curtis [1915-16] 1978, 11:39) for the ceremony. If that were true, perhaps this shrine was one of the remnants of ritual cannibalism that caught Meares' attention.

In 1903, the Mowachaht whalers' shrine was uncovered by George Hunt, the diligent part-native assistant of renowned anthropologist Franz Boas. The memorial was a moss-covered lodge hidden in the cedar and hemlock forest of a fog-shrouded island in Jewitt Lake, near the entrance to Nootka Sound. In the shelter, about 60 ghostly wooden figures, each measuring one to two metres in height, stared at Hunt with strange, mournful faces. At their feet were about a dozen human skulls. Others were perched on wooden stakes.

After negotiating for several months with two Mowachaht chiefs who had competing claims of ownership to the shrine, Hunt managed to buy the assemblage for $500 on the condition that it would be removed at night when nobody was around. In July 1904, Hunt carted off the memorial and shipped it to the Museum of Natural History in New York, where each skull and carved figure was numbered, labeled, and stored in a vault. To this day, the collection has never been displayed publicly. According to Hunt, the whaler's shrine was "the best thing I ever bought from the Indians."

In 1994, documentary filmmaker Hugh Brody helped produce *The Washing of Tears* (Darling and Green 1994), which recounted the history of the whalers' shrine and described current efforts by the Mowachaht and Muchalaht bands to revive their culture. In January 1995, the film premiered in Vancouver,

British Columbia. Maquinna's living descendants say the memorial was a secret source of spirituality, where the early whalers acquired the extraordinary spiritual strength, knowledge, and skill needed to catch and pull in huge whales.

The details of these clandestine, highly privileged ceremonies, which reached back to prehistoric times, have been forgotten or suppressed. But Dr. Roy L. Carlson, Professor of Archeology at Simon Fraser University, has unearthed evidence showing memorial or funerary feasts for renowned hunters involved "the literal feeding of the dead using spoons and bowls" (Carlson, 12). The historical record that we have examined so far indicates human heads and body parts taken in war, and trophy skulls could have been intended for use in other acts of ritual cannibalism during these memorials. As we will see in the next chapter, the alleged sacrifice of slaves could have added another dimension.

3

Eliza and Malaspina Fuel the Debate

This cruel man has eaten eleven children.

JACINTO CAAMAÑO

He told us that he had been destined to be a
victim and to be eaten by Chief Maquinna
together with many others.

TOMÁS DE SURÍA

AT THE BEGINNING of the 1790s the Spaniards tried to reduce socio-political tensions at Nootka, but allegations about the consumption of human flesh among the natives continued unabated. To make up for the debacle that Martínez precipitated in 1788-89, the Spanish regime in San Blas decided to undertake an entirely different approach in the struggle to achieve political control of the Pacific Northwest Coast. In the process, Lieutenant Francisco Eliza would establish a much more benevolent command at Nootka and the renowned explorer-scientist Alejandro Malaspina would make the first extensive inquiry into the reports of cannibalism that had been circulating for so many years.

In mid-August 1789, the new Spanish viceroy — Vicente Guemes Pacheco, Count Revilla Gigedo — landed in Veracruz with seven sterling naval officers and four surgeons assigned to the Pacific Northwest Coast. The assignments showed Madrid's commitment to occupying Nootka as former Viceroy Flóres had urged. The senior naval officer was Juan Francisco Bodega y Quadra. He served as commandant at San Blas until his death in

1794, spearheading Spain's intensive exploration of the north-west, which gained momentum in 1790.

Revilla Gigedo would emerge as one of the greatest viceroys to govern Mexico. On October 17, 1789, he took over from Flóres, facing two major issues: dealing with the captured Englishmen and their vessels in San Blas, and hanging on to Nootka. Giving the second challenge priority, he wrote Bodega in early December, instructing him to "relieve Martínez" and replace him with an officer "who might be more worthy of confidence" to occupy and fortify Nootka and explore inside the Strait of Juan de Fuca. Bodega placed Lieutenant Francisco Eliza in command of the most formidable force Spain had ever sent northward. He was to be assisted by two other newly arrived officers: Lieutenant Salvador Fidalgo and Ensign Manuel Quimper. The first item in Bodega's secret instructions to his new commandant stated that the expedition's primary objective was to fortify Nootka before some other power took over. Next, he was to explore the entire coast, including the Strait of Juan de Fuca. All the officers were ordered to compile detailed reports on the native civilization. On February 3, 1790, the Eliza expedition left San Blas.

Fortunately for Eliza, when he arrived at Nootka April 4th, the port was still unoccupied by either English or Russians. The Mowachaht, who considered the sheltered cove a prime campsite, pulled up stakes and moved. They had been alienated by Martínez's killing of Chief Callicum. But Chief Maquinna also had good reason to fear Spanish control. Meares' allegations that the chief had engaged in both gustatory and possible periodic ritual cannibalism had become a major issue among the Spaniards. Whether or not he was guilty, his continuance in power was threatened by the charges.

Most of the Spanish naval officers who served under Eliza continued to accept earlier reports that the natives practised gustatory cannibalism. Lieutenant Salvador Fidalgo believed his suspicions were confirmed when he was offered a child's preserved hand in barter for abalone shells. Horrified, Fidalgo ordered the native seller to depart immediately from the side of his ship

(Archer 1992, 37; Fisher 1993, 150: citing Fidalgo report). In describing native food preparation and eating habits, Eliza noted in passing that some slaves were fattened for eating during times of famine or at special ceremonies such as the annual observance of the first whale kill (Archer 1992, 37-38; Fisher 1993, 150: citing Eliza report).

Near the end of June, the naval officer Jacinto Caamaño arrived in command of the frigate *Princesa,* and he set to work assisting Eliza. Highly critical of the native lifestyle, Caamaño became a key figure in recirculating gruesome stories about Maquinna's alleged cannibalistic habits. Shortly after arriving at Nootka, he recorded in his diary that Eliza had received a disturbing report[1] from some natives:

There are only two chieftains who eat human flesh. One lives in Tahsis, at the foot of a very high mountain of this name, which one reaches by one of many arms of the sound and is about eight or nine leagues away. The other is called Maquinna: one of the most prominent and closest to our establishment.

This cruel man has eaten eleven children, which he bought for this purpose and raised to seven or eight years of age, executing this detestable act when it seemed to him they were ready, or his evilness prompted it.

Placing the unfortunate victim before him and closing his eyes, as if to symbolize the horror that such an abominable deed caused his nature and humanity, he began to beat the air with a club until one of the blows struck [the victim's] head. At once he quartered and cut it into strips, separating flesh from bones, eating it raw in great mouthfuls, shouting and making fearsome gestures and grimaces.

After we had confirmed this with Englishmen of the *Argonaut* [commanded by Captain James Colnett], Maquinna came by and we gave him to understand, as well as we could, the great evil in this and [we told him that] if we heard he repeated the practice, we would go to his village, burn it and kill everyone there.

This admonition had the desired effect. Previously it had been determined he should be whipped, but this was not put in practice to avoid driving the Indians away. After three or four days he brought a little girl to sell, whom I bought for a sheet of copper and gave the name Dolores. Since she was of the said age, I inferred that she was being kept for such a depraved objective. This he denied and he assured was only a charge made against him by those of other villages. What is certain is that before this they brought the legs and arms of children to our ships in order to sell them to us. (Caamaño 1938, 84-85)

Caamaño's diary entry raises some awkward questions. Did he record a report that Eliza actually received from natives, or did he simply plagiarize Meares' two-year-old tale, as Father Espi also seemed to have done? If English mariners confirmed the allegation that Maquinna sacrificed a specific number of slave children, why is their documentation of such remarkable information missing? Did any European ever see Maquinna perform the sacrificial acts that were alleged by Meares, Caamaño, and (probably) Espi?

Caamaño seems to have left us a paraphrased story, unconfirmed allegations, and no eyewitness evidence of either gustatory or ritual cannibalism. But his mention of Maquinna using a "club" to kill his victims is one of the rare references in any records to the ceremonial use of this type of weapon, which is widely identified as a "slave-killer" in museum collections. Caamaño probably did not know this at the time. But, given what we now know about this unique instrument, his reference to it tends to corroborate Eliza's report that Maquinna may have sacrificed slaves during the annual whale hunt ceremony.

To put Eliza's allegation in perspective, let us look briefly at the role of slavery in Northwest Coast Indian society.

* * *

Slavery and Social Status — The Spaniards purchased many aboriginal children on the Pacific Northwest Coast, justifying their actions as benevolent efforts to save enslaved youngsters from being killed and eaten. Meanwhile, their countrymen in the Californias were trying to create a huge work force of native slaves, but the scheme would prove ineffectual. Slavery among American Indians, including those on the northwest coast, had a 2,500-year-old functional role that was never fully understood or appreciated by the Spanish.

The Northwest Coast Indians maintained a sharp division between freemen and slaves — largely war captives. In the early 1800s, slaves made up 10 to 30 percent of the total populations of

Nootka Chief Tlupananul, *drawn by Tomás de Suría in 1791.*
As Maquinna's main rival, Tlupananul controlled central Nootka Sound
and the Tlupana Inlet groups. (Courtesy: Museo Naval)

various tribes. They were an oppressed class whose function included producing food for their masters by hunting and fishing, doing menial work around the village, and paddling huge seagoing canoes. They helped produce the wealth necessary for the potlatch and they relieved higher ranked people from subsistence activities. Regardless of their former status, all slaves were reduced to the level of productive capital. As a chief could destroy or give away any valuable possession at a potlatch to show his disdain for wealth, he could also sacrifice any number of slaves for the same reason.

Most authorities have said freemen on the northwest coast consisted of two categories: nobles and commoners. The privileged nobility was limited to chiefs, their wives, and their first-born children. But, because chiefs often had multiple wives and numerous offspring, the nobility was sizeable. All the other freemen were commoners. No two persons held exactly the same status, but a definite hierarchy existed. As a birthright, each individual occupied a unique position on a graded scale of kinship from highest to lowest.

Potlatches among the Mowachaht had three distinctive characteristics. Only chiefs hosted the ceremonies; commoners took charge of the feasts. There was a minimum of competition, destruction of property, or shaming of rivals. All potlatches were given for relatives and served to dramatize religious rites, formally pass on privileges, and reinforce lines of descent (Rosman and Rubel 1971, 87-88, 104).

During early prehistoric times and possibly as late as the pre-contact era, some slaves, taken as war captives, may have been sacrificed as part of social, hunting, or religious ceremonies on the Pacific Northwest Coast. But it probably had nothing to do with gustatory cannibalism. If such sacrifices occurred, the ritual was a functional aspect of the society's system for perpetuating itself economically, socially, and spiritually. This aspect of ritual cannibalism will be examined further in chapters four and eleven.

* * *

Southern Kwakiutl Chief, *drawn by José Cardero in 1791.*
(Courtesy: Museo de América)

The Malaspina Investigation — While Eliza was still in command at Nootka, the eminent explorer-scientist Alejandro Malaspina stopped at the outpost for two weeks in the fall of 1791. He was returning from an expedition to Alaska. Trained as a natural scientist, Malaspina had proposed a "politico-scientific" voyage around the world. In the end, he had to settle for another expedition in search of the Northwest Passage. But he and his fellow scientists would gather important geographic and ethnographic information about the northwest coast of America. In the process, Malaspina investigated each charge of cannibalism that had been levelled against Maquinna and his people. The remainder of this chapter is devoted to summarizing that broad investigation, evaluating the findings, and describing its immediate aftermath.

Some of the information Malaspina considered was collected by his subordinates. For example, Chief Natsapa, who had acquired considerable Spanish, assured Antonio Tova, one of Malaspina's officers who interviewed him at length, that the Mowachaht did not eat human flesh (Inglis 1992, 96). But Lieutenant Ramon Saavedra heard rumours from other natives that a shortage of salmon had forced Natsapa to travel northward to kidnap Nuchatlet boys for food (Archer 1992, 41; Fisher 1993, 152: citing Saavedra report).

Ciriaco Cevallos, one of two lieutenants who visited Maquinna unexpectedly at his camp at the head of Tahsis Inlet, remained skeptical about the non-existence of cannibalism. He reasoned that since "this chief knows that the Spaniards disapprove of, and perhaps have punished, this odious custom, nothing would be more natural than to deny it." He said: "This is a point that needs new information. Meanwhile, following the testimony of a traveler [Cook] whose authority cannot be more respected, it is necessary to believe that the Nootkas are anthropographi [i.e. anthropophagi]" (Cutter 1991, 101-02: translation of Cevallos log entry). As we have seen, the comments Cook actually made in his journal about cannibalism were limited, ambiguous, and tactful. But Cevallos, who had only been exposed to exaggerated statements attributed to Cook in the published version, concluded the British captain had left no doubt that "this custom which degrades and dishonours the human species was common in the year 1778 among all the inhabitants of Nootka" (Cutter 1991, 90: translation of Cevallos log entry).

Like most of the Spaniards at Nootka, Malaspina's officers suspected that Maquinna had cannibalistic tendencies. But the commander remained unconvinced. Troubled by the nagging question, the natural scientist made a detailed investigation of both past and contemporary reports. (The extent to which modern historians have relied on Malaspina's examination was noted in the introduction.)

Malaspina recognized that Captain Cook, "who viewed with truly philosophical eyes the customs of the nations which he visited, marveled at the great number of bones, skulls and human hands which were on various occasions offered in trade." However, Malaspina reasoned that uncivilized men often treated their enemies cruelly and that dismemberment alone did not incriminate the Mowachaht of the "extraordinary inhumanity" of eating human flesh "for mere lust" (Novo y Colson [1885] 1934, 2:219).

Malaspina also noted that Captain Meares had "methodically and fully asserted positive reasons to adduce the fact" of Maquinna's cannibalism (218). However, he suggested Meares may have slanted the picture by not reporting all the facts when he wrote about the bogus Dr. Mackay, who lived at Nootka for a year after Captain Strange had left him there in 1786 under Maquinna's protection. Mackay was the first European to live among the Mowachaht on their terms for any length of time. But soon after going ashore, he made two mistakes (Walker 1785-86, 180-81). First, he not only imprudently let Maquinna fire his musket, but he went so far as to take the firing mechanism apart and share the pieces with the curious natives. The parts disappeared, Mackay was disarmed, and his prestige was shattered. Next, he innocently broke a taboo by stepping over Maquinna's favourite child.[2] Treated as an outcast, he was forced to spend the winter living under trees and begging for handouts. The Mowachahts endured a severe food shortage that winter, and Mackay nearly starved. But apparently he had not feared being eaten by his host nor did he hear of other chiefs eating human flesh during the famine.

"It is to be supposed thus," said Malaspina "because surely Captain Meares would not have omitted such an important point in his article 'The Story of Mr. Mackay,' as it would tend to prove

[that] Maquinna and his subjects [were] cannibals" (Novo y Colson [1885] 1934, 2:219).

In June 1787, Mackay was finally picked up by Captain Charles Barkley and taken back to the Orient. But shortly after his return, the former ship's "doctor" drank himself to death, and he left no written record of his experiences among the Mowachaht.[3]

According to Malaspina, it was largely rumour that led Meares and most of those in the Spanish settlement to reach such uniform conclusions about cannibalism. He also pointed out inconsistencies in the reports.

For example, Malaspina noted that one child whom Maquinna sold to Eliza claimed that Maquinna "truly enjoyed human flesh, and that selection of the child for this horrible banquet depended on the one to which his hand pointed while his eyes were blindfolded." This seemed to confirm Meares' story. But Malaspina then pointed out that "there is no record of the ceremonies that Captain Meares describes or the use of adult men, or finally the participation of the other chiefs." He said: "Our officers have accused them and even threatened them, but they nevertheless continued to deny this deed with as much consistency as our people maintained in believing it" (Novo y Colson [1885] 1934, 2:219). He concluded:

> There is no other data with which to incriminate Maquinna except the simple account of a child of eight years, whose interpretation is doubtful. Different visits to his village have never provided the slightest indication of this terrible practice, or of the fragments of a recent sacrifice of this type. Finally, the more we saw the friendly character of the other chiefs, the more we were disposed to clear them of this inhuman act. (220)

One begins to see how the lurid story of Maquinna's alleged sacrifices was recirculated through gossip, rumour, hearsay, and the allegations of children.

To counter this kind of evidence, Malaspina cited a letter written by Joseph Ingraham, a young American mariner who had recorded his observations at Nootka in 1788-89. "We might add," wrote Malaspina "that Mr. Ingraham, the pilot of the *Columbia,* describing in a letter to [Captain] Martínez all that he had seen among these natives during a long winter, did not indicate the least suspicion of this horrible tendency in Maquinna" (Novo y Colson [1885] 1934, 2:220).

Ingraham, had served as first mate under Captain Robert Gray aboard the *Lady Washington.* As mentioned in chapter two, this ship had wintered at Friendly Cove in 1788-89. In July, Gray exchanged ships with John Kendrick at Nootka and sailed, with Ingraham aboard, for Boston via China aboard the *Columbia.* On its departure, Ingraham handed Martínez a long letter (Ingraham 1789). It gave a full account of Indian customs, a detailed geographic description, and a small Mowachaht vocabulary. Although Ingraham's cursory observations were largely a collection of hearsay by those who had visited the coast, his report nevertheless remained the best ethnographic information available until the Spanish made their scientific investigations in 1791.

As Malaspina noted, Ingraham's letter did not indict Maquinna as a cannibal, and the Spaniard relied on this document to defend the chief's innocence. But Ingraham's correspondence was so insubstantial it left little indication of how he viewed Maquinna or the Mowachaht regarding cannibal practices. To determine Ingraham's actual opinions on the topic, we have to turn to his other writings.

Unfortunately, Ingraham's journal of his voyage around the world on the *Columbia* in 1789-90 has been lost, so we do not know what he might have recorded in it concerning cannibalism on the Pacific Northwest Coast. But his next journal gave a revealing clue. In June 1791, Ingraham returned to Nootka in command of the brigantine *Hope* — the third American vessel to engage in fur trading there. Ingraham cruised among the Queen Charlotte Islands for two months, befriending several Indian chiefs. He described the Haida language and customs in some detail. On September 2, *en route* to Canton to sell his furs, Ingraham made the following journal entry:

I believe they are cannibals. Yet this arises from no ocular de-
monstration but from their own confession and declaration that
they had eaten men and that their flesh was good. There can be
little doubt, however, that people resembling those I had seen
to the southward [presumably the Mowachaht and their neigh-
bours] in so many particulars could not deviate from them in
this. (Kaplanoff 1971, 1:153-56)

Ingraham's shallow summary of hearsay makes it clear that he did
not question the stereotypical view of cannibalism held by most of
his fellow mariners. This would seem to make him one of the
weakest witnesses Malaspina could have selected to support his
contention that Maquinna did not eat human flesh.

Nevertheless, Malaspina became convinced that, if cannibal-
ism existed at all among the Mowachaht, it was only practised by
Maquinna. Pursuing his investigation, he turned to information
gathered from the natives:

In asking the young Teyocot, brother-in-law of Maquinna, what
were the foods of the chief, he always answered that it was con-
fined to fish, deer, herbs and roots, without ever even remotely
mentioning human flesh.

Nanikius [Chief Nanaquius], who at first answered our
questions in the affirmative, soon convinced us that we had mis-
understood him and he denied with horror even the idea of
such a feast.

Finally, Natzape [Natsapa] — to whom we were for a long
time a sad reminder of the arrival of Captain Cook at this port —
assured us that the hands, heads and bones presented aboard
the *Resolution,* were only fragments of the remains of enemies
and that the marks of a few bites on the hands were not unusual,
because the infuriated *michimis* (commoners) were used to vent-
ing their fury in this way. Neither he nor Maquinna would be
capable of making a banquet of human flesh, an idea which dis-
gusted him extremely, making him use the words *"pishek, pishek*
(bad, bad)" and even to tell Maquinna of the unjust suspicions
that we had formed concerning him. (Novo y Colson [1885]
1934, 2:220)

The most interesting piece of information here is Natsapa's disclosure that some of the body parts brought aboard Cook's ship in 1778 not only showed "burn marks" as he reported, but also "a few bites." But Malaspina concluded that this was just as indicative of the warriors' fury as it was of alleged gustatory cannibalism.

Next, Malaspina attacked Meares' logic in concluding that Maquinna was guilty of cannibalism because he had been in possession of a human hand and Mr. Millar's ring. First, he said Meares misinterpreted the chief's "confusion" as guilt. Malaspina reasoned that Maquinna could not have eaten the officer's flesh because the man had been murdered in another "kingdom" south of Juan de Fuca Strait. (Malaspina overlooked the fact that the "confusion" Meares noted in Maquinna's explanations actually described the *contradictory* nature of the chief's remarks, not his guilt.)

Second, Malaspina argued that, based on Meares' own characterization of Anapi and Callicum, it was unlikely they had feasted on human flesh. He also said Callicum was a more likely suspect than Maquinna because he had been "the one who used a bag of human fragments for a pillow." Meares had reasoned that the bones could have belonged to Callicum's "ancestors" (Novo y Colson [1885] 1934, 2:223).

Finally, Malaspina pointed to a contradiction. On the one hand, Meares had claimed that Maquinna had boasted about a recent cannibalistic banquet, which he attributed to "all the tribes of Nootka, except the beneficent Callicum." On the other, Dr. Mackay had reported a near famine in the winter of 1786, but it was known that the Mowachaht possessed numerous slaves who presumably would have been eaten by gustatory cannibals. Malaspina suggested the latter facts outweighed the implications of Maquinna's alleged boast (221). He concluded: "The assertions of Captain Meares on the question of cannibalism were precipitate" (220).

Case closed on cannibalism at Nootka? That is what historian Donald Cutter would have us conclude. But first, one must examine Malaspina's impartiality and credibility. Did he look at the evidence with an open mind or was he too preoccupied with discrediting Meares, whom he despised and mistrusted? On the one hand, Malaspina scoffed at the testimony of a youngster who feared for his life. On the other, he accepted at face value the evidence of Natsapa, Maquinna's subordinate chief, who was a major rival. It may have seemed unlikely that children would know much about the chief's secret rituals, but Natsapa was certainly not impartial.

Which of the two captains was in a better position to analyze Maquinna's character? Malaspina was a liberal-minded intellectual and a proud scientist. As a product of the Enlightenment, he tended to question previously held doctrines and values, and he believed strongly that empirical observation would lead to increased understanding and universal human progress. But he had only 15 days to study the chief and no knowledge of the native language. His investigation occurred after two traumatic events: Callicum's treacherous murder by a Spanish officer and the equally deceitful seizure of Nootka. So Malaspina's inquiry was probably impeded by suspicion and fear among the natives.

In contrast, Meares enjoyed months of intimate communication with Maquinna and other Mowachahts under the most auspicious circumstances. The wily fur trader's business practices were not always above board, but he was worldly wise and a savvy judge of people. Many mariners accepted his findings without question, but it was certainly in his interest to scare off potential competition with frightening tales of cannibalism and other cruelties by the natives.

The reader will have to decide which of these two men should be given the most credence. The point is, Malaspina's findings did not end the controversy. After his brief stay at Nootka, other mariners added their observations to the record. First-hand testimony about cannibalism continued to accumulate, piling up more and more circumstantial and hearsay evidence. All of it forces contemporary historians to raise some new questions about the Europeans' treatment of native people.

"Rescuing" Native Slaves — Some of the information Malaspina included in his report was personally embarrassing. For example,

Nootka Chief Tetaku, *from entrance of Juan de Fuca Strait, drawn by José Cardero in 1791. (Courtesy: Museo de América)*

he reported that Maquinna insisted on selling him a slave girl. The chief's persistence exposed the Spanish commander's ambivalence about the practice. Despite strong personal reservations about the purchase of slaves, Malaspina tolerated the trade, which was largely carried out by the priests. In Malaspina's opinion, too many children had been bought at the outpost, even though — officially — they were eventually only given to well-behaved men who had wives waiting back home (Novo y Colson [1885] 1934, 1:283; 2:230). When he left Nootka on August 28, 1792, Malaspina said his ships carried at least "22 children of both sexes," who were sold indiscriminately by Maquinna or lesser chiefs (230).

They usually obtained for each child one or two copper sheets or at times a rifle or a few yards of cloth. Father Don Nicolas de Luera, chaplain of the frigate *Concepcion,* distinguished himself particularly for his disinterested zeal in this kind of acquisition. Afterward he kept watch over their good habits and their social and Christian instruction. Ultimately he entrusted them for their dress, food, and subsequent instruction to those individuals of the crews who could take care of them and realize some benefit within their families from adopting these children. (231)

The friars believed that Spain's political and religious interest would be advanced by sending the youngsters to Mexico, raising them to adulthood in good Christian homes, and possibly returning them to their tribes as messengers of the new religion (Archer 1973, 30: citing Viana 1958).

The Spaniards may have rescued several orphans and saved some of their lives, but Malaspina apparently believed the trade in children should be stopped. Putting it diplomatically, he said his concerns arose "out of fear that those entrusted with these children might pretend, under guise of religion, to exert a kind of indelible mastery over these unfortunates." In short, the completely dependent youngsters could be forced into virtual slavery in San Blas or even made sex slaves by rank-and-file members of the all male expedition.[4] Did Malaspina's declared abhorrence of the trade in children spur his effort to prove that cannibalism was a myth? If the natives actually did not follow the practice, then continued purchase of children would not only become unnecessary, it would be repugnant. Malaspina's own actions make it even more difficult to understand his motivations. His position on the morality of this sort of commerce was ambiguous. In the end, he accepted six boys from Father Luera, who had bought the youngsters with guns.

The skilled artist Tomás de Suría, who accompanied the Malaspina expedition, said Luera bought the boys "for the purpose of teaching them the catechism and the doctrines of our sacred religion, and then baptizing them." He said the priest's "Christian charity gave us much satisfaction and stimulated us to follow his commendable project" (Wagner 1936, 274-75; Cutter 1980, 75). It is difficult to tell whether this represented sincere religious commitment or a convenient rationale for obtaining servants cheaply. On August 13, 1791, Suría noted:

> There was one [boy] whom the sailors called 'Primo.' He displayed quite a little vivacity and already could pronounce some words in our language. He told us that he had been destined to be a victim and to be eaten by Chief Maquinna together with many others, and that this custom was practised with the younger prisoners of war, as well as in the ceremonies which were used in such a detestable and horrible sacrifice.
>
> Having discovered a way to escape he took refuge on one of our ships. This same day, when it was already night, two children arrived, a boy and a girl, brother and sister, who had also escaped from the fury of these barbarians. They said that they came from the country of the Nuchimas [Kwakiutl]. . . . (Wagner 1936, 274-75; Cutter 1980, 75-76)

Primo's story reflects the rumours broadcast by Meares and other fur traders, which were recirculated by the Spanish officers and friars. As children like Primo provided few details of their escapes, awkward questions arise. Did the youngsters only learn about their colourful misadventures from their Spanish masters? Or did the youths invent these tales to ensure they were taken care of? Whatever motivated the Spaniards, they continued to purchase slave children, ostensibly to save them from cannibalism. After Eliza's return to Nootka from his only major expedition during his stay, his veteran first pilot Juan Pantoja reported that the natives enslaved enemies taken in war and that the chiefs occasionally ate some of the youngest captives:

> Fifteen Indians of both sexes from four to ten years of age have been obtained in exchange for copper and [abalone] shells. The principal land and sea officers undertook to raise and edu-

cate them. They are neither sons nor relatives of these natives but captives taken in wars. Some of the smallest are eaten, an inhumanity for which the commandant, Don Francisco Eliza, has reprimanded them with great severity, indicating that it is something very bad and telling them that if he found out that they were continuing this abominable cruelty he would punish them severely. (Wagner [1933] 1971, 161-62)

Later, the Spaniards purchased at least five more children. The price for all 20 came to 33 sheets of copper. According to Pantoja, "the naval officers, caulkers, carpenters, and some of the gunners [took] charge of their education and training" (Wagner [1933] 1971, 161-62).

In a letter dated July 7, 1792, Eliza reported with satisfaction that, during his three years in the Pacific Northwest, at least 56 children had been bought from the natives at Nootka, Clayoquot Sound, or Juan de Fuca Strait. He said three adult men and one woman had volunteered to return with him to Spain (Wagner [1933] 1971, 154, n154, 190).

Despite the Spaniards' excuses for enslaving native children, the results made their rhetoric ring hollow. Most of the youngsters died soon after their arrival in San Blas. To justify servitude, the Spanish mariners amplified the danger of being eaten that might have confronted these youngsters. Such rationalizations only made the issue of cannibalism more murky. Up to that time, no one had ever found any direct evidence of children being mutilated at Nootka. That would soon change with the murder of a Spanish servant boy.

4

Murder and Unfriendly Feasts

*We understood from the natives that they sometimes
made human sacrifices, and shocking to relate,
that they eat the flesh of such poor victims.*

JOHN BOIT

*Maquinna . . . informed me that it was an ancient
custom of his nation to sacrifice a man at the
close of this solemnity in honour of their God.*

JOHN JEWITT

BETWEEN 1792 AND 1884, reports of cannibalism among the
natives of Nootka Sound and elsewhere on the Pacific Northwest
Coast continued to appear in the journals of mariners, adventur-
ers, and settlers who came to the region. In 1792, the murder of a
Spanish boy sparked a new round of allegations. That same year,
several mariners finally began to acquire glimpses of aboriginal
feasts, celebrations, and ceremonies which seemed to include
some aspects of ritual cannibalism. Two British sailors, captured
in 1803, were forced to live as slaves among the Mowachaht for
two years. In 1817-18, a French mariner visited with Maquinna
and other chiefs, and he was shown the Mowachaht's secret whal-
ing shrine. From 1860 on, missionaries reported scattered inci-
dents of alleged cannibalism. In 1861, an early settler made the
first broad ethnographic study on the northwest coast. In 1878-79,
a Canadian geologist recorded an account of ceremonial canni-
balism among the Northwest Coast Indians. Between 1881 and

1883, a Norwegian mariner and curio collector scoured the Pacific Northwest Coast for native artifacts for a German museum. In the process, he added important details about ritual cannibalism to the growing ethnographic record. It is those late eighteenth and nineteenth-century reports to which we now turn.

The year 1792 was pivotal in Pacific Northwest Coast history. Nootka had drawn widespread attention as the focal point of an international dispute. The remote harbour was visited that year by some of the era's most noteworthy explorers.

While the Spanish established a foothold at Nootka, the Americans continued to record their observations about cannibalism among the natives. On the *Columbia's* second voyage, John Hoskins served as ship's clerk but he was actually spying for the owner Joseph Burrell. In this capacity, Hoskins kept a secret journal. Upon returning to Nootka in March 1792, he made the following assertion:

> That these people are cannibals is beyond a doubt, not from anything we saw, but from their own confession. And much credit is due to them for their diffidence in making it known. For it was not until after they were frequently questioned and an acknowledgement made on our part that it was the case with us, that they would own it. When again they were told we only said so to know if it was their custom, they appeared to be much abashed but with a modest firmness would not deny what they had before asserted.
>
> This inhuman custom is only practised on those whom the fortune of war throws into their hands and is conducted in the following manner.
>
> The men people are collected at the chief's house for the purpose of music and dancing. A number of those unhappy prisoners are at the same time present joining in the sport not knowing whom fate has decreed to be the victim on this occasion, each possibly consoling himself with the vain hope it is not his lot, or mayhap with the more pleasing idea that the time is come which will put an end to all his misery. In the midst of the music, several chiefs enter dancing after taking a few turns. (Howay 1941, 288-89)

At this point, Hoskins ended his journal abruptly. What happened next in the ceremony was left to speculation. Was it a cannibal society dance? On this, Hoskins left us in doubt. But he had already made it abundantly clear how the natives were tricked into saying they were cannibals.

Hoskins' comments were supported by John Boit, an officer on board the *Columbia* who wrote the only complete narrative of the ship's second voyage. Boit was the *Columbia's* fifth mate. On January 17, 1792, he described the ceremonial dance that he attended with Hoskins, which celebrated Chief Maquinna's gift to his eldest son of the name Chief Wikaninish. The latter was also Chief Callicum's brother-in-law.

> About noon upwards of 100 men assembled upon the beach in front of the village, with the King at their head. . . . Their faces was painted of different colours, and their bodies of a deep red. . . . The prossession moved slowly along the front, squatting on their hams. The others [were] standing erect, with three of the King's brothers upon their shoulders [on a platform], who where dancing and runing from right to left in that position while those under them was on the continual move.
>
> The King kept in front, giving the word of command. All their voices kept perfect tune with the rattling of the boxes. The rest of the inhabitants where seated along the beach viewing the performance.
>
> When the[y] arrived opposite the King's house, they enter'd single file, and I followed to see the transactions within doors.
>
> About 30 of the principall actors seated themselves in a circle, and was presented with a peice of board and a small stick. This they used instead of a drum. The whole company then began to dance and sing, and the musicians joining made itt very pleasing. But the smell was too strong for my organs. Therefore [I] soon drew off. . . .
>
> We understood from the natives that they sometimes made human sacrafices, and shocking to relate, that they eat the flesh of such poor victims. However I do not believe that this custom is very common and only happens on some very particular occasion. A prisoner of war is the person selected for this savage feast. (Howay 1941, 386-87)

Were Hoskins and Boit observing simulated man-eating or the real thing? Did the smell that drove Boit out of the chief's longhouse come from cooking human body parts, or was he simply oversensitive? Unfortunately, neither sailor stayed at the celebration long enough to tell us what actually transpired.

On May 13, 1792, the acclaimed Spanish captains Dionisio Alcala Galiano and Cayento Valdés arrived at Nootka from Acapulco. They anchored their twin schooners — *Sutil* and *Mexicana* — at Friendly Cove to prepare for their major exploration of Juan de Fuca Strait and Georgia Strait. The expedition had been organized by Malaspina to establish a definitive survey of these important waterways. It would be Spain's last exploration along the Pacific Coast after 250 years of leading the way in charting those waters. The voyage would lead to their celebrated encounter with England's Captain George Vancouver.

The officers who accompanied the famous Spanish captains reviewed past reports of cannibalism and speculated that the Spanish presence at Yuquot since 1789 had apparently checked what they considered an "abominable" custom (Higueras Rodriguez and Martin-Meras 1991, 131-32). In his original journal of the voyage, Captain Galiano recorded the following observations about anthropophagy, which were deleted from the official account:

> It is believed that some prisoners resulting from war had been destined by the victors to be sacrificed and used for food. In this respect, travellers with incontrovertible facts categorized them as cannibals, but, in the time that their actions were under our examination, there were no signs or word of such horrible cruelty.
>
> We tried to make Maquinna and all his subjects regard [cannibalism] thus, advising them that if they committed [this cruelty] they would forgo all our friendship and good treatment and we would rigourously punish anyone proven guilty of such an abominable offence. Europeans who trade with barbarous nations and bring to them all the evils of civilization, making them acquainted with many things of which they gain

Men's dance on the beach at Yuquot, ink and wash drawing
by Tomás de Suría in 1791. Tents are the observatory encampment set up by Malaspina. (Courtesy: Museo Naval)

considerable knowledge, must try to recompense them with whatever physical and moral benefits lie within their reach. (Kendrick 1990, 79)

Galiano tended to exaggerate friendly relations with the Indian people and he stressed "the dignity and good character of Maquinna." But his pretentious morality and patronizing attitude toward the natives typified the way many white mariners viewed native people: they were undoubtedly cannibals, but capable of adopting more "civilized" ways.

On June 5, Galiano and Valdés left Nootka and sailed south on their four-month-long voyage of exploration. They would return to Friendly Cove August 31 and sail for San Blas September 2.

The conviction among Europeans that some of the Mowachaht practised cannibalism was reinforced by a murder that rocked Friendly Cove September 14, 1792. The harbour was occupied by several Spanish and English ships, most importantly those of Capitán de Navío Juan Francisco Bodega y Quadra and Captain George Vancouver. As official representatives of their respective governments, each of these men had been ordered to implement the rather vague terms of the Nootka Convention signed in 1790. It resolved the dispute started by Martinez in 1789 and settled territorial claims on the northwest Pacific coast. Spanish colonialism in the region came to an end.

Edward Bell was a crew member aboard the *Chatham,* which accompanied the *Discovery* on Vancouver's expedition, and made a complete survey of the northwest coast, confirming English "rights" there. The two vessels arrived at Friendly Cove on August 28. Bell described the murder this way:

A fine little Spanish Boy — one of Mr. Quadra's servants, who had been missing about eight and forty hours, was found most barbarously murdered in a small bight within the Cove where the ships lay. A bloody knife was found lying near him.

It is supposed he was decoyed thither by some of the Indians, under the pretence of gratifying an illicit intercourse with one of their women. But no reason could be assigned whatever for the taking away his life. No quarrel was known [to have] happened between the Indians and him or any of the Spaniards. On the contrary, the Indians enjoyed a happier time since the Spaniards had been first there.

None of his clothes were to be found, but he was left naked with his throat cut in a dreadful manner from ear to ear. He had several stabs and cuts in his arms and on the backs of his hands, and the calves of his legs, and the fleshy parts of his thighs were most butcherly cut out and supposed to be eaten by the savage perpetrators of this act. (Meany 1915, 25)

Almost all of the evidence pointed to a straightforward killing, possibly by a vengeful relative or suitor of a native girl. Lieutenant Peter Puget, who commanded the *Chatham,* believed the boy had been involved in a sexual affair with an aboriginal woman, and he was not convinced that the Mowachaht were responsible (Archer 1992, n43; Fisher 1993, n154). But the missing chunks of flesh gave some of the European and American mariners grounds for suspecting deliberate mutilation.

Captain Vancouver's surgeon, Archibald Menzies, confirmed Bell's general description of the boy's condition and the suspicion that cannibalism had played a part in the murder:

His throat and the right side of his neck had been cut and mangled in a dreadful manner. There were some deep gashes on the inside of his thighs and apparently a small piece cut out of the calf of each leg, though it is probable that the contraction of the strong muscles composing that part might occasion the vacuity. This would be of very little consequence had it not been afterwards urged as proof that the natives, who were supposed to be the murderers, were cannibals and cut out these pieces for the purposes of eating them. (Newcombe 1923, 122)

Menzies seemed ambivalent about whether small chunks of flesh were cut out of each calf (not "thigh," as Bell reported) or whether these wounds resulted from normal muscle contractions around a deep gash. If hysteria about cannibalism had not been so rampant among his fellow mariners, it appears that Menzies might have pressed the second part of his diagnosis more forcefully.

An anonymous Spanish account of the incident, which became the official version of Galiano's journal, described several events that happened after Galiano's departure. It noted that a handkerchief lay near the murdered lad's body and that the lethal weapon was an English razor (Barwick 1911, 149). Both Bell and Vancouver remarked that when the murder was discovered, all the natives immediately departed the harbour. Vancouver concluded that this pointed to their guilt. Maquinna's people bore the brunt of suspicion (Vancouver 1913 [1914], 24; Vancouver 1798, 1:402).

The Spaniards who wrote this part of Galiano's journal were apparently Viceroy Revilla Gigedo and his staff in Veracruz (Kendrick 1990, 24-28, n204). They recorded that captains of all the foreign vessels anchored in the harbour vowed to avenge the atrocity. The next day, an American captain arrested two of Maquinna's servants, who were subsequently delivered to Bodega. But the Spanish commander decided they were innocent, set them free, and asked them to urge Maquinna to find the culprit.

Two days later, Maquinna paddled into the cove and berated the whites for arresting two of his people without any evidence of their guilt, and for suggesting that he had any connection to the murder. According to the anonymous Spanish writer, the chief then issued a subtle threat and tried to turn the incident to his advantage. Reminding Bodega of the many gifts they had exchanged, Maquinna allegedly launched into the following indignant soliloquy:

> Our reciprocal confidence has reached the point where we slept alone in the same chamber, a place in which, finding you without arms or men for defense, I could have taken your life, if a friend were capable of betrayal. It would do me and my dignity an injustice to imagine that if I wanted to break the peace I would order the assassination of a boy less able to defend himself than if he were a woman.

Do you not presume that a chief like myself would com-
mence hostilities by killing other chiefs and throwing the force
of his subjects against that of your soldiers?[1] You would be the
one whose life would be in greatest danger if we were enemies.
All of us [Vancouver Island tribes] united would comprise a
number so incomparably greater than the Spanish, English and
Americans together that there would be no fear of engaging in
combat.

Far from doing damage to the Spanish, I am ready to
avenge [the murder]. (Barwick 1911, 56)

Then the shrewd Maquinna alleged that the murder had been
committed by a band from across the sound. He asked Bodega to
loan him a launch and six swivel guns so he could "destroy those
bandits." The chief also cleverly invited Bodega to strengthen the
friendship the two men had formed by sending a contingent of
soldiers on the raid. Bodega politely declined both requests. In
the absence of solid evidence as to the killer's identity, he con-
cluded that vengeance was pointless and retaliation would under-
mine carefully cultivated relations with the natives. He let the
matter drop.

Vancouver and other English and American captains thought
Bodega acted too kindly toward the natives. In their view, he had
been duped. Vancouver said the Spaniard at least should have
held Maquinna hostage until the murderer was produced. "Mr.
Quadra was too good a man," wrote Bell. "He even treated the
Indians more like companions than people that should be taught
subjection" (Meany 1915, 25).

The grim murder convinced most Europeans at Nootka that
cannibalism among the natives was a reality, despite their contin-
ual denials. "Knowing well in what light we consider this species of
barbarity," wrote Bell "of course, when questioned on the subject,
they will not own it." He went on to report that, during the time
he was at Nootka, one of his officers "had a human hand, which
had not been a very long time cut from the body, thrown into the
boat to him from some Indians in a canoe" (Meany 1915, 39-40).

One of the most telling reports of cannibalism among the

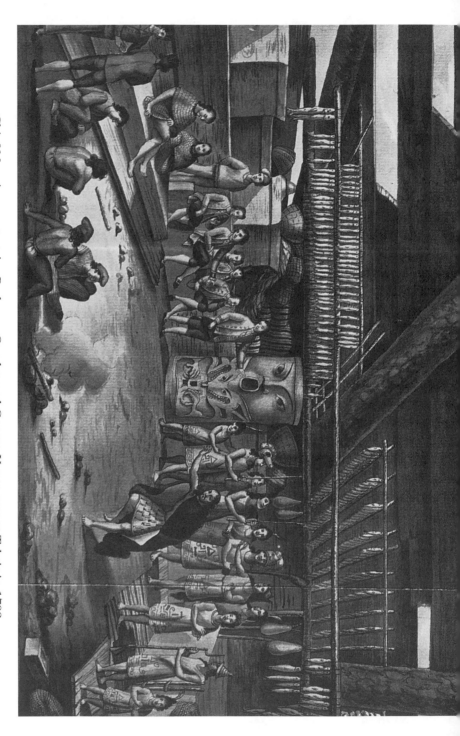

Chief Maquinna entertains Bodega y Quadra and George Vancouver at Tahsis in 1792, *improved version of drawing by Atanásio Echeverría. (Courtesy: Ministerio de Asuntos Exteriores, Madrid)*

Northwest Coast Indians came from one of Bodega's three scientists, José Mariano Moziño Suarez de Figueroa — official botanist on the Malaspina expedition. He was a creole who had studied theology, ethics, and mathematics in Mexican universities before graduating in medicine. He was considered one of the outstanding scientists produced by New Spain in the eighteenth century. Trained as a naturalist, Moziño observed the natives closely during his six-month stay at Nootka in 1792. He produced the most complete account of the Mowachaht's lifestyle at the time of their initial contact with Europeans. Moziño wrote:

> From the consistent reports that the Spaniards and Boston men have given us it appears to be proved in an uncontestable manner that these savages have been cannibals. In fact, they came on board the packet boat *San Carlos,* commanded by Lieutenant Don Salvador Fidalgo, with the cooked hand of a child, and took other limbs prepared in the same manner to other vessels.
>
> Certainly the abhorrence which they immediatcly perceived on our part, and the threats of punishment which they were promised for such execrable cruelty, have made them remove this viand from their tables. Or, better yet, the precious peace which they have enjoyed has not permitted them to be supplied with prisoners, the unfortunate victims who became entombed in their stomachs.
>
> Prince Hawitl [one of the scientist's informants] assured me that not everyone had eaten flesh, nor did they all the time, just the fiercest warriors when they prepared to go to war. I doubt the truth of this story, because this wise Indian knew very well how much we detested this custom, and now that he could not contradict what so many honest men had said, he wanted at least to diminish the gravity and circumstances of a crime that makes even nature shudder. (Wilson [1913] 1970, 22-23)

Considering the thoroughness of Moziño's study, which is still in use, it is unlikely he would have distorted any aspect of native culture. But his conclusions about the existence of gustatory cannibalism were surprisingly unequivocal. They were not based on his own observation and he rejected the explanation of an informant whom he usually considered reliable. Given the extensive documentation of trophy-taking that we have examined and the more elusive indications of ritual cannibalism that have begun to appear, it would seem that Prince Hawitl was closer to the mark.

After implementation of the Nootka Convention began in 1792, Spain gave up its claim to the northwest coast. The Spanish failed to develop economic reasons for remaining at Nootka. Without such a trading base, the Spaniards were incapable of taking on the task of converting the natives. By 1794, the isolated settlement was little more than a liability. Madrid sought negotiated frontiers that would protect the thinly settled Franciscan missions in California. When Spain went to war against Britain and France in 1793, the Mexican viceroys had to devote more of their resources to defending the settled coasts of Mexico and California. Spanish reports about the Indian culture, which had been thoroughly recorded during the flood tide of exploration, now all but ceased. Some of their findings, including the issue of cannibalism, also tended to be overlooked if not ignored as British and American influence dominated the settlement of the Pacific Northwest.

As the fur trade began to slacken so did the area's strategic economic and political importance. But in March 1803, another incident occurred at Nootka that added yet one more account of ritual cannibalism to the record, this time by an eyewitness. When the English brigantine *Boston* stopped to trade for furs, Maquinna and his warriors massacred the ship's entire crew, except for two sailors: armourer John Jewitt, 19, and an older seaman named John Thompson. Both men were enslaved by Maquinna for two years. Jewitt recorded his experiences in a secret journal, subsequently published in different versions, each of which captured the public's imagination.[2]

On December 13 and 21, Jewitt observed the beginning and end of an annual wolf dance initiation ceremony — the primary Mowachaht religious ritual.[3] "It terminated on the 21st with a most extraordinary exhibition," wrote Jewitt. "Three men, each of whom had two bayonets run through his sides, between the ribs, apparently regardless of the pain, traversed the room, backwards and forwards, singing war songs, and exulting in this display of firmness" (Stewart 1987, 119).

Offensive as it may have been to Jewitt, this kind of self-inflicted pain did not signify that the Mowachaht practised either human sacrifice or gustatory cannibalism. The three dancers were probably warriors, exhibiting their fortitude. Jewitt apparently witnessed authentic mutilation. In later years, such displays of bravery were often faked. As we will see, similar forms of trickery were also used in the cannibal dances. If Jewitt had been allowed to watch the rest of the ceremony that first winter, he might have become the first European to see these rituals and judge for himself how much cannibalism was simulated.

In the following year, Jewitt was given another opportunity when he and Thompson were invited to attend the full 14-day ceremony. Jewitt described it vividly:

> It was terminated by an exhibition of a similar character to the one of the last year, but still more cruel. A boy of twelve years old, with six bayonets run into his flesh, one through each arm and thigh, and through each side close to the ribs, was carried around the room, suspended upon them, without manifesting any symptoms of pain. Maquinna, on my enquiring the reason of this display, informed me that it was an ancient custom of his nation to sacrifice a man at the close of this solemnity in honour of their God, but that his father[4] had abolished it, and substituted this in its place. (Stewart 1987, 148-49; Alsop [1815] 1967, 133)

If, as Maquinna confessed, the Mowachaht practised human sacrifice at one time, were the sacrificial victims' body parts eaten during the religous ceremony or was such consumption only simulated? Jewitt's records do not help us answer that question.

The Frenchman Camille de Roquefeuil was the next mariner to find evidence that made him mistakenly assume the Mowachaht practised gustatory cannibalism. Between 1816 and 1819, he made a voyage around the world and stopped at Friendly Cove for a total of 19 days in September 1817 and September 1818. On both occasions he visited with Maquinna and other chiefs, including Omacteachloa, son of the deceased Callicum.

Roquefeuil recorded in his journal that on September 15, 1818, his ship's doctor, Mr. Vimont "found some human bones, which with other indications, led us to imagine that they were the remains of a repast of cannibals." The next day a chief Machoalick, who was a friend of Omacteachloa's, paddled out to Roquefeuil's ship in a large 14-man canoe:

> Omacteachloa and Machoalick passed the day on board and were very gay during the repast. I gave each a present and they endeavoured to express their gratitude and friendship towards me. I thought this would be a good opportunity to find out the secret respecting the bones which our surgeon had seen.
>
> I therefore went with him to the spot and questioned Machoalick, who confirmed our conjecture, that this place, some hundred paces in the forest, behind the abode of the chief, was consecrated to festivities. But I obtained no positive information on the principal point. He either could not or would not understand, whenever we asked how his countrymen treated their prisoners and whether they eat human flesh. He said the bones belonged to bodies unburied by the bears, which often disturbed the graves. . . .
>
> This place was destined to the repasts which followed the whale fishery. A large trunk in the wood served as a drum, on which Maquinna beat time and accompanied himself when singing. Machoalick entered into details on the subject, which we could not fully comprehend and which related to the ceremonies used by the natives before and after this undertaking, which is of so much importance to them. . . .
>
> I know not whether it was the idea of an abominable repast suggested by the accounts of Meares, which had possessed my mind and cast a gloom over all this scene. But I shuddered during this recital, made at the beginning of the night in a dark and deserted place by an enthusiastic savage. (Roquefeuil 1823, 33-34)

Machoalick was describing ceremonies surrounding the whale hunts led by Maquinna, who was famous for his skill and courage. His chief's hat, topped with a finial, was ornamented with whaling scenes. As a latecomer to Nootka, Roquefeuil was full of mistrust and preconceptions. He recorded his observations with candour but his comments about this incident show how easy it was for non-scientists to misread the significance of native ceremonies that involved ritual, not gustatory cannibalism.

During the next four decades, Northwest Coast natives saw the arrival of overland explorers, gradually adapted to the fur trading operations of the North West Company and the Hudson's Bay Company, and began adjusting to colonists who were intent on acquiring land. By 1849, the Hudson's Bay Company had moved its coastal headquarters from Fort Vancouver, on the Columbia River, to Fort Victoria. The company was given the task of colonizing Vancouver Island for Britain. In 1858, the mainland colony of British Columbia was established. The two colonies were not united for another eight years.

In 1861, Gilbert Malcolm Sproat, a pioneer businessman at Alberni, British Columbia, made the first comprehensive ethnographic study of the many Northwest Coast native groups. Sproat ran a sawmill and supervised the Alberni townsite, including its farming and trade. He learned the natives' language and lived among them. Not since Jewitt's captivity had a white person spent so much time with the natives — listening, watching, and taking notes. Sproat did his best to record what he saw and heard as accurately as possible. But his outlook was not objective. He remained locked in the racist view of native people that afflicted many European settlers. In summing up the native peoples' predicament, he said the "lazy savage" was victimized by a process of "natural decay" that resulted from contact with a "superior civilization."

Most of Sproat's experiences occurred far away from Nootka Sound and he did not witness any human sacrifices. But two incidents of "cold-bloodedness" convinced him that the natives were still practising ritual cannibalism:

I was told by a trustworthy eyewitness of another bloody act, committed at Clayoquot Sound by a native who is well known to me. My informant, while trading on the coast, stayed to sleep at the village. While at supper, he heard the death song. On going out of the house, [he] found the natives assembling to meet canoes on their return from a warlike expedition. . . . The men landed and danced on the beach, many holding high in one hand a musket, and in the other, several human heads.

A few captives were dragged by the hair towards the village. Amongst these were two children, a boy and girl of about twelve years of age, who had been captured by the Indian alluded to [as] 'Trader George,' the rich merchant of Clayoquot.

Approaching my informant in a state of great excitement, he said: 'Me strong. Me brave. Me very strong heart.' Suddenly, he drew his long knife and so quickly severed the girl's head that the blood spouted upwards and the body seemed to steady itself for a moment before it fell.

The demon danced with the head in his hand and pushed on the boy before him. This infernal crime was committed merely to show to the white man that the native warrior had a 'strong heart.' (Sproat 1987, 105-06)

Sproat said the second atrocity occurred within a few yards of his house. As the official magistrate, he proceeded to investigate the incident:

In December 1864, the Sheshaht [a Barkley Sound band], then occupying their village close to Alberni, put one of their women to a violent death. The day before, they commenced a celebration of a peculiar character which was to last several days, and the murder of the woman no doubt formed a part of this celebration.

The woman was stabbed to death by an old man in whose house she lived. [He] probably owned her as a slave and offered her for a victim. The body was laid out without a covering by the waterside about a hundred and fifty yards from the houses. There appeared to be no inclination to bury the body. It was only after the chief had been strongly remonstrated with, that

the poor victim's remains were removed after two days' expo-
sure.

I observed that even after this removal certain furious rites
took place over the very spot where the body had been exposed.
The chief feature of the celebration . . . was a pretended attack
upon the Indian settlement by wolves, which were represented
by Indians. The rest of the population — painted, armed and
with furious shouts — defended their houses from attack.
(Sproat 1987, 106)

"The horrid practice of sacrificing a victim is not annual," wrote
Sproat "but only occurs either once in three years, or else at
uncertain intervals. When it does happen, the sacrifice takes
place during the *Klooh-quahn-nah* season, which lasts from about
the middle of November to the middle of January."

Sproat said the *Klooh-quahn-nah* festival was observed annually
by all the Sheshahts after returning to their winter camp from
their fishing grounds. He described it as a time of celebration,
"during which tribal rank is conferred and homage done to the
chief." Sproat said the observances had lost their meaning and
could not be explained by the natives.

"Until this murder was committed under our eyes," said
Sproat "I was not aware that human sacrifices formed any part of
the *Klooh-quahn-nah* celebration. The Sheshaht at Alberni repre-
sent the practice as almost ancient. The fact that the other tribes
(about 20 in number) observe it, favours this supposition. Their
legends differ somewhat as to this practice, some saying it was
instituted by the Creator of the World, others that it arose from
the sons of a chief of former times having really been seized by
wolves."

Sproat said children were not acquainted with the "secret
institution" until they were old enough to be formally initiated. "It
is impressed upon them that the *Klooh-quahn-nah* must always be
kept up," wrote Sproat "or evil will happen to the tribe." He said
the ceremonies exposed children to "savage" preparations for
war, strange dances performed in hideous masks and accompa-

nied by unearthly noises, and occasionally, "the cruel destruction of human life."

"I have no direct evidence of the fact," wrote Sproat "but I believe that part of the course of those to be initiated would be to view, to howl over, and perhaps to handle, or even stick their knives into, the dead body of the victim, without showing any sign of pity or of horror" (Sproat 1987, 106-07).

Biased as he was, Sproat left us a colourful account of the winter wolf dance ceremony, which seems to have involved many aspects of ritual cannibalism, whether or not human flesh was actually eaten. The specific characteristics of these rites and analogous ceremonies that were practised on the Pacific Northwest Coast will be described in chapter six. Here we only glimpse what occurred.

During the period in which Sproat made his observations of ritual cannibalism on Vancouver Island, the Methodist mariner-missionary Reverend Thomas Crosby, was paying regular visits to numerous Northwest Coast Indian villages. Between 1871 and 1895, Crosby reported in his memoirs that, in earlier times, cannibal society members of the Haisla band at Kitimat ate dead human bodies:

> The various grades of medicine men or conjurers were organized into secret societies, initiation into which was considered an honor, and was solemnized by certain potlatching ceremonies. The principal degrees of honor were Fire-Eaters, Dog-Eaters and Man-Eaters [hamatsa].
>
> The Man-Eaters were a secret society of medicine men professing to eat human flesh. Sometimes they would exhume a body, tear it limb from limb, and stand before the public gaze professing to devour the flesh. The Man-Eaters, when initiating a doctor, went through a most cruel ceremony. To get power, the candidate for honors would go to the woods and be there for weeks, clothed in a bear skin, professedly fasting and having communion with the spirits. He would then come down through the village, and seizing hold of strong men's arms, tear the flesh off to the bone. It is needless to say that these Man-Eaters were a terror to all the people. (Crosby 1914, 319)

Whether his report was true or not, Crosby had not observed such ceremonies. He was simply passing on information obtained from native informants, many of whom had been converted to Methodism. But about 1875, Crosby may have nearly witnessed the arrival of a recently initiated *hamatsa*.

> On my second visit to [Kitimat], years ago, several of the young men had been converted and wished to have a teacher come and help them. After many days of evangelistic work among them, my party were getting ready to leave when one, Joe, came down to our canoe, and said he wanted to go to [Fort] Simpson with us.
>
> I said, "No, Joe, you must stay and help the other boys to be Christians and carry on meetings."
>
> Joe said, "I'd like to stay, sir, but the Man-Eater is coming from the mountains and he'll bite me."
>
> I said, "Surely not, Joe, surely no man will bite you."
>
> He rolled up his shirt sleeve and said, "Look here, sir; here is where I have been bitten many times," and to our surprise we saw that his arm was all deformed by old scars. (319-20)

It was the kind of circumstantial evidence Crosby needed to bolster his preconceptions about "shamanism and its evils." But, despite working among the natives as an ordained minister for almost 25 years, he never saw any *hamatsa* in action nor did he observe a single cannibal dance ceremony.

In another part of his memoirs, Crosby — quoting from a letter sent to the *Missionary Outlook* by the Reverend George H. Raley in 1898 — tells how some Haisla *hamatsa* tried to abduct an infant and a child.

> In [native missionary] Charlie Amos' brother's house (Noah Amos) wild dancers came right into our school and Charlie and his wife tried to stop them, but they were too strong for us. At last one of the men that ate dead bodies went to where Magnus ([native missionary] George Edgar's son) was in his hammock asleep and tried to get the boy and eat him alive. By the help of God, Mrs. Edgar, who was young and strong, was too quick for

him, caught the boy in good time and held him in her bosom.
The wild man went to Charlie's little baby and tried in the same
way to take it. Charlie's wife took hold of the man's head, for he
had long hair, and knocked him down; Charlie came and
helped her. There were fifty or sixty people in the house and
there was a good fight by all for about half an hour, some on our
side and some on that side. (253-54)

Crosby's accounts of *hamatsa* behavior among the Haisla were
only second-hand reports. But, except for his vague allegations
about human flesh being devoured, these stories subsequently
were substantiated in large part by a professional ethnologist. In
1930, Ivan Lopatin, assistant professor of anthropology at the
University of Southern California, spent four months at Kitimat
studying the social life and religion of the Haisla. Relying on two
native informants and three white residents, Lopatin inquired
about the accuracy of Crosby's reports. He found that:

> The [*hamatsa*] bit people indeed. The chosen parts for this were
> the shoulders and arms. It was considered a great honor to be
> bitten by the [*hamatsa*]; therefore, there were always some mem-
> bers of the Secret Society who wished to be bitten during the
> dance. Besides, people who were bitten were paid by the
> [*hamatsa*], each one usually receiving five or six blankets or a
> canoe. The [*hamatsa*] bit off a small portion of the human flesh
> and ate it. As to common folk and slaves, the [*hamatsa*] were not
> careful, but bit off pieces as large as they could. However, they
> did not devour them in fact, but tore and tortured their victims
> and by so doing brought themselves into a great state of excite-
> ment, which was the chief purpose of their wild dances.
> (Lopatin 1945, 87)

Lopatin noted that cannibal society rules required the *hamatsa* to
"tear the flesh of his victim from the bone" (86).

Crosby recorded one other incident of apparent ritual canni-
balism, which allegedly occurred in Stikine Tlingit territory. Cros-
by reported that Mrs. A. R. McFarlane, a Presbyterian missionary

appointed in 1878 to Fort Wrangell, from which all military troops had been withdrawn, "became nurse, doctor, undertaker, preacher, teacher, [and] practically mayor."

> She even rescued two girls from the horrors of the 'Devil's Dance.' Finding them naked in the centre of fifty frantic fiends, who with yells cut them with knives and tore off pieces of their flesh, she rushed into their midst and, after hours of pleading and threatening them with the wrath of the United States, she took the half-dead girls to her own house, only to have one of them recaptured and killed during the night. (Crosby 1914, 173)

Living alone at the remote outpost with a few whites and about a thousand natives, Mrs. McFarlane undoubtedly had some extraordinary experiences and she told a vivid story. But Crosby's second-hand account only added to the ever-growing mountain of hearsay.

While Crosby was sailing up and down the northwest coast seeking converts, the Canadian geologist and ethnologist George Dawson was making a thorough investigation of the area for the Geological Survey of Canada. In 1878 and 1879, he saw no consumption of human flesh, but he did find remnants of cannibalistic religious rites:

> It is unnecessary to say that no evidence of cannibalism properly so called is found among these people, though as a part of the ceremony of certain religious rites flesh was bitten from the naked arm; and in some cases it is said old people have been torn limb from limb and partly eaten, or pretended to be eaten by several of the coast tribes. No trace now remains in the Queen Charlotte Islands of the custom of taking heads. It was formerly common on the west coast of Vancouver Island. (Dawson 1880, 167-68)

As one of the last nineteenth-century accounts of ritual cannibalism among the Northwest Coast Indians, Dawson's reports set the tone of many commentaries that would follow. Seeing no more than feigned cannibal ceremonies — shocking enough for many white observers — most historians and ethnologists would conclude that either gustatory cannibalism had never existed or it had been abandoned. But almost all of them would fail to grasp the deep, hidden religious significance of the vestiges of ritual cannibalism that they saw or heard about.

A good example was Johan Adrian Jacobsen, a Norwegian seaman and avid collector of native artifacts for the Royal Berlin Ethnological Museum. The amateur ethnographer made collecting expeditions on the Pacific Northwest Coast from 1881 to 1883. His travel diary, *Reise an der Nordwestküste Amerikas,* written in German, was published in 1884. Using the Hudson's Bay Company station at Fort Rupert, near the northern tip of Vancouver Island, as a base camp, Jacobsen visited numerous Kwakiutl villages in October 1881. He was often assisted by the station manager's son, George Hunt: the man of mixed blood mentioned in chapter two who subsequently achieved his own recognition as an outstanding ethnographer.

According to Jacobsen, the Northwest Coast Indians were "some of the wildest and most robust specimens of mankind known" at that time.

> Practices of the ancient past, like murder, cannibalism, and other horrors, have been kept under control by British gunboats. . . . (Jacobsen c.1977, 29-30)
>
> In 1859 or 1860, Mr. Hunt watched with his own eyes while the Fort Rupert Indians bound a captured slave to a post and cut his abdomen open, whereupon the [*hamatsa*] filled their hands with the flowing blood and drank it. Later the slave probably was completely devoured. . . . [The] governor sent a gunboat to Fort Rupert to punish the Indians, who felt their strength was enough to offer resistance, and as a result the village was destroyed and all their canoes were burned. . . . (32)
>
> Now the "good old days" are over when they could kill slaves and prisoners of war and eat them without hindrance, but they have found another way, one might say more horrible, to gain

their ends. Nowadays before their great feast they eat the bodies of the dead; and not those of recent origin, but some that have been dead for one or two years. (30)

One must not regard cannibalism as practiced here . . . as a means of satisfying hunger or some need of the human body which only human flesh could satisfy. . . . To eat human flesh is considered an extraordinary privilege which only distinguished people can indulge in after a series of difficult and castigating preparations. A common person could never aspire to this, for one must be the descendant of a chief or other person of high rank to be initiated. . . . For this purpose it is not necessary that they have tasted human flesh, but they must have tasted human blood. This act is performed in the following way: a future [*hamatsa*] suddenly leaps out of the woods into the middle of the village, throws himself upon a person there, and bites him in the arm or leg and sucks the blood. . . . (30)

I saw several persons who had been bitten in this way, and when showing me their scars they assured me that the bite was not painful, for the [*hamatsa*] tears a little skin with his teeth and knows how to get some blood quickly so that in a few seconds he will have a mouthful. As one can see, there is very little left of this initiation ceremony. . . . (30-31)

With the drinking of some human blood the [*hamatsa*] has still not reached the highest rank because he has not yet eaten human flesh. The ceremony when this takes place is carried on with the [initiate] alone in greatest secrecy, and each [*hamatsa*] who takes part in it is permitted to add a carved wooden human skull to his mask. I saw an [*hamatsa*] who had no fewer than eight such skulls on his mask. When the corpse of which they take a few bites is old enough it is supposed not to be harmful, but in using a recent cadaver some have died of blood poisoning. (31-32)

Although he was not a professional ethnologist, Jacobsen's research provided strong indications that the remnants of older, perhaps ancient, forms of ritual cannibalism persisted on the Pacific Northwest Coast. In 1882, Jacobsen visited Nootka and watched a winter ceremony in Esperanza Inlet, north of Nootka

Sound. During the performance, the sacrificial ceremony described earlier by Hunt was pantomimed (64). Jacobsen also observed cannibal dance ceremonies performed by Koskimo and Quatsino natives in Quatsino Sound (71).

Given the linguistic problems and cultural differences involved, it is not surprising that the eighteenth and nineteenth-century accounts were sketchy, superficial, loaded with bias, and extremely limited when it came to providing insight into either the natives' world view or their outlook on ritual cannibalism. The new perspective was largely formulated by a stream of anthropologists who began studying Northwest Coast Indian cultures in the late 1890s. Before we see what they added to the picture, we need to pause and summarize the historical and ethnographic record that we have reviewed thus far.

5

Assessing the Record

*It appears to be proved in an uncontestable
manner that these savages have been
cannibals.*

JOSÉ MARIANO MOZIÑO

HAVING ANALYZED THE historical and ethnographic record
between 1744 and 1884, we can now evaluate the oft-alleged exis-
tence of gustatory cannibalism among the Mowachaht in particu-
lar and Northwest Coast natives in general. More importantly, we
can identify clues that reveal the more significant, multi-dimen-
sional practice of ritual cannibalism.

Two broad conclusions have emerged from the record. On
the one hand, the documentary evidence has failed to demon-
strate that any Northwest Coast Indians actually engaged in acts of
gustatory cannibalism. The natives — who were ready to accuse
other bands of eating human flesh — consistently denied the prac-
tice. The few who admitted it did so in peculiar circumstances. In
any case, no early visitors from Europe or America actually ob-
served such events, nor did the colonizers who came later. Con-
siderable circumstantial evidence was collected at Nootka Sound
by the early explorers and fur traders who congregated there. But
one does not find indisputable serial documentation of specific
instances of gustatory cannibalism which were observed by eyewit-
nesses.

On the other hand, the record has also failed to prove that some other kind of cannibalism never happened, as several historians would have us believe. It is clearly incorrect to assume, as did historian John S. Kendrick, that the historical record only contains one account — Moziño's — of alleged human sacrifice among the Mowachaht. In the previous chapters, we examined at least two dozen statements that bore directly or indirectly on the issue. They were written by men from five different countries over a 106-year period — mariners, priests, scientists, physicians, businessmen, and travellers. Their accounts cannot be cavalierly disregarded or simply dismissed. To the extent that these reports focused primarily on gustatory cannibalism, they were largely, as historian Christon I. Archer noted, "figments of the European imagination." But there was another aspect to many of these accounts that deserves closer examination.

The adventurers, explorers, and colonizers left us an impressive string of second-hand reports about alleged practices and considerable circumstantial evidence. Some of their accounts are sensational, many appear to be based on hearsay, and a few indicate that paraphrasing was common. Only four of these observers — Alexander Walker, John Mackay, John Jewitt, and Johan Jacobsen — qualify as eyewitnesses, and in each instance their testimony is flawed.

Yet the cumulative evidence that at least relics of some kind of cannibalism were still being practised in the late eighteenth and nineteenth centuries seems prodigious, consistent, and convincing. If the full record is taken at face value, it helps to explain the general, superficial, and incorrect conclusions that the early voyagers reached concerning the existence of gustatory cannibalism among the natives. Viewed in the context of the cultural clash that occurred at Nootka, those accounts leave a different impression today. First, they make it certain that the alleged cannibalism was not dietary in nature. Second, they force us to ask new questions. The most important are: Did any of these cannibalistic remnants represent previous or existing forms of ritual cannibalism? Did these rites involve actual as well as simulated man-eating?

My analysis of these reports, viewed against the context in which they were made, leads me to six conclusions about the issue of gustatory cannibalism.

1. *Only one account — Walker's — contained a valid first-hand, eye-witness observation of human flesh being consumed. But even his consci-entious probe, which was one of two pivotal reports, fails to resolve the issue.*

Several reports implicated Maquinna directly, but none was made by an individual who saw the chief eat human flesh without being provoked to do so by a European or American visitor. Three Franciscan friars claimed that Maquinna sacrificed and ate a slave, but they were probably recycling rumours started by Meares — a devious individual with a notorious reputation for self-serving exaggeration, distortion, and lies. Meares claimed the chief confessed to "how much he enjoyed banqueting on his fellow creatures." More significantly, Jewitt said Maquinna told him human sacrifice remained customary during annual winter cere-monies until his father abolished the practice some time in the past. But Malaspina argued that the entire case against Maquinna hinged on the questionable account of an eight-year-old child.

It should also be remembered that, despite numerous threats from Europeans who were offended by Maquinna's alleged gusta-tory cannibalism, the proud chief consistently and repeatedly denied engaging in the practice. He blamed rival chiefs and hos-tile bands for insulting him. Those who were quick to condemn Maquinna for his occasional displays of enjoying a practice that they found repellent, tended to overlook the possibility that he could have been either showing off his ferocity and prowess as a warrior or simply pulling the legs of gullible strangers.

Turning to Walker's testimony, we face a paradox. Two histori-ans (Archer 1980; Fisher 1982) have placed great weight on the fact that Walker was open-minded enough to revise his opinion about the Mowachaht being cannibals. They claim his self-con-fessed change of mind does two things. First, it shows that his ear-lier, direct observations did not leave him completely convinced. Second, it discredits the only unassailable eyewitness testimony.

They hypothesize that if Walker's journal had been published in a timely manner, two things might have happened: the numerous fur traders who believed they were observing cannibalistic practices might have had second thoughts; the Spaniards might have been more inclined to question the fur traders' tales.

But an equally strong case can be made for accepting Walker's initial observations and discrediting his later re-evaluation, which hinged entirely on Mackay's dubious testimony. In numerous respects, Mackay was demonstrably an unreliable, probably incompetent witness. He had a reputation for stupidity. By the time Walker talked to him, he was emotionally shattered, physically debilitated, and drinking himself to death. In any case, we do not have his own words. We only have Walker's record of Mackay's limited responses to a few questions and Walker's summary of the other things he claims Mackay talked about, long after the events occurred.

It is also noteworthy that Walker did not insert the significance of Mackay's alleged "evidence" into his journal until decades after the original incidents.

Walker's evidence provides potentially credible observations of some type of cannibalism. But it leaves the central question unresolved: If the Mowachaht engaged in any form of cannibalism, what significance did it have for them? After years of reflection, Walker must have recognized he had scratched only the surface of an answer, which probably had religious overtones. By his own admission, he had been unable to find out much about the natives' spiritual beliefs while he was at Nootka. This explains why he tried so hard to squeeze information out of Mackay, who was, up to that time, the only European who had lived among the Mowachaht. Otherwise, why would a man with Walker's respect for empirical evidence turn to someone whom he knew was both ignorant and undependable?

As subsequent ethnographic reports about ceremonial cannibalism indicate, Walker was headed in the right direction. The importance of his testimony is that he sensed something much more subtle than gustatory cannibalism might be involved.

The ethnographic accounts by Crosby (confirmed later by Lopatin), Dawson, and Jacobsen make numerous references to large chunks of human flesh being bitten for ceremonial purposes, and the consumption of this flesh is either suggested or taken for granted by these authors. Jacobsen asserted that corpse-eating had replaced the consumption of live bodies or body parts. Almost all of the information obtained by these three men was second-hand, based on informants, and circumstantial. But their findings provided strong indications that vestiges of older, perhaps ancient, forms of ritual cannibalism persisted on the Pacific Northwest Coast.

2. *All the reports involved circumstantial evidence and hearsay. They do not give us direct evidence from independent observers of serial acts of gustatory cannibalism.*

Only Meares obtained what might be considered expert testimony from two chiefs who said Maquinna feasted on a slave "every moon." To the extent that some kind of formal ceremony was involved, this might indicate ritual cannibalism. Maquinna's motives for these alleged acts, if they occurred, remain a mystery.

But anthropologist Joyce Wike suggests Maquinna may have aspired to the honour of being the cannibal of his time to outshine rivals and enemies (1984, 241). To make her point, Wike assumed that the various reports of the chief's performances referred to a single ritual. Then she pieced these fragments together into the following reconstruction of what she calls "Maquina's ritual cannibalism" (242-43), the sources of which are Meares (M), unknown persons (Uk), adults (Ad), and children (Ch).

A slave (M) or war prisoner was chosen (Uk, Ch) from a group or selected at random (M, Ch) by Maquina, blindfolded (M, Ch) or with his eyes closed (Ad). The group comprised younger prisoners of war (Uk), boys fattened (Uk), children (Ad, Ch) or children purchased for the purpose (Ad). They stood in a circle around him (Uk) or were pursued by him (M, Ad). This took place in his home (M) before spectators who were only men (Uk), including warriors (M), only the most valiant of these

(Ad), and subchiefs (M, Uk). The inferior chiefs sang a war
song (M), danced around the fire (M), fed the fire with oil (M),
prior to the main action by Maquina who held a club or "instru-
ment" (Ch). He then clubbed the victim, quartered and cut the
body into strips, separating flesh from bones, and ate it raw "in
great mouthfuls, shouting and making fearsome gestures" (Ad),
slit open the abdomen, cut off the arms and ate the flesh (Uk),
cut up the body in pieces and distributed them to his guests
(M).

Viewed as a whole, this contrived composite sketch of Maquinna's
alleged cannibalism bears many characteristics of ritual cannibal-
ism. But, as we have seen, the allegation developed over time and
it was all based on hearsay and gossip.

3. *If the consumption of human flesh occurred, there is no evidence
that it was practised by large numbers of people from all levels of society.*

Some reports suggest gustatory cannibalism may have been
widespread geographically throughout the Nootka nation, if not
the entire Pacific Northwest Coast, but the record does not sup-
port these assertions. Several writers were of the opinion that the
practice was restricted to the chiefs, but no one saw it happen.

4. *Eyewitness testimony indicates the natives treasured, traded, and
cooked human body parts — practices that could suggest gustatory canni-
balism was involved. But other explanations are equally plausible.*

No one reported seeing human bodies or body parts being
cooked. Several mariners and one scientist observed natives sell-
ing human heads and other body parts. Cook remained noncom-
mittal about the large number of human body parts that the
natives offered in trade. Strange dickered with Chief Callicum
over "three hands and a head." Hunter saw cured heads and the
head and arms of a recent victim offered for sale. Meares' crew
was offered a dried up "human hand" and their fellow traveller
Chief Callicum slept on a "bag filled with human skulls."
Caamaño reported Mowachahts trying to sell "the legs and arms
of children." Moziño saw natives bring the "cooked hand of a
child" onto his ship and other cooked limbs aboard other vessels.
Malaspina obtained confirmation from two chiefs that the natives

had, as Cook reported, brought "human skulls and hands" (allegedly showing burn marks) aboard the *Resolution*. Malaspina was told by Natsapa that the same hands also showed "a few bites." But Malaspina correctly argued that dismemberment did not incriminate the Mowachaht of eating human flesh.

All of this circumstantial evidence indicates, at the very least, that trophy-taking abounded, but there is no solid proof that human flesh was actually eaten.

The willingness of the Northwest Coast Indians to go to war to defend themselves and their distinctive lifestyle made it easy for highly biased, often frightened Europeans who did not speak the native language to perceive gustatory cannibalism in unfamiliar behaviour. As British and American fur traders and explorers rendezvoused at Nootka Sound, they read the same reports and passed on news and shipboard gossip about alleged consumption of human flesh by the natives. The factual evidence for these tales remained slim and shallow, but repetition and publication tended to legitimize the central charge.

As tales were recirculated, observations of trophy-taking were transformed first into reports of eating human flesh and then into instances of ritual slaughter by at least one chief. Uncritical Spaniards, such as Jacinto Caamaño and several friars, were duped into accepting a growing myth and perpetuating it.

In any case, none of these early mariners probed beneath the superficial observations and rumours to find out how the natives viewed cannibalism, especially when it came to eating certain appendages. Wike (1984, 245-46) suggests that the Mowachaht tested the Europeans' vulnerability and gullibility, or even attacked them covertly by offering body fragments which they knew were useless if not noxious or deadly. In these early encounters, each party mirrored the other's fears and desires.

5. *Some of the strongest circumstantial evidence indicates the chiefs probably engaged in some form of cannibalism, but their motive — which is critically important — remains unclear.*

Strange watched Chief Callicum eat human flesh on a dare. Meares saw Maquinna and Callicum returning from a battle with a basket of 30 heads. Ingraham said some Queen Charlotte chiefs confessed to eating their enemies. Caamaño, who seems to have obtained most of his information from fur traders, said only Maquinna and one other chief ate human flesh. Suría listened to the pleas of three child-slaves who supposedly were slated to be eaten by Maquinna and the Kwakiutl.

But few of these commentators questioned the motivation of their informants. They neglected to note that the various chiefs at Nootka were competing for the coveted role of principal middleman with the Europeans. Damaging a rival's reputation with rumours was certain to catch the ear of fearful visitors. Furthermore, by spreading such tales, English and American fur traders might have been trying to spoil friendly relations between the Spaniards and the natives so they could continue to control the lucrative market.

The essential question is: What motivated the natives to engage in these acts? Walker was the only early European who both left us his eyewitness evidence and revealed his limited efforts to probe the natives' motivations. He also told us Mackay observed Maquinna's people engage in the ritual sacrifice of enemies. According to Mackay, the preserved hands were "produced at their feasts as memorials of courage and achievement." What was the significance of these rites? Did it merely involve celebration of trophies or did it have a deeper religious meaning related to ancient concepts of ritual cannibalism? The nineteenth-century ethnographic accounts pointed toward the second possibility, but these reports were scattered and cursory.

6. *It is clear from the evidence that many Northwest Coast Indian tribes kept slaves, but there is no unbiased testimony that they were eaten by the Mowachaht or other groups.*

The Spaniards obtained some of these unfortunates, ostensibly to save them from being eaten. Martínez reported that, when he tried to buy some boys from Maquinna and Callicum, "they have always asked me if it was to eat them." He and his colleagues viewed the remark as a clear indictment of native motives.

But the charge also raises an intriguing ambiguity: How much of the natives' trade, first in human body parts and then in young children, was spurred by their assumption that the Europeans' interest in these items revealed their own cannibalistic inclinations? At a deeper level, did these perceived tendencies to favour native flesh represent a threatening supernatural force whose "hunger" had to be assuaged by either actual or ritual human sacrifice?

Summation — Taken together, the six conclusions above make it abundantly clear that the specific practice of gustatory cannibalism simply did not exist among the Northwest Coast Indians. But the historical and ethnographic records, on their own, do not allow us to make such a definitive statement about the issue of *ritual* cannibalism. At this stage of the examination, it is only possible to reach three tentative conclusions.

1. *The existence of ritual cannibalism among early Northwest Coast Indians appears probable, but the extent, importance, and function of that practice needs further investigation.*

Eating human flesh — simulated or actual — played some kind of role in the native culture, but it was poorly understood and badly misinterpreted by early Europeans. Enlightened men such as Malaspina tried to lower the barriers of ignorance that had led their predecessors to form misconceptions about the natives, but none of them gained sufficient knowledge of the new culture to appreciate the significant difference between gustatory and ritual cannibalism. By the end of the nineteenth century, a few ethnographers were beginning to collect scattered pieces of revealing information, but their analysis was shallow.

It is important to note that, of the two contemporary historians who have argued most forcefully that Northwest Coast Indians did not consume human flesh, one limited his analysis to dietary cannibalism but implied that ritual cannibalism existed, and the other stated emphatically that the latter was practised.

In 1980, Professor Christon I. Archer concluded his thorough study by conceding: "Although . . . some tribes had their own dark myths and cannibal dances, it was not the mystery and ritual of the shaman that caused the early European observers to draw their conclusions" (Archer 1980, 479). With the exception of Jewitt, the eighteenth-century Europeans left this influential aspect of native culture almost completely unexamined. Not until the late nineteenth century did Sproat, Crosby, Dawson, and Jacobsen finally begin to probe these rites.

In 1982, Professor Robin Fisher stated: "Clearly the Nootka did engage in ritual cannibalism for dramatic effect. Arm biting and the display of hands and skulls of slain enemies were all part of Nootka ceremonial. But this does not mean that human flesh was actually devoured" (Fisher 1982, 18). In other words, the Mowachaht did not practise gustatory cannibalism, but their ceremonies definitely included ritual cannibalism. Whether human flesh was eaten during these rites or whether such eating was only simulated, the significance of either ritual requires further discussion.

2. *The significant qualifications made by professors Archer and Fisher point up the need to use ethnographic information to illuminate the nature of ritual cannibalism, especially as it was revealed in winter ceremonials — which went largely unobserved by the early Europeans.*

Wike began to address this challenge by surveying, in essay form, the findings of key nineteenth-century ethnographers. But this format's limitations made it impossible for her to link these observations to the wealth of anthropological information that followed.

Portions of cannibal dance and wolf dance ceremonies were observed by Hoskins, Boit, Mackay, Jewitt, Sproat, and Jacobsen. Except for Jewitt and possibly Jacobsen, none of these men watched the entire ceremony. Moreover, none of the early mariners said they saw anything resembling ritual cannibalism because they were not familiar with the concept. According to Jewitt, Maquinna told him human sacrifice had formed an integral part of annual winter ceremonies until his father halted the practice. Early reports indicate ceremonial dances occurred at least annually. Sproat said they had become less frequent by 1861, had lost their meaning, and could not be explained by the natives. In the late nineteenth century, Jacobsen found winter cannibal dance ceremonies that included corpse-eating persistent and widespread.

3. *The reports tell us more about the preconceptions that the newcomers brought with them than they convey about a complex, controversial, and elusive concept that may have been cherished by the natives for hundreds of years. To understand and appreciate the latter, we must take responsibility for the former.*

Western explorers, conquistadors, priests, scientists, and historians fell into the trap of interpreting unfamiliar, allegedly primitive, cultures by imposing preconceived notions on the people they encountered. They tended to see what they expected to find. As a result, cannibalism operated more as a racial, and racist, discourse than as an impartially observed behaviour (Currie 1994, 74-77). The Europeans who settled the west coast of Canada in the nineteenth century, remained generally ignorant of the essence of Northwest Coast Indian civilization.

In the second part of this book, we will take a closer look at the cultural bias that kept our ancestors from understanding the general concept of ritual cannibalism. First we need to gain a more penetrating and complete ethnographic understanding of how ritual cannibalism was practised by the Northwest Coast natives. To lay the foundation for that perspective, we now turn to the covey of anthropologists who followed in the wake of the explorers and colonizers.

6

The House that Billowed Red Smoke

In olden times, when the hamatsa was in a
state of ecstasy, slaves were killed for him,
whom he devoured.

FRANZ BOAS (1895, 439)

THE PRECEDING CRITIQUE of allegations about cannibalistic practices among Northwest Coast Indians from 1778 to 1884 has pointed to the need for a more penetrating investigation of ritual cannibalism. That inquiry began in the late nineteenth century as missionaries sought new converts in what had once been relatively secret corners of the world, and anthropologists probed the lives of native people there. Both sets of newcomers came across what they believed were cannibalistic cults flourishing in many places. We will see that what they discovered was a stunning, sophisticated form of ritual cannibalism which had been practised on America's northwest coast for centuries.

Toward the end of the nineteenth century, one of the first trained anthropologists to study Northwest Coast natives in depth was the distinguished scholar Franz Boas. He worked in the area between 1886 and 1931. Using native informants whose personal reminiscences reached back to about 1850, Boas tried to trace aboriginal history backward to the beginning of the nineteenth century and reconstruct ancient cultural patterns. As a scientific

129

investigator, Boas disciplined himself to follow a method that was intended to prevent jumping to conclusions. He concentrated on transcribing the language, recording a large number of legends that he heard, describing the ceremonial dances that he observed, and documenting reports and explanations given by informants who recounted events they had seen or heard in the past. He postponed interpreting the information until he had accumulated massive amounts of raw data. Boas concluded that some of the ceremonies he had seen represented a highly refined form of ritual cannibalism.

Boas' monumental work would not have been possible without the assistance of George Hunt, the gifted son of a Tlingit Indian noblewoman and a Scot who worked for the Hudson's Bay Company. Hunt's contributions as translator, informant and liaison proved indispensible. He became a skilled researcher in his own right. Together, the two men collected a mountain of ethnographic information. It remains our best source of evidence. But it tends to be overlooked, neglected, or ignored by many contemporary Western historians and even anthropologists. Historians shy away from information that is based on oral tradition, legends, folklore, and native informants. Some cultural anthropologists — preoccupied in the last 25 years with important methodological issues related to interpreting the acts and emotions of unfamiliar peoples in remote times — question the thoroughness of Boas' professed objectivity,[1] and scorn Hunt for exploiting his own culture. In contrast, several native archivists and writers have said they owe Boas and Hunt a debt of gratitude for recovering as much information about the Kwakiutl culture as they did.[2] Regardless of one's perspective, the mountain of material collected by the two men remains a rich source of study, if it is approached carefully. In part, that means remaining aware that one is reading and looking through Boas' lens.

To gain any understanding of ritual cannibalism among Northwest Coast natives, one must make a thorough reexamination of Boas' findings, beginning with his descriptions of native ceremonies and his explanation of their legendary roots. The

George Hunt and family with Franz Boas at
Fort Rupert in 1894. *Photograph by O.C. Hastings.*
(Courtesy: American Philosophical Society, Philadelphia)

winter ceremony took different forms among several tribes. But none of them made it more complex, elaborate, and dramatic than the Kwakiutl, who would later reclaim the name Kwakwaka-wakw. Their ceremonial, and especially the spiritual beliefs behind it, will be described in detail in chapter eleven. Here, we present a general explanation of the *hamatsa* ceremony's legendary roots and a composite description of its outward forms.

The Hamatsa Ceremony — Among the Mowachaht at Nootka, the winter ceremony was called *tsayeq (tseka)*,[3] *lokoala,* or *nonlem* — names that were also common among the Kwakiutl, Haida, Tsimshian and Salish tribes. As we have seen, the Mowachaht featured the wolf dance. The complex winter rituals were usually associated with admission to an elite secret society, the most influential and respected of which was that of the cannibals — the *hamatsa.*[4] Their societies also possessed the most highly prized dances. These factors led Boas to investigate the legends behind these rituals, and trace their roots (Boas 1895; Boas 1935, 140-46).

"The idea of the existence of a spirit who is killing people, is present among all the tribes," said Boas. "The Kwakiutl state uniformly that the custom of devouring men was introduced among their tribe about sixty years ago [i.e. about 1835], and that it was derived from the Heiltsuq or Heiltsuk, a Kwakiutl group that resided from Gardner Canal to Rivers Inlet. There is no doubt that the custom originally was confined to the small territory of [that band]" (Boas 1895, 664). He later said one *hamatsa* dance was received in the early nineteenth century from the Bella Bella along with four slaves, one of whom was eaten during the performance (Boas 1921, 861). At an even later date, Boas noted that during "the first half of the nineteenth century," various parts of the ceremony were received piecemeal by the Kwakiutl "through a number of marriages" (Boas 1932, ix).

Northwest Coast natives had a long history of acquiring attractive customs from each other through intermarriage, trade, warfare, and other means. By 1914, Boas had uncovered even more impressive evidence for an ancient *hamatsa* tradition among the northernmost of the southern Kwakiutl. The marriage history of the leading Gwasilla family in Smith Inlet, which covered 23 generations (Boas 1921, 836-85), indicated that its first *hamatsa* dance was held during the tribe's initial winter ceremonial (848-51; Goldman 1975, 213-14). According to the family's reckoning of its lineage, this would have been sometime between 1575 and 1600. They acquired rights to the dance through a marriage gift from their neighbours to the south, the Nakwaxda'xw, of Seymour Inlet (Boas 1921, 850). The Nakwaxda'xw also provided "two slaves as food for the cannibal-dancer" and his female companion. The account states that "the two slaves were killed to be eaten" and that the cannibal-dancer and his partner did so. As we will see in chapter eleven, the Nakwaxda'xw still perform the *hamatsa* ceremony.

It was impossible to keep such a powerful idea from spreading, especially during periods when native groups were subjected to strong external social pressures. The maritime fur trade begun by the Europeans and Americans stimulated inter-tribal trading, warfare, and increased dissemination of cultural traits, including ritual dances. As noted above, in 1835, an elite Kwakiutl war party attacked their northern Heiltsuk relatives and acquired the coveted *hamatsa* dance and the right to perform its powerful cannibalistic rituals (Boas 1895, 425-27, 664; Boas 1966, 258). The Kwakiutl replaced a previous ceremony which consisted of more limited cannibalistic imagery with the highly prized new performance. With various modifications, the dance spread rapidly to other bands and villages and is still performed today in places such as Alert Bay during winter ceremonies.

Ritual cannibalism was grounded in ancient legends, which were common throughout North American Indian tribes. The legend of how the Heiltsuk's cannibal society began tells that a woman gave birth to a number of dogs, who, transformed into men, discovered the secrets of *Baxbakwalanuxsiwae* — only to be eaten by him.

According to the various legends, *Baxbakwalanuxsiwae* ("He who is first to eat man at the mouth of the river," "Man-Eater-at-the-North-End-of-the-World" or simply Man-Eater), lived in a rock that opens on the high slopes of *Naualakum* (Supernatural-Face-Mountain), which is located in the heavily forested inland region at the north end of the world. Man-Eater was a bear-like monster, whose entire body was covered with gaping, bloodstained mouths. Blood-red smoke billowed continuously from the chimney of his remote dwelling. His room was covered with red cedar bark. He shared it with his terrifying wife *Qominaga,* who, dressed in red and white cedar bark, procured his meals. Her female slave, *Kinqalalala,* rounded up the victims and collected corpses. In the house was a box containing whistles, rings, and the four cannibal masks: *Qoaxqoaxualanuxsiwae,* (Raven-of-the-North-End-of-the-World), *Hoxhogwaxtewae* (Hoxhok-of-the-Sky), *Gelogudzayae* (Crooked-Beak-of-the-Sky), and *Baxbakwalanuxsiwae.*[5]

Two of these mythical birds perched at the door of the foul-smelling house. Raven had the privilege of plucking out the eyes of its master's victims with its long beak. The giant crane *Hoxhok,* which constantly craved human flesh, used its even longer pointed beak to crack the victims' skulls and pick out their brains. *Nenstalit,* or Grizzly-Bear-of-the-Door, also stood guard.

One of Man-Eater's first mythological victims became the original *hamatsa,* or cannibal. The dramatic, gory re-enactment of that myth formed an essential part of Kwakiutl life. The spirit of Man-Eater initiated several *hamatsas* into the private cult. They were driven by a violent desire to eat human flesh. Man-Eater took the neophytes to live at his house in the woods for about four months. After two months, the gaunt, hysterical novices began appearing outside their village, shrieking, "hap, hap, hap" (eating, eating, eating). Piercing whistles warned residents that the *hamatsas* were filled with the cannibal monster's spiritual power, some of which was good and some bad. The savage parts had to be tamed before the *hamatsas* could be accepted back into human society.[6]

Each *hamatsa* returned to the forest and asked his *kinqalalala,* or shaman, to procure food for him. The most important legendary *kinqalalala* was *Winalagilis,* the Warrior-of-the-World who acted as spiritual guide and healer to *Baxbakwalanuxsiwae.* He rarely appears in Indian tales, but this tall, thin black man with a small head and batlike eyes was believed to be constantly travelling about in his invisible canoe.

The cannibal dancer's *kinqalalala* was always a female relative. She linked the human realm with the world of spirits. The natives believed that animals with great spiritual power assisted the shaman to cure illness, to predict the future, and to drive out evil spirits. Animals such as the eagle, killer whale, bear, and salmon were instruments of the gods. The food that the *kinqalalala* supplied came from corpses, which had been carefully soaked in salt water and smoked.

Finally, the *hamatsa* charged back into the village and attacked all those he could catch, biting pieces of flesh out of their arms and chests. To keep him from attacking people in this state of ecstasy, a group of men known as *heliga* surrounded the novice and shook rattles (actual or carved skulls) to calm him down (Boas 1895, 437-39).

Boas said ceremonial cannibalism among the Heiltsuk originally took one of three forms: "A slave was killed by his owner and then was torn and eaten by the cannibals; pieces of flesh were torn with the teeth from the arms or the chest of people; corpses were prepared in a particular manner and devoured by the cannibal" (664). Boas linked both the secret societies and their ceremonies with warfare.

One such ceremony began with a female master of ceremonies carrying a corpse into a longhouse. This *kinqalalala,* impersonating the slave in the original legend, was followed by several *hamatsas* who were scheduled for initiation. When the *kinqalalala* placed the corpse on a drum, all the old *hamatsas* jumped down from the roof and rushed into the room. After the naked dancers ran around the fire four times, the *kinqalalala* cut slices of flesh from the corpse, took four bites and distributed other pieces to the *hamatsas*. As they swallowed the meat whole, the audience kept count.

The young initiates engaged in two dances. In the first, the bare-skinned dancers followed the *kinqalalala* in squatting positions, looking excitedly for human flesh to eat and crying "Hap." When the dance ended, the new *hamatsas* disappeared into a room at the rear of the longhouse. Known as the *mawil,* it was supposed to be the house of the cannibal spirit *Baxbakwalanuxsiwae.* On its front was painted either the spirit's face or that of his servant, the raven. When the *hamatsas* reappeared, they came out of the painting's mouth.

Painting on the front of a *mawil, representing the face of* Baxbakwalanuxsiwae, *sketched by Franz Boas' artist in 1895.)*

In their second dance, the *hamatsas* wore blankets and stood erect. They marched to the beat of batons, taking high steps. Their supplicating hands trembled violently. Typically, their faces were painted black. Some had two curved red lines on each cheek, which either showed where Man-Eater had rubbed off their skin or indicated they were living on blood.[7]

As the dancers saw certain objects in the legend or heard key words referring to corpse, ghost, skulls, cut-off-heads, or maggots, they fell to the ground in ecstasy. When the ceremony ended, the *hamatsas* repaid the owners of the slaves whose flesh they had eaten by giving them blankets.

According to Boas, the ritual and its underlying legend had its source in the advantages that came from membership in the secret *hamatsa* cannibal society. The excitement of the ceremony caused a young initiate who had fasted for some time to hallucinate and "see" the spirit sung about in the myth. Upon returning to reality, the *hamatsa* told about his experience and gained new stature.

Once initiated, the *hamatsas* were virtually licensed cannibals. As privileged meat-eaters they formed an elite group with a special obligation. Their duty was to maintain accord with Man-Eater by sharing his passion for human flesh. But their responsibility was surrounded by taboo.

Human Sacrifice — A thorough reading of Boas' study reveals that the ritualistic cannibalism he observed seems to have been grounded, at an earlier time, in actual human sacrifice. According to Boas, in ancient times, slaves were killed for an ecstatic *hamatsa* and he devoured them. Boas recounted a story told to him by Hunt, whose father and a Mr. Moffat,[8] had observed such a ceremony at Fort Rupert:

> When a *hamatsa* had returned from the woods, a slave, a man of the Nanaimo tribe, named Xuntem, was shot. They saw him running down to the beach, where he dropped. Then all the *nulmal* [messengers of the *hamatsas*] of the Kuexa tribe went down to the beach carrying knives and lances. The bear dancers and the *hamatsas* followed them. The *nulmal* cut the body with their knives and lances and the *hamatsas* squatted down dancing and crying, 'hap, hap.' Then the bear dancers took up the flesh and, holding it like bears and growling at the same time, they gave it to the highest *hamatsa* first and then to the others. (Boas 1895, 439)

To commemorate this event, the tribe carved the face of *Baxbakwalanuxsiwae* in a rock on the beach where the slave had been eaten. Boas said he found several other, much older, carvings near this one (440).

Boas also recorded another eyewitness statement about a slave being killed in Nahwitti (at Cape Scott on Hope Island) in about 1867. "A female slave was asked to dance for the *hamatsa*," he

Southern Kwakiutl guests at a feast hosted by anthropologist Franz Boas in 1894. *Those sitting on the platform wearing hamatsa neck and head rings are members of the secret cannibal society. Photograph by O.C. Hastings. (Courtesy: Garfinkel Publications, Vancouver)*

wrote. "Before she began dancing, she said: 'Do not get hungry, do not eat me.' She had hardly said so when her master, who was standing behind her, split her skull with an ax. She was eaten by the *hamatsa*" (440).

Boas noted that the observer's name was Qomenakula and that the man was alive at the time the anthropologist published his study.[9] According to Boas, the man told him fresh human flesh was much more difficult to eat than a dried corpse. "When the *hamatsa* had bitten a piece out of the arm of one of his enemies," said Boas "he drank hot water after having swallowed the flesh. . . . Nowadays, when the ceremonies have lost much of their former cruelty, they do not actually bite the piece of flesh out of the arm, but merely pull the skin up with their teeth, sucking hard so as to remove as much blood as possible, and then with a small sharp knife cut off secretly a piece of skin" (440).

According to Boas, a *hamatsa* sometimes returned from the woods carrying the corpse of a deceased relative, which he devoured after the dance. He said the bodies were specially prepared. "The skin is cut around the wrists and ankles," said Boas (441) "as they must not eat the hands and feet. It is believed that else they would die immediately."[10]

Anthropologist Ronald Olson found that human sacrifice was allegedly featured in ceremonies held by the Haisla at Kitimat sometime between 1860 and 1875. The Haisla were a northern Kwakiutl people who occupied the region where ritual cannibalism was believed to have originated on the Pacific Northwest Coast. A distinguished Haisla chief named Sanaxet reportedly conducted his first cannibal dance ceremony by eating two slave children. Olson obtained the information in 1935 from five native informants at Kitimat and Rivers Inlet.

> Only rarely are commoners honored by being bitten by the [*hamatsa* or cannibal society member]. . . . This biting is really severe, large chunks of flesh being removed. I have seen old men show scars of half-dollar size which were received fifty years ago. Ordinarily (at least in later times) these bites of flesh are

not swallowed by the [*hamatsa*] but are surreptitiously removed from his mouth by one of the noble women attending him, who places them in a basket she carries under her robe. A famed incident is related how on one occasion some sixty or seventy-five years ago Sanaxet during his initial [*hamatsa*] dance was presented with two child slaves by a Tsimshian chief. These Sanaxet seized and bit, eating the flesh, until both were dead. (Olson 1940, 177)

Sanaxet's alleged conduct seems to replicate the way Maquinna was said to have performed sacrifices seven or eight decades earlier.

The issues of consuming human flesh and corpse-eating were also addressed by the famous ethno-photographer Edward S. Curtis. Relying heavily on Boas' documentation, Curtis shot a large number of controversial photographs among the Kwakiutl between 1910 and 1915. One series included depictions of a wild-looking *hamatsa* initiate from the Koskimo band emerging from the woods, biting a man's arm, carrying a mummy, placing the corpse on wooden stakes above a small fire pit in his hut, and brandishing several human skulls.[11] Most of Curtis' photographs were not taken of live events. He recruited willing natives as models, dressed them in traditional costumes amidst various authentic props, and often had them strike dramatic poses.

"The Kwakiutl declare that the *hamatsa* eats human flesh. . . ," wrote Curtis ([1915-16] 1978, 10:221). "But there is grave doubt whether cannibalism ever existed in British Columbia. . . . Of the Kwakiutl men who can be induced to discuss the subject, all except one [George Hunt] say that substitution has been invariably practised in modern times, adding, however, that 'long ago' human flesh was eaten." But Curtis tried to have it both ways by featuring the native ethnographer's gruesome stories. He proceeded to give four of Hunt's more extraordinary, "substantially verbatim accounts" about the "recent existence of ceremonial cannibalism."

The first incident Hunt recounted (Curtis [1915-16] 1978,

10:240-41) referred to the winter dance held by the Nahwitti in 1867, which Boas had described 20 years earlier. Only seventeen-years-old at the time, Hunt arrived at the village in charge of a Hudson's Bay Company trading sloop and found the cannibal dance ceremony underway. He said a secondary chief named Nunkamais slew the young female slave, burying a hatchet blade in the back of her head.

> Yumqus, an old [*hamshamtses,* predecessor of the *hamatsa*], roughly tore the hatchet from the wound. . . . Then he opened the abdomen and disembowelled it, and cut off the head, which he gave to the initiate. He dismembered the body and distrib-uted the pieces among the [*hamshamtses*]. . . . Others slit the flesh into long ribbons, cutting clear to the bone, and severing the strips at the ends. The [*hamshamtses*] then dangled the strips one by one above their mouths and swallowed them without chewing. They watched one another and exhibited rivalry, each endeavoring to eat more than the others. When they could eat no more, they took the remnants to their seats and laid them down, and after the dance, so the chief told me, they boiled the meat and ate all. . . . At the end of the feast a chief passed me with blood-smeared face, and smiled as he exclaimed, "Sweet food."

According to Wike (1984, 245), this seems to be the only ethno-graphic reference to humans being cooked on the Pacific North-west Coast

The second cannibal ceremony that Hunt witnessed occurred in 1871 among the Owikeno, when an *hamatsa* of long-standing named Awati gave a winter dance at Fort Rupert (Curtis [1915-16] 1978, 10:222-34). Hunt said Captain Alexander W. Moffat, Hudson's Bay agent at Fort Rupert also observed parts of the cere-mony. Hunt and Awati's other young attendants were sent to a burial ground to find a "suitable mummy" for the Owikeno *hamatsa* to eat. His name was Gwakiils — a huge, 260-pound man, with a legendary appetite for human flesh.[12] The attendants had to make sure that the corpse was "not mouldy nor rotten, but dry."

To compete with Gwakiils at eating the corpses of a young boy and a woman, Awati would need the help of two other *hamatsas.*

> . . . Awati, carrying his mummy, was moving backward toward the house, showing the body to the [Owikeno] *hamatsa,* so as to induce him to follow. . . . He moved slowly round the fire, and just behind it he stopped and faced the door, watching Gwakiils and moving the corpse as if playing with something he held in tender regard.
>
> . . . When Awati was behind the fire after the fourth circuit, Gwakiils leaped upon the mummy, took it in his arms, and twisted the head. But the skin was too tough to be twisted off, and one of his attendants came quickly and cut it. Then Gwakiils tore off the head and tossed it to Awati, and himself carrying the headless body he began to sing. . . .
>
> The [Owikeno] singers took up the words, and then Gwakiils stopped and went through the usual gestures and movements of the *hamatsa.* He rolled his eyes, held up his palms, rocking the corpse from side to side, thrust out his lips as if with great desire, then laughed hideously. Next he ravenously licked the body from one end to the other, and . . . seized a knife and rapidly cut the dry skin of the arms, legs, and trunk into long narrow strips. One by one he tore them off, raised them at arm's length, threw back his head, lowered one end of the strip into his mouth, and with a single movement of the throat and tongue he swallowed it.
>
> Awati was holding the head, and did not seem to know what to do. He tried to bite out a piece of the skin, but could not; then an attendant gave him a knife, and with it he cut the skin into small squares and began to swallow them hurriedly. He was afraid. Before he had finished, Gwakiils had stripped the bones of the body. I stood just behind Awati and only two steps from Gwakiils, and clearly saw everything.
>
> After the [Owikeno] *hamatsa* had stripped the bones, separated and licked the joints, and swallowed every particle of the dry integument except that of the palms and the soles, his sister . . . came forward . . . [and] . . . picked up the bones one by one and thrust them inside her robe, and then stood there

beside [Gwakiils] while he seized the skull from Awati's hands. Only a part of one cheek was eaten. Gwakiils put his fingers under the edge of the skin and with a jerk tore off the entire covering of the skull. . . . He tore off the lower jaw and licked it, and pretended to pick off bits of flesh, though there could have been none on it. He threw it down, and his sister put it in with the rest of the bones. Then he picked over the skull, and tried to break it on the floor, so as to get at the cavity. An old man, his father, came forward with a small axe. . . . He took the skull from his son and laid it carefully on its side. . . . The old man chopped it in two pieces, one of which Gwakiils quickly seized and placed carefully in one hand, while with the other he as carefully picked small objects from the floor, put them into his mouth, and ate with great delight and much smacking of lips. I think these objects were the thin brown shells left by maggots. Next with his right hand he scooped out from the half of the skull whatever was in it, probably maggot shells, poured them into his open mouth, and ate them with a crunching sound which I could plainly hear. . . .

Hunt went on to describe how Gwakiils sucked water through all the long bones of the corpse, how the old *hamatsa* had difficulty digesting what he had swallowed, and how he drank salt water as an emetic. In Hunt's eyes, Gwakiils must have seemed like a champion corpse-eater. But he evidently had stiff competition. According to Hunt, Hamasaka, principal *hamatsa* at Fort Rupert, told him in 1910 that he had participated in 32 corpse-eating feasts (242).

The third winter dance described by Hunt (239-40) was held in 1875 by the Owikeno, who invited the Nakwoktak from Nugent Sound to attend. The guests arrived by canoe, but they did not bring the customary corpse.

After they had entered the dance house, their hosts brought forth a mummy and it was eaten in the usual way. During the feast Yahyekulagyilis [the principal *hamatsa*] was evidently revolving something in his mind while he regarded a female slave belonging to one of his companions. Soon he directed one of his attendants, in a whisper, to go and ask the owner if he would take a hundred blankets for his slave. This was a generous price, and was quickly accepted. . . . After the mummy was eaten, [Yahyekulagyilis] rose and led the other *hamatsas* in a rapid dance round the fire. Four times round they went, and then suddenly he leaped upon the slave woman, who fell on her back. Quick as a flash he fastened his teeth on her throat. She struggled, and scratched his face, but he kept his hold, and two other *hamatsas* seized the woman's legs.

When she ceased struggling, Yahyekulagyilis cut a hole around the navel, severed the intestine, placed an end between his teeth, and ran about the fire dragging out the intestine like a rope. While he was doing this, another *hamatsa* was cutting the woman's throat and catching the blood in a wooden dish, which was passed among the *hamatsas* until the blood was drunk. Then the flesh was cut into pieces and distributed, and as there were many *hamatsas* among the Owikeno, there was no difficulty in consuming all the flesh and leaving only the bare bones.

This kind of eyewitness testimony from Hunt and other native informants convinced Boas that the consumption of human flesh by *hamatsas* was practised in the nineteenth century, and that it was indicative of a much older ceremonial rite. Obviously, Curtis was impressed by Hunt's vivid accounts. He conceded that it was "quite possible, even probable, that in earlier days slaves were sometimes killed . . . and corpses were dismembered." But he argued that "at that point the genuineness of the performance probably ceased" and simulation took over (Curtis [1915-16] 1978, 10:221-22).

The fourth winter dance that Hunt described for Curtis ended in either tragedy or multiple murders (241-42). About 1892, the Tlawitsis on Turnour Island invited all the tribes to their ceremony. But the throng did not display the usual spirit of happiness. When an *hamatsa* named Tsahahstala announced that he would get a corpse to cheer up the crowd, about one-third of those present objected to the "old-fashioned" practice. The dissidents wanted to give away property or break coppers. But

Taming of an *hamatsa* initiate reenacted.
*Photographs by George Hunt, 1902. (Courtesy: Department of Library Services,
American Museum of Natural History #22866 and #22858)*

Tsahahstala insisted on using a mummy, and subsequently one was found and prepared by an old man who knew how to do it properly. According to Hunt, seven *hamatsa,* including Tsaha-hstala, waited in anticipation.

> A Nimpkish man was the first to begin eating. No sooner had he swallowed his first piece than his head fell forward and rested on the piece of mummy in his hands. His attendants raised his head to see what was the matter, and he fell back dead. They carried him out at once. A Tlawitsis named Kyemkalus was stricken next. His head fell forward, and then he himself tumbled backward. They carried him out. Then the other Nimpkish, a young man, perceiving what was happening, ran out, got a dish of oil, and drank it. He became very sick, but did not die. Tsahalistala was just starting to run like a *hamatsa* round the fire and out, when he too fell dead. The Mamalilikulla *hamatsa* arose, presumably to go out, and dropped in his place, and the other Tlawitsis fell dead. The people sat stunned for an instant, then silently arose and [filed] out. The dead were disposed of secretly in the night, for the people were ashamed that death had occurred in the very midst of the winter dance. It was reported that [*Baxbakwalanuxsiwae*] had taken the spirits of these men.

Hunt concluded that those who had objected to the feast had poisoned the corpse.

Wike (1984, 252) claims Hunt's story suggests that "corpse-eating was not stopped by threats nor by the conversion of prominent people to Christianity (as in the north), but instead became covert" after the six *hamatsas* were deliberately poisoned by natives opposed to the old ways. Whether the pressure came from outside or inside native communities, or from both directions, the practice of eating corpses soon vanished.

The Haida's secret society held a ceremony each winter that was similar to the Kwakiutl performance. But it had virtually disappeared by the end of the nineteenth century. "The ceremony was repeated many times in a village during a winter," wrote Curtis in 1916. "It has been practically obsolete since about 1875, though sporadic performances were given about 1888" (Curtis [1915-16] 1978, 11:143). But Curtis also questioned the authenticity of actual cannibalistic practices. "No informant out of many interviewed on this point believes that the Kwakiutl or any other tribe ever actually ate human flesh," he wrote, overlooking the stories Hunt told him one year earlier. "At Skedans village about the middle of the nineteenth century an old slave woman dancing in front of the [initiate] was clasped by him and killed by a stab in the abdomen. But no flesh was eaten" (n144).

Curtis is also known for emphasizing the significance of head-hunting among the Northwest Coast Indians. "Astonishment has been expressed that head-hunting existed among the North American Indians, notwithstanding the fact that every explorer of the North Coast region mentioned this custom," wrote Curtis in 1915. "The taking of heads was a common practice along the Pacific Coast from the Columbia River to the Arctic" (Curtis [1915] 1975, vii-viii). This assertion became the premise for his romanticized, highly controversial documentary film, *"In the Land of the War Canoes,"* made in 1922. But, as noted in chapter five, the prevalence of head-hunting, other forms of dismemberment, trophy-taking, and ritual slaughter did not mean human flesh was actually consumed.

In 1930, Boas began shooting his own documentary, *"The Kwakiutl of British Columbia,"* which contains staged demonstrations and reenactments of all aspects of daily life, including the *hamatsa* dance. Boas and other anthropologists would explain how the idea of eating human flesh functioned within the Indian culture. But, like their European predecessors, none of these men and women witnessed actual acts of humans being eaten. Also, most of them wrote about the subject long after such behaviour had been restricted to seldom held, highly ritualized ceremonies, which were never fully understood by most native people. Responsibility for interpreting the deeper meaning of these ancient rituals, practised only by secret societies, had always been retained by a few ritual specialists. For all these reasons, native spirituality remained cloaked in mystery and viewed with suspicion by white society.

The Anti-Potlatch Campaign — By the end of the nineteenth century, the ritual cannibalism that highlighted winter ceremonies had inflamed Canadian public opinion against potlatching to the point that even Boas' highly competent assistant would be arrested for mutilating human bodies.

The gap of misunderstanding between native spirituality and white religion had widened steadily. Missionaries branded the potlatch as "evil," the "work of the devil," and the primary hindrance to what they called the Indian's "progress." To Victorian missionaries and Indian agents, progress meant emulating white farmers and becoming steady workers who did not make enough money to support any major vices. But the potlatch, in many cases, had turned into a form of economic warfare that sometimes got out of hand. Church leaders and government officials deplored the prostitution and bootlegging that they claimed natives pursued to finance extravagant potlatches. The ceremonies also were the only independent, self-organized means of coming together left to the Indians. As such, potlatches represented both a potential religious and political threat to those who were charged with managing aboriginal communities.

Determined to eradicate Indian traditions and force natives to assimilate, the Canadian government had added an article to the Indian Act in 1876 that prohibited potlatching, the shamans' society winter ceremonies, and spirit dancing. As mentioned in chapter four, the native village at Fort Rupert was destroyed by a gunboat bombardment in 1865 after *hamatsas* killed a slave. The ethnographer Jacobsen had the impression that external threats and the bombardment inspired the *hamatsas* to substitute corpses for living bodies (Jacobsen c.1977, 29-30). Neither the historical nor the ethnographic record support this claim, but outside pressure from white authorities was omnipresent throughout this period. The first winter ceremonial that Boas observed at Nahwitti (Cape Scott-Hope Island) in October 1886 was performed under the threat that a gunboat would appear (Rohner 1969, 33).

Revised in 1885, the anti-potlatch law made it a misdemeanor, punishable by two-to-six months in jail, to engage or assist in a potlatch. In 1895, the statute was recast again, specifically to ban cannibalism and animal sacrifice. But the potlatches that Canada tried to ban did not correspond with those which the First Peoples performed. The colonizers' ignorance of native customs plagued the anti-potlatching campaign which persisted for more than 50 years.

The prejudicial messages that fuelled the attack were detailed recently by Christopher Bracken, a graduate student in English at the University of British Columbia (Bracken 1994). He branded the effort to kill the potlatch "an act of cannibalistic nationalism" (ii). He said the misguided attempt to enforce the anti-potlatch law was driven by a concept that interpreted Canada's relation to the First Nations as one of incorporation and assimilation.

"This law that aim[ed] to put the First Nations of British Columbia to death by helping white Canadian society swallow them alive [was], in effect, a law against eating others," said Bracken (148, 215-16). "To facilitate its project of [social] assimilation, the Dominion government . . . had to outlaw the act of [physical] assimilation itself. . . . Who, in the context of Canadian postal-colonialism, [were] the true cannibals — the [natives] or their colonizers?"

Writing in 1967, anthropologist Philip Drucker noted that the Tsimshian and Haida (both of which included few if any cannibalistic rites in their ceremonies), the Nishka, and even some Heiltsuk gave up the "macabre Dancing Society performances" because of pressure from missionaries and Indian agents (Drucker and Heizer, 1967, 31). But it did not stop similar potlatches in other tribes. Drucker said the isolated Mowachaht maintained their relatively conservative wolf dance version of the winter ceremony,[13] and the southern Kwakiutl "enthusiastically continued their 'heathen' practices . . . and, in connection with many potlatches, their cannibal dancers (hamatsa) bit flesh from the arms of their fellows in a horribly gory fashion, and gormandized on human corpses in what must have been . . . one of the world's more appalling forms of public entertainment"(32). As Drucker noted, whether the performances were real or make-believe, they "rarely failed to shock and horrify white spectators."

McIlwraith reported that in 1922, among the Bella Coola (Nuxalk) there was only one man who still had the "unusual pre-rogative of eating corpses." He said "ritualistic devouring of corpses was well known . . . in former days," but "the actual eating of a body was practically unknown" (1948, 107).

With most of the anti-potlatch campaign directed at the Kwakiutl, this group finally modified its cannibal ceremony. Ironically, George Hunt apparently played a key role in sparking the change. Drucker recounted the following story (Drucker and Heizer, 1967, 86-87) about Hunt's experience.

Early in 1900, Hunt visited a Kwakiutl village on a trading trip, arriving in the middle of a cannibal feast. All the active *hamatsa* were present. As an inactive, but initiated member of the society, Hunt was given the special privilege of carving up the corpse and serving it to the dancers. But someone informed Indian agent R.H. Pidcock that his special constable — Hunt — had broken the law.

Hunt was charged with violating a clause of the anti-potlatch law that prohibited the "mutilation of human bodies." When the case went to trial in Victoria, numerous Kwakiutl testified on his behalf, affirming that the alleged corpse was merely a dummy. Hunt was acquitted.

Soon thereafter, a super-council of chiefs announced publicly that in the future only dummies, not real corpses, would be used in the *hamatsa* ceremonies. They also said biting of flesh from the arms of living persons would be simulated (Drucker and Heizer 1967, 87). By implication, the chiefs seemed to concede that, pre-viously, dead bodies may have been used and live flesh eaten on occasion. But the council's assurances achieved the desired result: the controversy cooled down.

The Potlatch as Theatre — By 1936, enforcement of the anti-pot-latch statute had disappeared. But it was not repealed until 1952, after extended negotiation and pressure by the Native Brother-hood of British Columbia.

Throughout the twentieth century, anthropologists continued to endorse Boas' interpretation of the *hamatsa* ceremony's significance, but they became increasingly skeptical about the legacy of ancient flesh-eating practices reported by Boas. They came up with a variety of elaborate, less controversial explanations for what went on during the ceremonies.

One of these anthropologists was Drucker. Overlooking the apparent concession about flesh-eating made by the council of chiefs, he took a position in 1955 that he contradicted 12 years later. "It is highly improbable that corpses were actually used," noted Drucker. "The Kwakiutl were past masters at producing realistic tricks for stage effects. The smoked carcass of a small black bear, for example, fitted with a carved head, would look convincingly like a well-dried human body at a distance by firelight" (Drucker 1955, 151). Yet, as we have seen, Drucker stated in 1967 that southern Kwakiutl *hamatsa* ate what appeared to be "human corpses" (Drucker and Heizer 1967, 32). He left the apparent contradiction unresolved.

The naturalist Vinson Brown, who wrote the ethnographic novel *Peoples of the Sea Wind* in 1977, suggested that all the complex acts of eating human flesh contained in the Kwakiutl ceremonies were cleverly staged tricks, designed to terrify enemies, maintain internal order, and control evil forces. According to Brown, the mock cannibal's "victims" were preselected and promised rich rewards for their cooperation. Instead of biting them, the cannibal carried a tiny knife hidden in his hand, which he used to nick his supposed victim.[14] To simulate spurting blood, the *hamatsa* squeezed a small bladder of seal's blood hidden under his victim's sleeve. The dead slave carried in by the *kin-qalalala* was actually a carved dummy. The chunks of "flesh" swallowed by the *hamatsas* came from a freshly slaughtered seal, whose head and flippers had been replaced by a head, arms, and legs that appeared human. These were attached by a secret method. Ghost voices were piped in from offstage through hollow kelp stems. Monsters emerged magically from hidden tunnels. False heads carried by small boys dressed like women were chopped off. Women who were burned to death in a box, actually escaped through trap doors. Puppets flew across the dance house, manipulated by hidden strings (Brown 1977, 85-88; Drucker 1955, 150-51).

Brown's explanations of the elaborate stage props employed by the Kwakiutl around the turn of the last century are certainly plausible. They are also substantiated by other observers (Goddard 1924, 128-29; Drucker 1955, 150-52; Curtis [1915-16] 1978, 11:143-44). The skill of the Kwakiutl in designing sensational stage effects was unsurpassed among North American Indians (Drucker 1955, 150). But these writers were only commenting on the historic period. Unlike Boas, they did not concern themselves with either the prehistoric legends that undergirded modern ceremonies or the ancient practices that probably preceded them.

The twentieth-century anthropologists and the ethnographer Brown tried to decipher a complex ceremony that involved profound, subtle, deeply personal concepts which were much more complicated than the superficial trickery on display. But their analysis only scratched the surface. It would be a mistake to conclude from these relatively recent observations that, in prehistoric times, nothing more than magic tricks were employed and that all eating of human flesh had always been simulated. To speculate sensibly about the kind of practices that the Kwakiutl engaged in before the eighteenth-century European and American adventurers arrived on the Pacific Northwest Coast, we have to rely on Boas' older, somewhat dry, and frequently neglected studies.

Brown had a flair for description that brought to life a strange, mysterious, and vanishing way of life. But he felt compelled to soften the harsh reality of the Kwakiutl culture's most controversial feature — ritual cannibalism. In the introduction to *Peoples of the Sea Wind,* Brown outlined his intent. "Many outworn and false ideas about native Americans, bred and nurtured by the white conquerors of this continent to justify their conquest and their treatment of those they conquered, now need to be put aside if we are truly to understand and appreciate the varied and wonderful peoples who once owned this land," he wrote. "Instead, let us be free and curious as the wind that blows. . . .

Where the sea wind went in centuries past, we also shall go and see and hear what used to be."

The challenge is to make such an inquiry without demonizing aboriginal people with unsubstantiated labels, but also without idealizing them by glossing over controversial realities. One must extrapolate from all the existing evidence to theorize about what might have occurred in the distant past. Based on the entire body of evidence we have examined, it seems probable that human lives were sacrificed, but it can't be proved. Real corpses were probably used, but it is unlikely we ever will determine whether they were actually consumed or the eating was faked.

In general, these issues are unresolvable. But that should not deter us from our inquiry into the deeper motivations that sustained ritual cannibalism. The sensationalism surrounding marginal concerns has clouded the picture for centuries. As a psychological preoccupation, the alleged ingestion of human flesh became an intellectual distraction and an obstacle to open-minded investigation. Persistent efforts to prove that such practices existed, have kept observers from focusing on the much more important central question: What did the symbolic remnants of ritual cannibalism signify?

Answering that question from outside the native culture will not be easy. To probe it fairly, we need to develop a much wider background of understanding and appreciation. To broaden our perspective, we will address two new topics: the origin and function of the cannibal concept in Western civilization; the religious significance of ritual cannibalism among the Northwest Coast Indians. The rest of this book is devoted to exploring these two themes. The former will require intensive examination and analysis. Armed with greater sensitivity and more information, we will be in a better position to probe what the *hamatsa* ceremonies meant for the people who actually experienced them in the past, and what they mean for today's native participants.

PART TWO

■

WHITE FLAMES

Cannibalism is the fundamental form
of institutionalized aggression — it is impossible to
comprehend the true nature of human culture without
understanding its role in human history.

ELI SAGAN (1974, 144)

7

Cannibalism: The Prime Taboo

*The ambivalence [towards incest or the death of
someone loved] intrinsic to cannibal behaviour is
reflected in the fact that almost all cannibal activity
is circumscribed by forms of ritual that have as their
purpose the integration of cannibalistic acts into the
normal activities of the tribe.*

ELI SAGAN (1974, 14)

THIS PART OF THE book shifts the focus from documentation
of cannibalism among early Northwest Coast natives to the deli-
cate, sensitive tasks of analysis and interpretation. That change in
the discourse presents an ethical and intellectual dilemma. As
Westerners, how can we analyze the impact that ceremonies fea-
turing ritual cannibalism had on people belonging to a native cul-
ture, if we do not first clarify our own perception?

As anthropologist Clifford Geertz reminds us, we look back at
the legendary "first contact" encounter between eighteenth-cen-
tury European explorers and Northwest Coast natives "through
the haze of the modern order of life [and] from our particular
positions within that order." What we know about both groups of
people engaged in this meeting comes to us sifted through the
perspectives of those who have told us about it. "We make of them
what we can," says Geertz "given who we are or have become.
There is nothing fatal in this, either to truth or fairness" (Geertz
1995, 6).

But, when the issue being studied is as controversial as canni-
balism, I believe non-native writers attempting to interpret "first
contact" encounters have a special obligation to take their post-
colonial inheritance into greater account. What methodology
should we employ in trying to make sense of the acts, thoughts,
and emotions of other people in remote times? I suggest that
Boas, as one of three anthropologists who set the terms of dis-
course for much contemporary ethnographic practice,[1] pointed
the way. Just as he disciplined himself to postpone interpreting
native customs until he had accumulated a huge amount of raw
data, so we have an obligation to suspend judgment while we (1)
increase our knowledge of the different — sometimes contradic-
tory — ways in which the idea of cannibalism has evolved and
mutated in Western thought, (2) take responsibility for our cumu-
lative biases about this subject, and (3) address the critical differ-
ences between native spirituality and Western religious dogma.
The next four chapters will focus on this preparatory work. Then
we will be ready to address the spiritual significance of ritual can-
nibalism for the individual *hamatsa* and for his community.

* * *

The first step is to summarize the most rudimentary scientific
information about cannibalism that now exists, highlighting im-
portant points of agreement, disagreement and ambiguity.

The notion of cannibalism roams the dark shadows that sur-
round the tiny clearings of our conscious minds. The widespread
belief that cannibals lurk just beyond one's culture has existed
throughout history. Aboriginal people, such as the Mowachaht,
often asserted that those who ate human flesh lived across the
inlet or in the next valley. Euroamericans have presumed that
those who consume human flesh are savages inhabiting remote
lands on the fringes of the modern world. For eons, the over-
whelming majority of the world's population has been carnivo-
rous, consuming almost every type of living creature. But most
people have shunned one type of meat: human flesh. Eating one's
own kind remains the ultimate taboo. Of all human acts, it is the

most shocking. We are culturally programmed to find it revolting. Our disgust reaches far back into the collective mind, beyond reason. In this distant inner jungle, matter and spirit merge in dreadful confusion.

We cannot be certain how the taboo against eating human flesh evolved, but anthropologists have advanced two broad theories. Those who favour economic determinism suggest it began in the following way. As long as early people remained wandering hunters and plant-gatherers, with only limited control over their food supply, it is probable that they sometimes turned to part-time cannibalism out of necessity — for instance, during a famine. But when some people learned to cultivate the soil, they settled down and became farmers or pastoral nomads tending herds of domesticated animals. With plenty of alternative foods available, nomadic herders reserved the eating of human flesh for solemn ceremonial occasions. Farmers faced a more difficult problem: they often ran out of meat but could not risk either the social breakdown that would result from eating members of their immediate community or the danger of antagonizing neighbouring groups. They banned the eating of human flesh for practical reasons (Tannahill 1975, 17). Proponents of this theory say it was on this political foundation that the gradual development of law and religion erected a complex moral code, which made the consumption of human flesh taboo.

But the taboo is viewed differently by anthropologists who rely on psychoanalytic interpretations of human behaviour. They assert that cannibalism had much more primitive, non-economic, sacramental origins. They say such ceremonies were not outlawed for centuries. In some societies, such as the Aztec, human sacrifice may never have been shunned. Those who take the psychoanalytic perspective say morality and religion had primordial origins that reach far beyond the development of agriculture.

Despite the deep-seated taboo against eating human beings, the practice has allegedly occurred since prehistoric times — sporadically and in widely scattered locations all over the earth. But identifying those places has been a matter of heated dispute among anthropologists for almost 75 years, and it continues today. A brief overview will put the argument in perspective.

In 1923, the pioneer American anthropologist Edwin Loeb published a short, speculative paper outlining what he claimed was the evolutionary development of cannibalism and human sacrifice. After examining 140 "tribes or entire localities" around the world, he concluded that 54 practised cannibalism, 80 engaged in human sacrifice, and 36 followed both customs (Loeb 1923, 6). According to Loeb, a "blood sacrifice complex" linked five customs: cannibalism, blood sacrifice, finger sacrifice, circumcision, and human sacrifice. Claiming these customs were all "geographically and causally related," Loeb said the complex centered on tropical regions and occurred mainly in aristocratic societies (24, 6, 9).

"Cannibalism was unusual in North America and of secondary origin among the civilized people of Central America," said Loeb. "It must be presumed that the complex was brought to America across the Bering Strait, for in this manner alone could the isolated circumcision of the Athabaskan tribes be explained, as well as the cannibalistic societies of Nootka Sound" (27). Based on this tenuous connection, some anthropologists have theorized that the Kwakiutl and other Northwest Coast groups descended from inland hunters thought to have come from the same region as the Athabaskans (Sanday 1986, 114).

Loeb's theories were vague, poorly documented, and told us more about the imaginations of twentieth-century anthropologists than they did about the actual existence of cannibalism among humankind. But our ideas about the subject are rooted in both fact and fantasy. And some investigators have made generalizations that make Loeb's ideas seem moderate. For example, in 1966, the socio-biologist Robert Ardrey wrote a book about the origins of territory among animals, in which he stated categorically: "Cannibalism has been a prevalent pastime throughout all of the human record" (Ardrey 1966, 263).

The actual prevalence of cannibalism remains open to debate. As the anthropologist William Arens has cautioned: "Extinct bones, like extinct cultures, always seem to provide the best evidence for cannibalism. . . . Like the poor, cannibals are always with us, but happily just beyond the possibility of actual observation" (Arens 1979, 125, 166). He conceded that it is impossible to prove cannibalism never existed. But he argued it was far more significant that no reliable observers have ever reported seeing it happen, even among the Aztecs. He concluded that cannibalism is as imaginary and fantastic as witchcraft.

Arens' challenging assertion about the improbability of cannibalism is often echoed by anthropologists and historians who may be looking for a way to sidestep this complex issue. We will not take that route. Our analysis will scrutinize the validity of Arens' simplistic views, and distill from them the one avenue of promising inquiry that he opened for examining the significance of ritual cannibalism among early Northwest Coast Indians. To put that investigation in perspective, we first must examine the findings of anthropologists, paleontologists and historians concerning various types of cannibalistic practices. In the process, we will see how Arens disputed some of the key examples. His opinions will be critiqued more fully in chapter ten.

* * *

If humans have practised cannibalism, when and where did it happen? Many anthropologists believe that Pekin man (*Homo erectus*) ate human brains and the marrow from the long bones of his fellows some 400,000 years BCE. Scattered evidence of ceremonial brain-eating has been linked to Neanderthal times (Tannahill 1975, 14-16), which began about 230,000 BCE (Gore 1996, 19). But usually bodies were buried and skulls were propped up separately as memorials. Cut marks on a skull from Krapina Cave in Croatia suggest to some paleoanthropologists that Neanderthals had a taste for human flesh. Others believe the marks point to ritualistic cannibalism. As Neanderthals also smashed open the large bones of human limbs, some scientists believe these people ate both the meat and the marrow as a means of sustenance (8, 27).

Solo man of Java, an early *Homo sapien,* also is said to have practised brain-eating about 150,000 BCE. The idea that the body had a soul, which was located in the head, and that it possessed a life-essence, led to the practice of headhunting and to the cult of skull collecting that were widespread throughout the prehistoric world. Enlarged openings around the base of some skulls reinforced the brain-eating hypothesis.

But many paleontologists, including Franz Weidenreich, the leading student of Pekin man, reject this speculative conclusion in favour of other explanations for the damaged skulls that were found (Weidenreich 1943). One theory holds that predators dragged the skeletal remains into vacant caves. Another concludes that the brain was carefully removed through the larger opening, so the skull could be kept intact and used as a funerary object (Arens 1979, 124-25). We are left with another unresolved issue.

According to University of Minnesota anthropologist E. Adamson Hoebel, prehistoric Minnesota Indians engaged in brain cannibalism. In southwestern England, archaeologists unearthed a pile of bones in a cave in 1987. The scientists cited it as evidence that some Stone Age Britons practised cannibalism about 12,000 years ago.

The historical record contains an even longer list of alleged cannibalistic practices in many parts of the world. The Greek historian Herodotus is often considered the first to depict other cultures. In the fifth century BCE, he informed his readers that an unknown people living beyond the frontier of civilization resorted to eating their own kind. The practice was called anthropophagy, a combination of the Greek words *anthropos* (man) and *phagein* (to eat). The term would last until the end of the fifteenth century, when (as we will see in chapter nine) careless reports by the navigator Christopher Columbus caused Europeans to popularize another word — cannibal. Down through the ages, colourful reports came from historians, explorers, travellers, and military men who ventured to far off countries.

Only in comparatively recent times have anthropologists

attempted to survey the evidence of cannibalism and differentiate one type from another. They denote three kinds of anthropophagy, depending on the dominant motivation involved: *ritual, gustatory* (or dietary), and *survival* cannibalism.

In its *ritualistic* form, cannibalism involves the belief that eating some portion of the victim's body, which contains a special quality of that person, enables the feaster to *incorporate* that "soul-stuff" into his self. Boas found remnants of this type among Northwest Coast Indians.

The Australian aborigines' Walloonggura ceremony involved initiation rites that addressed both the cannibal, patricidal impulses of young, assertive males and the benevolent aspects of the archetypal father. During a long period of instruction, initiates were forced to live about a month on only the freshly drawn blood of the older men. In earlier times, the blood was allegedly obtained from a man who was killed for the purpose, and portions of his body were eaten by the novices. "Here," said psychoanalytic anthropologist Géza Róheim (1945, 41-43, 231-32), "we come as near to a ritual representation of the killing and eating of the primal father as we can ever get."[2] (The significance of the first patricidal meal will be examined further in chapter ten.)

During the nineteenth century, Maori cannibalism was linked to ritual warfare. The sacrificial victims were captives or slaves. By eating these "fish," a chief acquired control over the land of the vanquished. Fijian chiefs exchanged "raw" women and "cooked" men at communion feasts. Some of the sacrificial victims were rebels and dissidents. As "food for the gods," those who were offered up assumed divine status (Lewis 1986, 74).

The Tupinamba Indians of Brazil's Amazon jungle allegedly practised an elaborate form of ritual cannibalism. As was common in many cultures, victorious chiefs required their captives to "marry" into the tribe. The former enemy was called "loved one." These prisoners were fêted and given unmarried women companions. After enjoying a long period of luxury status, the captives were ritually slain and eaten. The communion feast often culminated in orgiastic sex (Lewis 1986, 74-75).

Earliest known portrayal of New World inhabitants: *a sixteenth-century woodcut depicting cannibalism and "free love" among South American Indians. Dated 1505, it shows one person gnawing on a human arm while other parts roast over a fire. (Courtesy: New York Public Library)*

Western scholars commonly cite the Tupinamba as an indisputable example of man-eating, because the practice was carefully documented in the sixteenth century by eyewitness accounts of Portuguese Jesuit missionaries. But Arens disputed this classic case by pointing out that the priests seem to have paraphrased each other and based their opinions on the questionable report of a single shipwrecked German seafarer — Hans Staden — who wrote a book about his experiences on the South American coast aboard a Portuguese trading ship (Letts [1557] 1929). Arens said it was a case of plagiarism, not serial verification of cannibalism by independent eyewitnesses (Arens 1979, 22-31).

The ancient Aztecs of central Mexico carried human sacrifice to a greater degree of complexity than any other people. Almost all anthropologists believe it involved cannibalism. But Arens contended most of his colleagues failed to scrutinize the limited documentation carefully. He argued that conventional opinion rests heavily on the accounts of biased friars and ruthless conquistadors like Hernando Cortés, none of whom actually observed the acts which they reported (Arens 1979, 60-66).

The Aztecs placed their connection with the universe above everything. They believed that their world would be destroyed if the gods Quetzalcoatl and Tetzcatlipoca were not offered enough human hearts. Onlookers were allegedly invited to share portions of the flesh so they could identify themselves with the gods. In the years leading up to the Spanish conquest, the Aztecs became obsessed with the notion that they were living on borrowed time. Demographer Woodrow Borah, a specialist on ancient Mexican cultures at the University of California, Berkeley, has estimated that during this period, 250,000 people were sacrificed and eaten every year. The victims were usually prisoners captured in battle. Anthropologists say the Aztecs treated their sacrificial victims with respect for the sacred role that they supposedly played in pacifying the gods.

People who consume human flesh because they think it is healthful or tastes good are said to engage in *gustatory* (or dietary) *cannibalism*. In his widely used textbook, E. Adamson Hoebel, says the practice has occurred occasionally in historical times. "It was common in [the South Pacific] and parts of Africa, especially among Congo tribes," he claims, without citing his source. "In both places, prisoners were penned and fattened for the feast." He claims this type of anthropophagy also occurred in parts of South America, but not among North American Indians (Hoebel [1966] 1972, 155). But Arens remained skeptical. He said there is no first-hand documentation to support the instances of "man-eating" cited by Hoebel.

Survival cannibalism is the last resort of starving people. To save their lives, the Eskimos resorted to this practice, but only after great suffering. Potentially, people are food. Beneath our disgust for eating human meat, we recognize this reality. Under extreme circumstances we can not only accept the necessity of consuming another person's flesh, we can even accept our dead bodies being eaten by another if that offers them a chance of survival. In such circumstances, even theologians generally agree that the determination to maintain life supersedes mores.

The historical novelist Rudy Wiebe points out that there are a number of books about survival cannibalism at sea, which contain an "enormous amount of documentation as to what really did take place." He claims "the English [seafarers] were particularly susceptible to these kinds of horrors" (Robertson 1995, 23).

In Wiebe's thoroughly documented novel, *A Discovery of Strangers,* he recounts the story of Sir John Franklin's first ill-fated Arctic expedition, which became lost in 1821 while searching for an overland route. Eleven of the 20 men Franklin commanded died in horrifying and suspicious circumstances. But it was not until 1848, when the bones of some of Franklin's sailors were found on the Arctic tundra around Starvation Lake, that the issue of cannibalism surfaced. Some of the bones bore knife marks, indicating that the bodies probably had been cut up.

When Wiebe flew into Starvation Lake in 1988 to research *A Discovery of Strangers,* he heard for the first time about bush pilots and other people eating "long pork" after they had crashed. Turning to Eric Partridge's *Dictionary of Slang and Unconventional English,* Wiebe found "long pig" — pidgin English for human flesh. The term came from the Fiji Islands, where natives thought "long pig" (*puaka balava*) tasted better than real pig (*puaka dina*) meat (Robertson 1995, 23; Tannahill 1975, 149). In 1992, acclaimed travel writer Paul Theroux (1992, 187) jokingly claimed that "the people-eaters of the Pacific [have] evolved, or perhaps degenerated, into Spam-eaters" because Spam had so much of the "porky taste of human flesh [or] 'long-pig.'"[3]

Isolated instances of survival cannibalism continue to occur.

One of the most celebrated occurred in 1972, when a plane carrying a Uruguayan rugby team to Chile crashed high in the snow-capped Andes. The survivors, after their sparse rations ran out, realized that their only hope of staying alive was to eat human flesh. In his acclaimed 1974 book, *Alive,* author Piers Paul Read paid special attention to the social structure that evolved among the group. A warrior class emerged that was counterbalanced by a civilian government which looked out for the welfare of the weak and wounded.

Whether cannibal societies engaged in the practice for ritual or gustatory reasons, most tried to restrain the socially destructive habit of developing a taste for human flesh by looking outside their kinship group for people to eat. Anthropologists call this tendency exo-cannibalism. Some Northwest Coast Indians allegedly feasted on slaves captured in war. But in some aboriginal societies exo-cannibals preferred to eat portions of vanquished warriors of an opposing tribe. Through this sensational act, the victor not only reenacted his triumph but incorporated his rival's spiritual power. Missionaries sometimes served the same purpose.

In January 1993, dissident Chinese writer Zheng Yi, smuggled documents out of China which revealed allegations of exo-cannibalism involving hundreds of men and women who, in the name of revolutionary purity, violated one of humanity's strongest taboos. Between 1966 and 1976, the atrocities — officially condoned and encouraged — took place in public, forcing onlookers to prove their fidelity to the Cultural Revolution by eating "class enemies." The practice was widespread in the Guangxi Autonomous Region in southern China.[4]

Endo-cannibalism — the practice of eating one's kin — is driven not by aggression but by a need to perpetuate the group. As part of mourning, a cadaver's flesh is consumed to keep the person's spirit and accumulated wisdom "alive." One anthropologist dubbed it "compassionate" cannibalism (Lewis 1986, 73). The most recently popularized, but controversial example was recorded among the Fore people of Papua New Guinea. In 1976, D. Carleton Gajdusek, M.D., won a Nobel Prize in physiology and medicine for discovering the cause of *kuru,* a fatal neurological disorder. Dr. Gajdusek pinpointed a genetic deficiency that allegedly stemmed from eating undercooked flesh of humans who had died of the illness. The Fore had a reputation as brain-and-intestine eaters who restricted their ritual cannibalism to family funerals.

Once again, Arens challenged the generally accepted view, by claiming that "Fore cannibalism has never been observed by an outsider" (Arens 1979, 109). He also raised serious questions about the validity of Dr. Gajdusek's findings. After scrutinizing the doctor's research records, Arens reached two startling conclusions: during Gajdusek's 10 months among the Fore, he recorded no actual evidence of cannibalism; his laboratory work demonstrated that "the disease he was trying to cure was caused by an active virus rather than a genetic weakness" (107, 109).

On the other hand, Arens conceded that "it is impossible to prove that cannibalism was not a factor in the *kuru* syndrome." But he stressed that Gajdusek's hypothesis was based entirely on circumstantial evidence and contradictory ethnographic information. Arens also noted that no one has suggested other suspected "slow-virus" maladies — Parkinson's disease, multiple sclerosis, and certain strains of measles — are transmitted among Westerners by cannibalism (114).

Despite Arens' reservations about the Fore, the list of alleged cannibals in the New Guinea highlands is almost endless. As recently as 1950, another highland tribe reportedly followed a practice that was similar to the Fore. Gimi women ate the dead bodies of husbands to release the men's souls, freeing them to rejoin ancestral forest spirits.

Allegedly, another form of commemorative cannibalism was practised by the Trobriand Islanders. The corpse of a recently deceased man was exhumed, dismembered by his sons and other male relatives, and eaten. The bones were kept as relics, commemorating the dead.

* * *

This summary of the common types of cannibalism raises some important questions for our study.

If the basic evidence for man-eating is as scant as Arens claimed, are the conventional categories used by anthropologists valid? The answer seems to be "yes," for three reasons. First, existing case studies show there is more evidence than Arens would have us believe. Second, the standard classifications are based on identifiable behavioral differences. Third, these differentiations keep us from lumping "telltale signs" together into a single, oversimplified phenomenon and assuming — as the early European explorers did — that cannibalism obviously exists.

Does the ethnographic data have to be reexamined in each instance? Definitely. The traditional categories are general, superficial groupings which have to be substantiated by circumstantial and direct evidence in each instance. In a given culture, more than one type of cannibalism may be involved. As we saw in part one, carelessness can confuse one with the other or cause one to be overlooked entirely.

Does it make sense to classify societies by the way they allegedly practised cannibalism when there seems to be insufficient eyewitness corroboration, or is there a better way to study the phenomenon? Direct evidence is always desirable, but it is not always available or essential. As we noted at the end of chapter six, attempts to prove beyond a doubt that human flesh was actually ingested in every instance can prevent researchers from focusing on the more important issue of *interpreting* the circumstantial evidence. The most helpful aspect of the traditional categories used by anthropologists is that they encourage investigators to examine motive.

But Arens argued that the old categories should be abandoned and replaced by a new approach. He suggested looking at the different ways societies *think* about cannibalism. He postulated three negative perspectives and one, less obvious, positive outlook. First, Arens said some groups view neighbouring societies as cannibals, thereby defining superior and inferior status and distinguishing between civilization and barbarism. Secondly, he noted that some societies use the concept to chart cultural development or "progress." Thirdly, he found that some groups save the label for selected people in their own society, to explain the persistence of evil and calamity. Finally, Arens noted that, in many societies, these three negative views of cannibalism are often employed simultaneously with far more subtle symbolic messages in the realm of religion, where "the [profane] notion of eating human flesh and blood is transformed into the most sacred of all acts" (Arens 1979, 159-60).

The French author-economist Jacques Attali has called this positive process "therapeutic cannibalism." He says human history, individually and collectively, reflects a constant quest for eternity, a continual striving for immortality. All societies have sought to perpetuate themselves. From the time when humans first banded together, designated authorities have developed different strategies and institutions for warding off evil and eliminating death. In analyzing this process, Attali concluded that every society has engaged in formal, organized acts of cultural "healing" designed to separate evil (that which threatens life) from good (that which the society values most) by either "consuming" or containing the malevolent force's power. "To struggle against evil," said Attali "is always to eat evil — the order is always cannibalistic" (Attali 1979, 15).

As I have indicated, the standard categories of cannibalism used by anthropologists remain useful. But mere classification can also lead to shallow interpretation. Arens' suggestion that researchers should shift their attention to examining the way different groups of people *think* about cannibalism offers a fresh, productive line of inquiry. Most importantly, his recognition of the need to take the "therapeutic" aspect of ritual cannibalism into account goes to the heart of this book's study.

To understand how and why this profound religious process was overlooked by early Europeans and Americans during their encounters with Northwest Coast Indians, we next probe the widely divergent world views held by these two groups of people. As Boas and other anthropologists demonstrated, the natives believed the first, most essential form of human struggle involved ingestion of the cannibal spirit. But Westerners, who had almost no appreciation of ritual cannibalism's spiritual significance, were preoccupied with condemning and suppressing ceremonial practices that seemed alien, shocking, and frightening. This divergence in beliefs came into sharpest focus around the religious practice of symbolic sacrifice.

8

Clash of Cosmologies

Then Jesus said to them, "Believe me when I tell you
this: you can have no life in yourselves, unless you
eat the flesh of the Son of Man and drink his blood.
The man who eats my flesh and drinks my blood enjoys
eternal life, and I will raise him up at the last day.
My flesh is real meat indeed and my blood is real
drink. He who eats my flesh and drinks my blood, lives
continually in me, and I in him."

JOHN 6: 54-57

DESPITE ARENS' SKEPTICISM about the probability of canni-
balism around the world — which will be countered in chapter ten
— my reading has convinced me that ritual cannibalism has
existed in many different cultures. But wherever human flesh may
have been eaten, the physical act was replaced long ago by sym-
bolic sacrifice and the consumption of a spiritual essence. The
people in question often honoured a myth about a remote past,
which included a "once-upon-a-time" account of eating human
flesh. In metaphor at least, these sacramental, "therapeutic" acts
are a staple of many religions. Too often, little effort was made to
understand these legendary events and appreciate the role they
played in maintaining the society's world view. It was easier to
brand those who held these strange beliefs as "cannibals." This
was especially true when the intruders also cherished a powerful
myth which contained equally mysterious cannibalistic overtones,

such as those imbedded in Christianity. During the age of European exploration, the ensuing clash of cosmologies proved most dramatic when people calling themselves Christians encountered two Amerindian cultures: the Aztecs of Mexico and the Northwest Coast Indians. An eighteen-hundred-year-old European religion with a powerful millenialistic message came into direct conflict with even more ancient Amerindian forms of spirituality which had their own beliefs about the impending end of the world and the arrival of a better existence. Our study focuses on the collision between Christianity and the Northwest Coast natives.

The subtle links between endo-cannibalism and ritualistic forms of human sacrifice have posed awkward problems for Christian missionaries in many cultures. Devout Christians, believing in the miracle of transubstantiation, too often stopped hearing the literal meaning of "take, eat, this is my body, this is my blood" — established as doctrine in 1215 by Pope Innocent III after more than a thousand years of debate within the Church. The sacrificial communion celebrated in the Catholic eucharist — the ritual reenactment of the incarnation — was often misinterpreted by native people as a cannibalistic ritual. Among the Northwest Coast Indians, ritual cannibalism had a particular religious significance, and Catholic communion was too similar in form and function to avoid confusion. Both "Mass" and the name given to the consecrated bread of the eucharist came from Latin. Significantly, "Host" was derived from *hostia,* or "sacrificial victim" (Tannahill 1975, 58).

To avoid the risk of using the altar to precipitate cannibalistic visions, the clever Anglican missionary, Father William Duncan, who worked among the Tsimshian Indians in the 1860s, deliberately eliminated the rite of communion from his services. Duncan also dropped other aspects of Christian ritual or symbolism that he suspected would assume a talismanic virtue in the eyes of newly converted natives. To minimize signs of superior rank similar to a chief's ceremonial regalia, Duncan declined to wear the priest's vestments in the pulpit. He cautiously postponed baptism until he was convinced the candidate would not misconstrue its intended meaning. Because of the remarkable influence totem pole carvings had on the Tsimshian, Duncan avoided all religious paintings and sculpture. In each instance, Duncan feared that the act or symbol might be misunderstood by natives whose primary way of interpreting new beliefs was to adapt them to old ideas (Barnett 1942, 24).

Anthropologists call the process of reinterpretation *transference*. When new traits, complexes, and ideas are introduced to a culture, they are sized up and either rejected outright or accepted and modified in terms of the meaning they have for those who receive them. It is one of the most difficult processes for observers of unfamiliar cultures to understand and interpret. This is particularly true for "professional civilizers," both past and present. "This applies to teachers, Peace Corps volunteers, economic-development programmers, public health workers, and missionaries, whose numbers are steadily increasing," said the anthropologist Hoebel (1972, 80). "When this principle is ignored, the consequent mischief worked is often monumental."

This brings us back to the numerous reports about cannibalism among Northwest Coast Indians by eighteenth-century European explorers and nineteenth-century colonizers. Did their fervour to civilize savages blind them to the actual meaning ritualistic cannibalism had for the natives who practised it? Did the Europeans' world view so cloud their vision that their observations should be dismissed?

Every culture has its own way of looking at experience. "Without comprehension of world views," said Hoebel "there is no comprehension of mankind" (492). There was a wide divergence between the world views of the Northwest Coast natives and those of the Europeans who first encountered them.

When it was necessary, most Europeans could draw a line between their religious and secular beliefs. Their world view was predominantly rational and mechanistic in its conception of an orderly universe that operated according to discernable scientific laws. Europeans believed in the possibility of human progress.

They were convinced that humans could change and improve the world's material, biological, and social conditions. They believed in success, which was marked by personal achievement and material rewards. Their strong sense of individual responsibility combined with a religious tradition of human sinfulness tended to provoke anxiety and self-criticism. They viewed the past largely as an indication of what the ever-changing future could yield.

To the extent that Europeans were influenced by Christianity, they believed that the source of spiritual power or force was concentrated in a single benevolent God, residing in heaven. Many of those who professed Christianity thought seriously about the unseen world only during times of periodic worship or trouble.

But the Northwest Coast Indians believed the influence of malevolent supernatural forces was everywhere and constantly at work. Almost every aspect of their lives was connected with spiritual power. Their motives for personal development, work, self-control, and war were all tied to the unseen, vigilant, sometimes hostile spirit world. Their unique, rich "guardian spirit complex" was an ancient phenomenon, which had deep cultural, social, and psychological significance for every individual.

The natives' world view was built on the belief that spiritual force pervaded the world and might reveal itself in anything from the cry of a loon to a flash of lightning. They believed spirit beings created the world and gave it order. But it was a dangerous, threatening universe, full of cannibal monsters. It could only be controlled by compulsive, symbolic acts. Among the Northwest Coast Indians, far more than with the Aztecs, religion and tribal life — both collectively and individually — involved highly personal obligations that called for constant watchfulness, courage, and acceptance. Lurking in the background was the disconcerting knowledge that supernatural powers favourably disposed to the tribe's ancestors might change their attitudes toward the present generation if they were not appeased. The secret was to obtain protection from certain powerful intermediate spirits, such as *Baxbakwalanuxsiwae.*

Artistic masks were used in ceremonies to give dancers the

Hamatsa's multi-headed mask from Fort Rupert,
*carved about 1914 by Charlie James of Alert Bay for his step-son
Mungo Martin, shows the three major avian attendants of Man Eater:*
Cannibal Raven, Hoxhok, *and* Crooked Beak. *Multiple masks represent the
appearance of Man Eater's cohorts as a corporate entity and show the inability
of men to hide from a supernatural being who can see in all directions.*
(Courtesy: Museum of Anthropology, Vancouver, A3653)

power to change identities and cross over time to re-experience ancient but enduring encounters between animals and spirits. In the cannibal dance, the performers portrayed the experiences of an ancestor who left his village, wandered in the wilderness, and met a terrifying spirit called *Baxbakwalanuxsiwae.* He was attended by three supernatural cannibal birds: Raven, *Hoxhok* and Crooked Beak. After some encounters with these creatures, the *hamatsa* escaped and returned to his village in a wild, frenzied state. He had to be tamed — to be brought over that invisible boundary that separates the human and spiritual realms. At that moment, the dancer recapitulated his ancestor's original experience — the boundaries collapsed between human beings, animals, and spirits; between past and present; between ancestor and descendant.

Other artistic implements used in the dance illustrated this same concept of collapsing boundaries. For example, a rattle might show a face, composed of the eyes, mouth and cheeks of other animals, all sharing the same boundary. During the cannibal dance, masked dancers shook these rattles to help the *hamatsa* cross boundaries and relate to supernatural spirits (Wyatt 1992, 11-12).

One could not make a connection with such a wild and terrifying spirit as Man-Eater by simply seeking it. As Boas pointed out, some Northwest Coast tribes formed elite secret societies, whose members ate human flesh as part of an elaborate ceremony designed to establish positive relations with the spirits. But the ritualized vision-quest and possession also carried a lurking sense of guilt. Returning to the tribe after a long initiation period, the *hamatsa* participated in a dance that was designed to purge the evil part of the cannibal's spirit, so living with him would be safe. The exorcism involved swallowing whole chunks of human flesh. Between each mouthful, the *hamatsa* swallowed salt water. He was later forced to regurgitate all the meat. The *hamatsa's* cleansing was over, but he had to adhere to numerous taboos for several months (Hogg 1980, 61-66).

The aboriginal perspective was permeated with an acceptance of powerful supernatural forces, a sense of unity between human and animal realms, and a belief in the possibility of magical trans-formations. It had almost nothing in common with the outlook of Europeans, who remained largely ignorant of native views. This enormous gap was bound to engender misunderstanding, distrust and conflict.

Another way to examine the cultural clash that took place between Europeans and Northwest Coast natives over the issue of cannibalism is to consider the divergent views that the two cul-tures had formed of the ideal personality type.

The anthropologist Ruth Benedict has characterized the Kwakiutl Indians' view of the "good man" as a "Dionysian configu-ration" (Benedict 1934, 78-79). She contrasted this image with the "Apollonian configuration," exemplified by the Zuni Indians of New Mexico. Their view of the ideal person was similar to the Greek notion, which influenced Western concepts of heroism.

According to Benedict, Dionysians pursue life's meaning through "the annihilation of the ordinary bounds and limits of existence." Peak experiences are those moments when one escapes the boundaries of the five senses and breaks through to a higher level of awareness. In both daily experience and ritual, the Dionysian seeks to press through superficial acts toward an intense, frenzied psychological state of excessive emotion. It involves feelings of ecstasy similar to drunkenness and hallucina-tions. Quoting William Blake, Benedict said the Kwakiutl believed that "the path of excess leads to the palace of wisdom."

In contrast, the Apollonian not only distrusts excessive emo-tional states, he often does not understand them. Consequently, he makes every effort to outlaw them from conscious life. According to Benedict, he "knows but one law — measure in the Hellenic sense." In other words: stick to the middle road, stay within familiar territory, and do not indulge in disruptive psycho-logical experiences.

Benedict asserted that, among the Northwest Coast Indians, excess and spectacle were essential attributes of the ideal man. To maintain his stature, a chief had to demonstrate constantly his greatness and the inferiority of his rivals. Benedict said this nearly uninhibited self-glorification led to ever more impressive payments of property and wealth. Extravagant potlatching became the universal method for maintaining social and political order. Some said this form of economic power was used as a substitute for war (Duff 1964, 59). According to Benedict, it institutionalized what she claimed were the megalomaniacal attitudes that dominated many aspects of a chief's life.

If Maquinna and Callicum represented the epitome of a "good man" among the Mowachaht, any ritual cannibalism that they may have practised probably had an enormous influence on their followers' general character, outlook, and behaviour. A chief's influence over his subjects derived from the belief that their general welfare depended upon his ritual intercession with the supernatural forces. He was viewed by both the nobility and commoners as the proprietor of all resources within the tribe's territory and controller of everything produced by his people (Warren Cook 1973, 66).

Finally, another chasm that separated Europeans and Northwest Coast natives focused on the fundamental concept of humanity's relationship to the land. The Europeans viewed land as property that was owned by the individual, who had a right, if not an obligation, to exploit its resources. Conflict, conquest, and domination — tempered by certain civil and religious beliefs — were simply necessary "civilizing" tensions and the inevitable consequences of progress.

Native conceptions of land and property involved a fusion of civil and religious beliefs, which gave aboriginals a collective interest in lands that belonged to them as a people by occupation and tradition. They had basic cultural and spiritual ties to the land and these values were grounded in ancient myths and legends. Humans, the creatures of the forests and seas, the supernatural forces, and the land were in unison. Humanity's paramount role was one of maintaining harmony and ensuring that the universe remained in balance. These divergent ideas about land, the environment, and personal responsibility would pose a profound and lasting abyss between indigenous people and European interlopers.

How could outsiders from Europe hope to overcome their radically different view of a human being's place in the world, of individual greatness, and of humanity's relationship to the land to understand, let alone appreciate the function that ritual cannibalism played among the Northwest Coast Indians? Nothing made it more difficult for the intruders to maintain an open mind than their preconception that the entire New World was occupied by "savages."

To appreciate the impact of that bias on the European mentality, we will have to take another long step backward in time. In the process, we will finally see how the term cannibal entered Western discourse and how it coloured Western thinking. Once that process is explained and its implications are understood, then we can try to probe the way Northwest Coast Indians thought about the subject.

Fallacy of the "Savage"

We profoundly fear what we cannot understand and control.

ANON

Lost among the peoples, I will gather you. Scattered over the world, I will muster you and give you the land of Israel for your home. To it they shall find their way and rid it of all that is foul, all that is abominable. . . . Wherever men's hearts are set on their own foul abominations, the Lord God says, they shall bear their punishment.

EZEKIEL 11: 17-21.

Chacun appelle barbarie ce qui n'est pas de son usage.

MICHEL DE MONTAIGNE (FRAME [1588] 1976, 152)

WE HAVE SEEN HOW European mariners, traders, priests, and early settlers who came to the Pacific Northwest Coast in the eighteenth and nineteenth centuries became convinced that they found signs of gustatory or dietary cannibalism among the natives. Because of their preoccupation with this phenomenon, it is not surprising that almost all of them failed to notice more subtle, private, and carefully hidden indications of ritual cannibalism. Because of their superficial, often biased understanding of native cultures, they confused one form of cannibalism with the other. But to comprehend why this tendency to misinterpret certain aboriginal customs was so prevalent, and why it persists even today, we need to know how the bias developed. What was the ori-

gin of the cannibal concept? How has this idea functioned in
Western civilization? Has the outlook of Westerners been clouded
by a so-called "cannibal complex"? If such a disorder exists, how
has it influenced Western thought?

As the anthropologist Alfred I. Hallowell observed, it is peo-
ple, not cultures that clash. The friction that ensues is caused by
conflicts in deeply held personal attitudes and beliefs, many of
which are profoundly shaped by cultural orientations. In the his-
tory of Western civilization, one of the most explosive notions has
been an artificial separation between two terms: "civilized" and
"savage." This view did not develop overnight. It formed during
three centuries of contact between widely divergent cultures.

The fifteenth-century encounter between Europeans and
Amerindians proved decisive for both. For Europeans, it acceler-
ated the forces of empire-building and mercantilism. For Amer-
indians it meant cultural and political upheaval. Some highly
sophisticated civilizations, founded thousands of years before the
European conquest, were invaded and culturally plundered —
robbed of identity, belief, language, and ritual.

When members of the old and new worlds met, first impres-
sions set lasting patterns by which their followers viewed and eval-
uated each other. Because Europeans often found it relatively
easy to establish control in the New World, most of them found it
unnecessary to alter their assumptions about the strangers they
encountered. The more vulnerable Amerindians were quick to
modify their reactions as they sought ways to adapt to these peo-
ple and their remarkable technology. By viewing the New World
through a one-way window, Europeans tended to form intellec-
tual biases that would distort their outlook for centuries. Alleged
and actual instances of different kinds of cannibalism would
become a key feature of this skewed perspective.

"The fact that such [subjective] views had little to do with real-
ity did not mitigate their fundamental importance in coloniza-
tion," wrote journalist-historian Olive Patricia Dickason in 1984.
"By classifying Amerindians as savages, Europeans were able to
create the ideology that helped to make it possible to launch one

of the great movements in the history of western civilization: the colonization of overseas empires" (Dickason 1984, xiii).

After making two voyages to the West Indies in 1492 and 1493, Christopher Columbus portrayed a land populated by naked natives living in a state of primordial innocence who were waiting eagerly to be elevated and enlightened by the superior race of "men from heaven." When he encountered a tribe of Caribs, who he had been told ate human flesh, the Genoese captain sent a few of them back to Spain as slaves in hopes that they would benefit from the experience. During these expeditions, Columbus probably did not believe the Caribs consumed their own kind. He did not observe any such practices directly. His information was based entirely on stories by the Arawaks — longstanding enemies of the Caribs. Initially, Columbus scoffed at these reports. He even noted in his journal that the natives thought he and his men were cannibals because the Europeans showed so much interest in the subject (Arens 1979, 44-54). Bartolomé de Las Casas — the great writer of the early sixteenth century who sailed with Columbus on one expedition, preserved the navigator's log, and travelled widely in the New World — categorically denied that the Caribs ate human flesh (Las Casas 1971).[1]

Columbus' benign picture of the Amerindians did not last long. Europeans had long accepted the notion that many of the world's unknown lands were occupied by monsters, including creatures that ate humans. A European prejudice that savages ate like dogs (L. canis) and the Spanish transliteration of Carib into Canib led to the appellation "cannibal" (Dickason 1984, 10; Tannahill 1975, 78; Hulme 1986; Henige 1991). Both the term and the reputation that went with it struck fear among the Spanish explorers.[2]

When the Florentine merchant-navigator Amerigo Vespucci described his voyage to America in 1501, he told of an incident where a sailor sent ashore to charm or solicit some native women was killed and eaten by the maidens while his shipmates watched.

"I spoke with a man who told me he had eaten 300 men," wrote Vespucci, who attested to seeing preserved human flesh hanging from house beams. "Of this be assured, because I have seen it," he said. "I tell you also that they wonder why we do not eat our enemies, as they say human flesh is very tasty" (Dickason 1984, 10).

An incident in Vespucci's voyage of 1501. *This woodcut illustrated a German translation of Vespucci's letters published in 1509.*

Spanish voyagers would echo Vespucci's assertion for three centuries. They were consistently struck by two characteristics that distinguished Amerindians from themselves: nudity and cannibalism. By the time Columbus died in 1506, Amerindians were widely referred to as "cannibals." In his last will and testament, the famous navigator bowed to public opinion and applied the popular term to the "Indians" he is credited with discovering.

One more incident regarding the Caribs shows how the misapplied label clouded European-Amerindian relations. In 1622, Antonio de Herrera y Tordesillas, historian to the King of Spain, recorded a popular story that was making the rounds toward the end of the sixteenth century. It told of some Caribs who died after eating a priest and, thereby, finally made that island a safe place for missionaries to visit (Dickason 1984, 21). It was assumed that the natives had become convinced the clerics were protected by a powerful spirit. But Bishop de Herrera viewed the Amerindians' concept of guardian spirits as devil worship. Like many early European commentators who assumed the New World natives ate each other for food, the bishop overlooked the religious role of ritual cannibalism.

Only a few observers went so far as to adopt a more moderate, but condescending tone. "They are men and women disposed as we are," wrote Antonio Pigafetta, an Italian gentleman who sailed on the three-year voyage around the world with Ferdinand Magellan. "Although they eat the flesh of their enemies, it is because of certain customs" (22).

Faced with Columbus' irrefutable evidence that people existed in the New World, Pope Alexander VI ruled in 1493 that the Amerindians "being in peace, and, as reported, going unclothed, and not eating [human] flesh," were human and capable of being Christianized. But many Spanish clerics held that the natives were brutes, incapable of learning the mysteries of faith. On his second voyage in 1493, Columbus took 13 priests with him; none of them could find any sense of God or religion among the Amerindians (Dickason 1984, 29).

This bias was reinforced by Francisco Lopez de Gomara, who served as private chaplain and secretary to Hernando Cortés after the ruthless conquistador returned to Spain in 1540. Lopez claimed that the Amerindians were devil-worshipers. The charge represented majority opinion among sixteenth-century Europeans and formed a keystone of the rationale for colonization advanced by Spanish officials. Papal injunctions condemning mistreatment, enslavement, and deprivation of Amerindians had little effect (Dickason 1984, 30-33). Spanish conquest continued unchecked as churchmen engaged in largely one-sided, but nevertheless heated debate over native rights. The question at stake went to the heart of world problems that still plague us today: What right do more advanced nations have to dominate, enslave, and exploit less technically developed peoples?

The leading proponent of the minority position was the Dominican friar, Bartolomé de Las Casas — the father of native rights in North America. He asserted that Amerindians possessed inherent rights because they had souls. The only thing that justified imposing European power upon native sovereignty was the obligation to offer New World peoples, without compulsion, the benefits of a higher set of values, i.e., Christianity. He also argued that resistance to Spanish colonization was blamed on cannibals (Las Casas 1971, 126). This linkage would be used to legitimize Spain's barbaric reaction to all those who defied her authority.

On the other side was Spain's top Aristotelean philosopher, Juan Gines de Sepúlveda. He argued that Amerindians had no rights because they were heathen, cannibalistic savages. Europeans were obliged to conquer and subjugate these inferior creatures.

In 1515, Spain's King Ferdinand II of Aragon convened the first royal commission on the Amerindian question, but he died before the tribunal finished its task. In 1550, King Charles V called another conference to address the issues of aboriginal sovereignty versus the right of European conquest. After a long, heated confrontation between Las Casas and Sepúlveda, the Spanish debates culminated in 1551. Las Casas won the moral debate, but the practical outcome remained unclear. Meanwhile, Spanish conquest rolled on (Dickason 1984, 56).

The debate spread to other European countries. In 1556, Johann Boem enlarged his *Omnium Gentium Mores* — a basic study of worldwide customs and manners first published in 1520 — to include information about contemporary explorations, including a large section on America. Viewing human history as a slow rise from bestiality, Boem began his account with the Flood, which had scattered Noah's three sons around the Old World. Noah's son Shem peopled Asia. Ham's descendants settled in Africa. Japhet's family spread across Europe. These Old World savages allegedly consumed human flesh, especially the Tartars — descendants of Japhet — who roasted and ate their enemies. Aristotle had reported similar tendencies among the Black Sea Scythians. But where the New World "savages" belonged in this genealogy remained a matter of heated and unresolved debate. Cannibalism was one of the key characteristics used to link them to descendants of one of Noah's sons (Dickason 1984, 32-34).

Boem reflected prevailing convictions in holding that cultural diversity and diffusion indicated a process of degeneration. But Loÿs Le Roy, a sixteenth-century professor of Greek at the University of Paris, argued that cultural multiplicity represented an opportunity rather than a threat. New cultures clearly offered challenges for spreading Christianity. He cited the Spaniards' courage in exploring unknown seas and facing the terrors of cannibalism (Dickason 1984, 48-49).

Renaissance Europeans, while still clinging to a conviction that the universe represented a single order, had stumbled upon the New World. They had a difficult time explaining how other, disparate civilizations could have developed without having been in contact with each other. Throughout the sixteenth and seventeenth centuries, Europeans clung to the idea that Amerindian societies were primitive, unevolved, and even static. What proved the point was the contrast between the civility of European customs and the crudity of American practices. Even such an independent thinker as the French philosopher Michel de Montaigne supported this view. In his essay *On Cannibals*, he argued that cannibalism and human sacrifice were characteristic of immature societies. But he also noted that "each man calls barbarism whatever is not his own practice" (Frame 1976, 152).

Europe's golden age of discovery and its large-scale encounter with previously unknown native people is often credited with the formation of the European concept of the "noble savage" — uncivilized human beings living in a natural state who could be either virtuous or debased. But the idea had been around since Greek and Roman times. Faced with new cultures, Europeans overlooked the advanced civilizations of Mexico, Central America, and Peru and branded all of them "barbarian" — modified savagery.

La femme et l'homme sauvage, *as conceived by François Deserpz in*
Recueil de la diversité des habits, *1567. Such portrayals of noble savages —*
hairy, naked, but clearly human stone-age people — reveal the tension
in European minds struggling to incorporate the existence of
Amerindian cultures in a world view that had little room for such ideas.
(Courtesy: Bibliothèque Nationale, Paris)

Renaissance Europeans filled their dictionaries with refined definitions for the word "savage." They focused exclusively on negative aspects such as "not tamed," uncivilized, and ferocious. A leading French dictionary of 1691 defined a savage as a person without religion, law, civility or a regular habitation. The author said America was almost exclusively peopled by naked, hairy savages and most of them were cannibals. In common use, the words "savage" and "cannibal" became interchangeable (Dickason 1984, 64).

Few Europeans tried to look at the flaws in their own society through the eyes of Amerindians. But Montaigne recorded a revealing conversation between himself and three captive Tupinamba Indians — notorious "cannibals" who had been brought from the Amazon jungles of Brazil to France and paraded before the boy-king Charles IX in 1562.

> The King talked with them for a long time; they were shown our ways [of living], our splendor, and the aspect of a fine city. After that, [I] asked their opinion, and what they had found most remarkable. They . . . said . . . they had noticed that there were among us men full and gorged with all sorts of good things, [while] their other halves were beggars at their doors, emaciated with hunger and poverty. They thought it strange that these needy halves could endure such an injustice, and did not take the others by the throat or set fire to their houses. (Frame 1976, 159)

Whether Montaigne was putting his own words into the mouths of the three natives or they actually voiced such views remains unclear. In either case, Montaigne was able to stretch the metaphor of consumption that underlies cannibalism and use it to reflect on European values.

During the seventeenth century most European commentators called all Amerindians savages. The French cosmographer Pierre d' Avity broke down savagery into "five degrees of brutality." Surprisingly his long list did not include cannibalism, which he classified as a mental illness. D'Avity also omitted cruelty, a

label commonly applied to Amerindians that often served to con-
note cannibalism (Dickason 1984, 66-70).

Integrating the Amerindians into what Europeans considered
an acceptable Christian social order became a major challenge
for political and religious leaders during the sixteenth and seven-
teenth centuries. With a highly developed administrative appara-
tus in place, Spain was the first nation to launch into conquest
and colonization of the Americas. Her move to exploit sudden
access to alluring sources of wealth sparked heated debate about
the theoretical and legal bases for establishing European sover-
eignty in the New World.

Papal bulls attempted to carve up the new lands among com-
peting powers and establish ground rules. But theologians and
missionaries disputed the Pope's right to exercise his dominion in
such an arbitrary manner and they quarrelled over the rationale.

In 1532, Francisco de Vitoria, Dominican professor of moral
theology at the University of Salamanca, delivered a series of lec-
tures about the bulls of demarcation, Spain's imperial claims, and
the rights of Amerindians. Many consider Vitoria the founder of
international law. He said the Pope lacked civil or temporal
dominion over the earth, the authority to transfer that power to
the Spanish emperor, and the right to seize aboriginal territory
and set up new governments. Vitoria granted the aborigines theo-
retical dominion, but he supported the commonly held doctrine
of the Christian right to preach the gospel and to use force if the
pagans refused to listen. He even claimed that discovery had
given Spain exclusive rights to spread God's word and to pursue
trade by force of arms. Further, Spaniards had the moral right
and obligation to rescue Amerindian people from such oppres-
sive practices as human sacrifices and ritual cannibalism.

Vitoria enunciated the first clear statement of aboriginal
rights. But he qualified it with a broad justification for interven-
tion. Thus, he established the official rationale for Spanish con-
quest and colonization that eventually resulted in the death of an
estimated fourteen million natives in the Americas and the oblit-
eration of their rich and varied cultures (Dickason 1984, 125-31).

Demographers' estimates of the number of Amerindians who died of disease or violence during the first century of conquest run as high as 90 percent of the indigenous population — about fifty million people. In his blistering exposé of European domination, *Stolen Continents,* travel writer Ronald Wright says at least ninety million native people died (Wright 1992, 14). Although many scholars dispute these high estimates, it was the worst genocide in history.

The victorious Spaniards rationalized the holocaust by redefining the vanquished as either innocent savages or mindless barbarians, and, in either case, "cannibals" and "natural slaves." English literature professor Maggie Kilgour has noted that "the definition of the other as cannibal justifie[d] its oppression, extermination, and cultural cannibalism (otherwise known as imperialism) by the rule of 'eat or be eaten'" (1990, 148). By converting the threatening "other" into an object of consumption, Europeans created a tenuous alibi for unprecedented pillage and plunder. If the existence of advanced civilizations in the New World failed to trouble sixteenth-century Europeans, the destruction of these societies would plague them for ages. The crime against humanity has made the West's progress toward civilization long and painful.

As European powers used these so-called territorial rights of discovery to impose their power in the New World, they became less and less inclined to recognize aboriginal rights. From the beginning, the focus was on one issue: who owned the land? It would remain the most important question in the history of relations between Indians and non-Indians in North America. To elevate their base desire to acquire land to the level of a social and political "obligation," the Europeans formulated a lofty rationale for systematic and ruthless exploitation. The logic was deceptively simple. For primitive people to transcend their "savage" state and enjoy the benefits of civility and righteousness, it might be necessary to help them overcome or even destroy both their traditional environment and the customs that adapted them to it. Both the land and the people had to be civilized. "Coming to Christ" by turning to agriculture and "working for a living" on undeveloped land were sure signs of "progress" (Chamberlain 1975, 4-7).

Cannibalism, as a characteristic of the "savage," was used to justify armed force. Simultaneously, its gradual disappearance among the "infidels" was taken as proof that European "civility" was improving the lot of Amerindians. Where the horrible practice allegedly persisted, it was viewed as a special challenge for renewed missionary zeal.

The replete cannibal. *From* L'Amérique historique, *1638. Cartoon-like caricatures of Amerindian people perpetuated the myth of the savage long after first encounters with many advanced cultures challenged these illusions. (Courtesy: Bibliothèque Mazarine, Paris)*

By the seventeenth century, missionaries bent on making Amerindians conform to Christian standards had developed numerous techniques for making conversions stick. No group was more successful than the Jesuits, who adapted judiciously to the ways of the Amerindian people they were trying to convert. They were among the first to recognize that too sharp a distinction had been drawn between "civilized" and "savage." To increase their ability to evangelize, they made numerous minor adaptations to a viable culture that had its own logic. But when it came to spiritual views as fundamental as the American Indian's concept of guardian spirits, the Jesuits remained as inflexible as any other order. Notions like that amounted to devil-worship.

On the Pacific Northwest Coast, Europeans encountered diverse aboriginal societies during the last half of the eighteenth century. Large numbers of non-native people had little respect for aboriginal people and held an ethnocentric, stereotyped image of the Indian as a savage inclined to practise cannibalism. That bias was used to justify suppressing aboriginal people, subjugating them, converting them to a new religion, exploiting their natural resources, and occupying their lands. In the nineteenth century, many white people continued to regard native customs as either quaint or unwelcome obstacles to Euroamerican trade, colonization, domination and assimilation. But the process also yielded a grudging recognition of persistent cultural differences.

Ultimately, acceptance of the legitimacy of Amerindian culture only complicated evangelization. Toward the end of the seventeenth century, even the Jesuits replaced the practice of working within the framework of native cultures by a concerted effort to destroy them completely and supplant them with Christianity. That approach persisted, in one form or another, into the twentieth century. In the late 1800s, Bishop Paul Durieu of British Columbia was still trying to stamp out winter ceremonials and guardian spirit dances, which he referred to as "familiar spirits" (Jilek 1974, 1). Devastated by disease and cultural disintegration, Northwest Coast Indian tribes clung desperately to their ancient traditions. For example, between 1830 and 1900 the Kwakiutl population declined by almost 90 percent (Walens 1981, 154), yet potlatching not only persisted, it increased. Some anthropologists claim the Kwakiutl believed that the souls of their people were being taken to feed the bodies of an ever increasing number of white men. Threatened with consumption by external forces, the natives intensified their efforts to assuage Man-Eater's voracious appetite (Sanday 1986, 120; Walens 1981, 1540) — a theme that will be revisited in chapter eleven.

The whites who tried to wipe out the ancient guardian spirit complex did not realize how deeply they were reaching into Indian attitudes and behaviour. Their religious and educational brainwashing crusade, inspired by a false dichotomy between "savage" and "civilized" human beings, continued relentlessly. They failed to eradicate traditional beliefs, but their impact on native society was devastating.

During the early twentieth century, the young science of anthropology finally began interpreting the guardian spirit complex as an elaborate form of totemism — belief in a mystical relationship between an individual or clan and an animal (or plant), which is understood to be the clan's original ancestor, and therefore not to be eaten by clan members except on ceremonial occasions. As anthropologists gained greater understanding and appreciation of native religions, they presented a wealth of comparative analysis that gradually opened Western minds to the cultural, social, and psychological significance of these ancient belief systems. That examination has revived debate about the existence and function of ritual cannibalism among all native people.

10

The Myth of Man-Eating

Anthropophagy is one of the unchallenged "facts" of anthropology.

Anthropology and anthropophagy, as views of the external world, have had a comfortable and supportive relationship. It is possible that in their present form, one could not exist without the other.

The idea and image of cannibalism expands with time and the intellectual appetite. Only the fleeting quality of the documentation remains constant.

WILLIAM ARENS (1979, 8, 162, 165)

TODAY, NO SERIOUS examination of aboriginal cannibalism can take place unless it comes to terms with the challenging opinions of anthropologist William Arens. As noted in chapter seven, this skeptical professor sent shock waves rolling through academic circles in 1979, when he published *The Man-Eating Myth* — a provocative critique of the time-honoured, universally accepted notion of cannibalism. His frontal assault on ideas that were commonly held by both anthropologists and laymen brought a breath of fresh air to the scholarly community. He stirred up healthy debate and forced his colleagues to reexamine their findings. But most importantly, he shifted the focus from the object of study — primitive people who were too often presumed to be cannibals — to the observer's criteria and role. How that point of view was shaped by the experience of most Westerners is precisely what we have been systematically exposing in the last two chapters.

Arens argued that, among his twentieth-century cronies, this largely unquestioned way of looking at certain aspects of aboriginal behavior constituted a "cannibal complex." The same bundle of unexamined notions about cannibalism perpetuated many of the biases that blinded the early mariners, explorers, scientists, priests, and settlers who came to the Pacific Northwest Coast.

By advancing a simplistic, sensational, iconoclastic thesis, Arens shattered many preconceptions and forced the scientific community to take stock of its theories and methodology. But, as we will see later in this chapter, his argument had two major flaws: it was overstated and it focused almost exclusively on gustatory cannibalism.

The "Cannibal Complex" — Arens charged that all the vast commentary by laymen and professionals about cannibalism contains no solid evidence that man-eating ever existed as an accepted custom in any society. "I could not be so forthright on this matter if I had ever encountered in person or in print a single anthropologist who had personally witnessed the act," said Arens (Arens Apr. 2, 1979). He conceded that the ancient Aztecs of central Mexico practised human sacrifice extensively, but he argued it was presumptuous to conclude the victims were eaten.

The mountain of case studies about purported cannibalism that has accumulated over the centuries prompted Arens to subject some of the most popular and best documented cases to careful examination. As we saw in chapter seven, these included the classic, spectacular examples that are commonly cited: the Congolese of Africa, Fijian chiefs, the Fore of New Guinea, the Aztecs, and the South American Tupinamba. Except where sheer survival was involved, Arens was unable to uncover adequate historical or scientific documentation of cannibalism as a socially approved custom in any culture. "Rumours, suspicions, fears, and accusations abound," he said "but no satisfactory first-hand accounts" (Arens 1979, 21).

What Arens did find was a "cannibal complex" among those

who reported the phenomenon they were programmed to perceive. He claimed it had been spawned and perpetuated by collective prejudice. In place of direct observations by reliable sources, the evidence of cannibalism rested on second-hand descriptions. Abandoning standard methods of scientific inquiry, too many tribe-trotting anthropologists had failed to question the validity of these reports, which were "primarily accounts by single individuals of isolated events among obscure peoples on the fringes of time and space." Arens found that the investigators, intent on proving a point, had based their hypotheses on circumstantial evidence and ethnographic information that was often both incomplete and contradictory. According to Arens, none of these anthropologists actually saw the acts that they ascribed to various groups. In every instance, the cannibalistic behaviour they reported had actually ended "long ago," before contact with the civilized world, with pacification, or just before the professional observer arrived (38, 43, 112, 132 180, 145, 35).

"For layman and scholar alike, the idea of cannibalism exists prior to, and thus independent of, the evidence," concluded Arens. "We assume cannibals exist, but not because the act has been physically observed, since the evidence is lacking. Therefore, the assumption rests primarily on the accusations made by one group or individual against another" (22, 154).

Arens' analysis showed that "all cultures, subcultures, religious sects, secret societies, and every other possible human association have been labeled anthropophagic by someone." He found that the notion of "others" as cannibals, not the act of "man-eating," is the actual worldwide phenomenon. "The significant question is not why people eat human flesh," said Arens "but why one group invariably assumes that others do." He concluded that this myth, which has no solid basis in historical reality, persists because it contains and transmits "significant cultural messages for those who maintain it" (139, 182).

Down through the ages, the cannibal label has been used by various cultures as a powerful ideological weapon. Among aboriginal people, it served to distinguish one group from another and reinforce other means of separation. Western civilization has also found comfort in the notion of barbarians just outside its gates. By linking the concepts of cannibalism and savagery, we have been able to distance ourselves from so-called uncivilized cultures, to rationalize the existence of previously unknown and sometimes remarkably advanced cultures, to justify the domination and exploitation of these people, and to assuage our guilt by redefining the vanquished. By denying the accused their humanity, the powerful cannibal label sweeps away most cultural attributes and classifies the suspects as subhuman.

"For reasons peculiar to each era," said Arens "the Aztecs as a specific complex social system and the Fore as representatives of the last preserve of savagery on the present fringe of Western civilization were converted into cannibals by the most prominent and respected ideological systems available at the time. The Aztec case in the sixteenth century was supported by the weight of explicit religious morality and scholarship in conjunction with the contributions of the first ethnographers. The Fore instance of the twentieth century is shored up by the medical sciences and the now-institutionalized discipline of social anthropology" (114-15).

According to Arens, the appellation *cannibal* has captured the imaginations of too many social anthropologists looking for new and exotic cultures to investigate. If this excitement were not enough, these gurus have also developed a vested interest in maintaining their almost shamanistic role as licensed mediators between the Western world and the strange cultures they study. The stigma of alleged cannibalism and its transformation into the popular notion of savagery enhance the need for these specialists to act as expert middlemen in the ideological domain. They find themselves playing a tricky and unusually influential role. "At this intellectual juncture," said Arens "the anthropologist simultaneously generates and mediates differences. . . . Such a delicate position depends upon maintaining a requisite minimal degree of crude cultural tension and opposition between 'we' and 'they'" (166, 169-70, 182-84).

As a result, those scientists who should be making critical

assessments about cultural differences are too often merely reviving, reinventing, and defending the idea of savagery and disregarding the lack of evidence. "The general tone of modern anthropological commentary on cannibalism emerges as little more than nineteenth-century reinterpretations in contemporary scientific jargon," said Arens. Numerous social anthropologists are recycling old, unquestioned reports of cannibalism and simply tacking on exotic new theories that purport to reveal the true, hidden meaning of these alleged practices. By employing the latest scientific methods, barbaric behaviour is made comprehensible and even excusable (142, 166, 183).

Arens accused his colleagues of using "liberal and pseudo-scientific" explanations for cannibalism to instruct laymen in the complexities of other cultures. He claimed that their "blasé and seemingly detached objective" analysis of "man-eating" also suggests a "moral relativity" that enhances the image of a professional mind at work which, free of cultural blinders, can view cannibalism as "nothing more than a curious custom." He cited introductory textbooks as the clearest illustration of anthropology's dependence on this "aura of bemused scientific detachment" about "man-eaters." Arens said these books perpetuate the cannibal complex from one generation to the next by making unqualified assertions about its prevalence and citing examples that require closer scrutiny (167, 174-75).

Although the need for intellectual and scientific rigour by anyone studying cannibalism could not have been stated more forcefully, Arens' argument is vulnerable in at least three respects.

First, in being selective about the areas he examined, Arens omitted any discussion of the Pacific Northwest Coast — source of the world's most elaborate, thoroughly documented examples of ritual cannibalism. Arens also ignored places like New Zealand where the Maori had a well-established reputation for cannibalism, and he treated ritual cannibalism among the Tupinamba superficially.

Secondly, Arens declined to investigate some of the original manuscript references to cannibalism, including those examined in the first part of this book. Regarding the Tupinamba, he failed to come to grips with Hans Staden's sixteenth-century book, *Hans Staden: The True Story of His Captivity 1557,* written among these people, and he did not even cite the classic works on this subject by Alfred Métraux: *La Réligion des Tupinamba* (1928) and *Réligions et magies indiennes d'Amerique du sud* (1967).

Thirdly, by simultaneously relegating cannibalism and witchcraft to the realm of imagination, Arens erected another barrier to understanding and appreciating the significance of ritual cannibalism. In his effort to expose all unsubstantiated reports of cannibalism, he inadvertently deprecated the religious aspects of those rites, which were vital to many aboriginal groups.

In 1986, the anthropologist Peggy Reeves Sanday took up Arens' challenge to reassess all the reputed examples of cannibalism that had been cited over the years. She made a detailed examination of 156 selected tribal societies, 109 of which yielded enough information to suggest the existence of ritual cannibalism. Out of this sample, she found 37 cases that were most convincing, one of them being the Kwakiutl. Conceding that none of the 37 represented "undisputed examples of actual cannibalism," Sanday urged readers to look for "suggestive trends" of physical acts that have cultural and symbolic meanings (Sanday 1986, 4-5, 9-10). One critic has noted that she concentrated exclusively on non-European cultures and overlooked the cannibalistic overtones of the Christian mass (Currie 1994, 72). Contemporary Western scholars, as well as the early explorers, can be Eurocentric.

Although most of Sanday's evidence was not based on firsthand reports, she sided with the army of anthropologists who branded Arens a maverick. "A search of the literature convinces me that Arens overstates his case," she wrote. "Although he is correct in asserting that the attribution of cannibalism is sometimes a projection of moral superiority, he is incorrect in arguing that cannibalism never existed. Contrary to his assertion that no one has ever observed cannibalism, reliable eyewitness reports do exist" (Sanday 1986, 9). She cited an exchange of letters to the

Hamatsa dancer, *inspired by the cannibal spirit* Baxbakwalanuxsiwae,
is possessed with the desire to eat men. Photograph by Edward S. Curtis, 1914.
(Courtesy: Garfinkel Publications, Vancouver)

editor by Arens and fellow anthropologist Marshall Sahlins, in which the latter presented excerpts from some eyewitness reports by nineteenth-century Pacific travellers (Sahlins and Arens 1979, 45-47).

In 1986, even more convincing *physical* evidence was unearthed by two groups of archaeologists at prehistoric sites in Ethiopia and southeastern France. Clusters of human and known food-animal bones and the presence of microscopic cut marks on the human remains convinced the scientists that gustatory cannibalism definitely existed (Villa 1986, 431-37; White 1986, 503-09).[1]

But the information that is most illuminating about the function and significance of ritual cannibalism, especially on the Pacific Northwest Coast, did not have to be dug up. Thanks to Boas' pioneering fieldwork, it has been available for more than a century. But too often, preoccupation with the more obvious, negative aspects of gustatory cannibalism has kept Western scholars from investigating positive, more subtle, symbolic, religious meanings. They lacked an unbiased, unified way of looking at witchcraft, spirit-possession, shamanism, and cannibalism.

Man-Eating's "Charisma" — The anthropologist Ioan Lewis agreed with Arens' view that anthropologists have tended to exploit the notion of "cannibalism" to promote and protect their uniquely privileged role as specialized scientists. But he disputed Arens' assertion that the idea of *cannibal* has mainly functioned as a means for distinguishing between "us" (the civilized) and "them" (savages). He dismissed entirely Arens' notion that just as witchcraft only exists in people's imaginations, cannibalism must be equally fantastic and mythical. Lewis argued that the real significance of ritual cannibalism can only be understood by determining the mode of thought behind such practices. That also requires removing cultural blinders.

According to Lewis, too many anthropologists have relied on secondhand reports in their accounts of man-eating. As a result, "many modern anthropological studies inadvertently tend to entrench and further legitimize deep-seated Eurocentric assumptions concerning the prevalence of cannibalism in tribal societies"

(Lewis 1986, 63). Lewis argued that many contemporary anthropologists have unwittingly reinforced a misconception spawned in 1913 by the influential founder of psychoanalysis, Sigmund Freud.

In his stirring cosmic fable *Totem and Taboo*, Freud offhandedly introduced the spectre of cannibalism to dress up his compelling theory of primordial incest, which he believed is the origin of totemism and religion. Like many Victorian scientists, Freud equated "savagery" with "cannibalism," and he tended to accept at face value scholars' reports of native practices in various places around the world. But his effort to get behind the mask of ritual cannibalism by probing its psychoanalytic origins made a major contribution to our understanding of primitive spirituality. With both of these factors in mind, let us turn to a brief summary of Freud's theory.

According to Freud, the earliest state of human society consisted of Charles Darwin's "primal horde," which had no interest in totemism. The only order that existed was imposed by a violent, jealous father who kept all the females for himself and drove his sons into exile and sexual celibacy as they matured.

In Freud's version of the Oedipus myth, the patriarch's rebellious sons — being "cannibal savages" — celebrated the liberation that stemmed from murdering their tyrannical father by *eating* him. "The violent primal father had doubtless been the feared and envied model of each of the brothers," said Freud. "In the act of devouring him they accomplished their identification with him, and each of them acquired a portion of his strength."

Subsequently, the sons regularly commemorated and replicated the original act by the ritual slaughter and consumption of a totemic animal. Freud said this mythical totemic feast, "which is perhaps mankind's earliest festival," marked the crucial turning point in the evolutionary development of human beings — the "beginning . . . of social organization, of moral restrictions, and of religion" (Freud 1946, 141-42).

"[The sons] hated their father, who presented such a formidable obstacle to their craving for power and [to] their sexual desires," said Freud. "But they loved and admired him, too." After they killed him, that affection gradually turned into remorse and guilt. To make amends for their deed, they forbade killing the totem animal — "the substitute for their father" — and renounced the totem's benefits by giving up their claim to the women who had thereby been set free. In this way their "filial sense of guilt" gave rise to the two basic taboos of totemism: murder (patricide) and incest. According to Freud, these were "the only two crimes with which primitive society concerned itself" (143).

Freud reasoned that totemism was the first attempt at religion. It arose from the sons' attempt to allay their collective guilt and to appease their father by "deferred obedience to him." According to Freud, all later religions have attempted to solve the same problem of reconciliation. "All have the same end in view," he said "and are reactions to the same great event with which civilization began and which, since it occurred, has not allowed mankind a moment's rest" (145).

According to Freud, this "tension of ambivalence," which was implicit in the "father-complex," persisted in totemism and most subsequent religions. "Totemic religion not only comprised expressions of remorse and attempts at atonement," said Freud "it also served as a remembrance of the triumph over the father. Satisfaction over that triumph led to the institution of the memorial festival of the totem meal, in which the restrictions of deferred obedience no longer held. Thus it became a duty to repeat the crime of parricide again and again in the sacrifice of the totem animal, whenever, as a result of the changing conditions of life, the cherished fruit of the crime — appropriation of the paternal attributes — threatened to disappear" (145). As we will see in chapters eleven and twelve, this aspect of totemic religion had particular relevance to the ritual cannibalism that developed among the Northwest Coast Indians.

Freud said these fraternal impulses profoundly influenced social development for "a long time." They gave rise to "sanctification of the blood tie" and emphasis on the solidarity of life within the clan. Freud reasoned that, by guaranteeing the lives of all clan members, "the brothers were declaring that no one of them must be treated by another as their father was treated by them all jointly." Thus a socially based prohibition against fratricide was added to the earlier religiously-based prohibition against patricide. "The patriarchal horde was replaced in the first instance by the fraternal clan, whose existence was assured by the blood tie," said Freud. "Society was now based on complicity in the common crime; religion was based on the sense of guilt and the remorse attaching to it; morality was based partly on the exigencies of this society and partly on the penance demanded by the sense of guilt" (146).

It is clear that Freud was attempting to penetrate the mode of thought that led to totemism — exactly what Lewis identified as the key challenge in understanding ritual cannibalism. Perhaps the most dynamic aspect of Freud's provocative theory is the "tension of ambivalence" that pervades totemism, persists in religion, and surrounds the cannibal complex. Throughout history, the epithet "cannibal" has been employed by people in various parts of the world to distance themselves from outsiders, to voice contempt for the "uncivilized" and uncouth, or to express hostility toward oppressors. But the label has also been used to show respect for people of status who possessed exceptional powers. "Man-eating's" double-edged imagery derives its fascination and its evocative power from intimate physical experiences that are common to all human beings (Lewis 1986, 64).

Most anthropologists have tended to treat practices such as witchcraft, spirit-possession, shamanism, and cannibalism as separate types of extraordinary experience. According to Lewis they are "actually closely related expressions of mystical power, or 'charisma,'" that are invoked by many aboriginal people to conquer and transform malign forces. He said that too many anthropologists have been preoccupied with the evil connotations of these essentially religious experiences. He argued that open-minded investigators should accept accurate reports of "man-eating" as an ethnographic "fact," take a "generally disbelieving stance, and formulate informed theories about the *ideology* of cannibalism" (Lewis 1986, vii-ix, 71-72).[2]

According to Lewis, cannibalism, as either idea or actual practice, usually occurs in a ritual setting. Ritual cannibalism is a form of sacrificial communion. The forbidden act of eating human flesh enables the one who consumes it to acquire vital energy or power. "The problem is not, as Arens claims, that of explaining why people attribute cannibalism to their neighbours and enemies," said Lewis, "but rather of understanding those cultures in which cannibalism is (or was) actually practised as an integral part of ritual life" (Lewis 1986, 76-77).

In applying this perspective to Northwest Coast Indians, most anthropologists have emphasized the functional role that ritual cannibalism played in maintaining status, rank and social order. Few of them have stressed the psychological, religious, or ideological significance of these ceremonies. Only a handful of anthropologists have delved deeply into the subject. One of them developed a penetrating, balanced, and comprehensive picture of Kwakiutl cosmology. The next two chapters summarize this group's findings.

11

The Hamatsa Reality

I went all around the world to find food.
I went all around the world to find human flesh.
I went all around the world to find human heads.
I went all around the world to find corpses.
　　　　　　A HAMATSA SONG (BOAS 1895, 459)

I have the magical treasure,
I have the supernatural power,
I can return to life.
　　　　　　A TSONOQUA'S SONG (BOAS 1966, 373)[1]

HAVING DEMONSTRATED THE need to examine the psychological, religious, or ideological significance of ceremonies involving ritual cannibalism, let us return to the Kwakiutl as a representative, thoroughly documented case study of this phenomenon. It was exemplified by the elite cannibal society's initiation ceremony, which featured the *hamatsa* dance. We will first try to analyze how an individual *hamatsa's* outlook might have been affected by participating in these rites. That will give us a basis for appreciating the connections between the initiate's personal experience and the group's general world view.

For a *hamatsa*, what was the psychological and spiritual impact of participating in a ceremony that featured ritual cannibalism? In chapter six, we examined the common outward forms that such ceremonies followed in different Northwest Coast Indian groups, the symbolism involved, and the mythology behind the celebration. But we did not look at how these experiences shaped the beliefs of active cannibal society members within a single group.

Most of the information about secret societies among the Northwest Coast Indians came from the Kwakiutl band, which continued to be studied by twentieth-century anthropologists, many of whom observed highly refined, symbolic forms of earlier performances. Over time, adaptations were made to match the cultural traits of different groups. But the function and meaning remained consistent.

Recall that the Kwakiutl obtained a new *hamatsa* dance from the Heiltsuk in about 1835 (see chapter 6). One researcher has suggested that the Heiltsuk had used their winter ceremonial, which featured a cannibal dance that was greatly admired by many other groups, to cope with the impact of European encounter and new trade patterns (Harkin 1988, 83-100).

"It provided the Heiltsuk with a model of possession, consumption, and containment by a foreign [seemingly] supernatural source which [both] destroys life [and displays] spiritual power and material wealth," says Aaron Glass, a graduate of Reed College in Portland, Oregon who is working at the University of British Columbia Museum of Anthropology (1995, 29). "Like supernatural creatures, the Europeans brought wealth and disease, life and death" (30).

According to Glass, the *hamatsa* dance symbolically reconciled the conflict between traditional Kwakiutl society and European influence, which included both positive and negative aspects. "The initiate . . . was consumed by, surrounded by, and contained by *Baxbakwalanuxsiwae,* representing the colonial European society," theorizes Glass. "As he is tamed and vomited from the cannibal, reborn with new social means, so too shall the natives be absolved from deleterious white rule to return to their own ceremonial and economic activity" (29).

But social tensions increased as the nineteenth century progressed. "As the Europeans were politically and spatially assimilating the [Amerindians], the [Kwakiutl] were conceptually and symbolically assimilating the whites," notes Glass (31). "By constantly assimilating European presence, the [Kwakiutl] resisted being consumed themselves. By becoming food for each other [sustaining each other spiritually], they refused to become food for the Other" (34).

Euro-Canadians continued to cause increasingly serious disruptions in traditional life. The fur trade subsided, settlers moved northward, missionaries attempted to wean the natives from "pagan" ways, and government officials tried to mold them into "productive workers." The native population was decimated by disease, alcohol abuse, and alienation. In reaction, the *hamatsa* dance became increasingly elaborate, violent, symbolic, and secretive.

But colonization and the pressure of secularization also caused a major change in both daily life and ceremonial behaviour among the Kwakiutl. According to anthropologist Helen Codere (1961, 451), age-old beliefs in the supernatural and the energy once invested in war-like activity shifted to a concentration on material wealth and potlatching. Codere (451, 474) and Wike (1952, 97) say this was a key part of the decline and gradual disappearance of traditional religious practices that occurred in the mid-nineteenth century among all Northwest Coast Indian cultures, except, presumably, the Coast Salish.

"By the end of the nineteenth century, the Kwakiutl ritual had been considerably modified," wrote the historian Reay Tannahill in 1975. "Dogs were substituted for corpses and, instead of biting bits out of people the *hamatsa* merely shaved off a sliver of skin and sucked it. Nowadays, the ceremonial dance has even become something of a tourist attraction" (Tannahill 1975, 119). Instead of killing and devouring slaves, a "copper" (copper shield, or figurative body) was thrown on the ground in front of the fire to tempt the cannibal dancer. Each copper was worth several thousand blankets. The practice continues today. Each time a copper is purchased, it increases in value. Some have come to represent vast wealth. The author has attended two winter potlatches in Alert Bay, during which small coppers were cast at the feet of cannibal dancers, who feigned temptation. Chief Harry Assu, chief of the Lekwiltok tribe of the Kwakiutl, described a transfer of coppers at a huge potlatch held in June 1984 by the We-Wai-Kai band at Cape Mudge to honour his dead wife (Assu 1989, 111-13). The exchange of coppers was followed by the Red Cedar Bark ceremony, which Assu said involved the reenactment of "the dark side of our history." It featured an *hamatsa* dance, the rights to which Assu had obtained from James Sewid, a respected Kwakiutl from Alert Bay who was instrumental in perpetuating cannibal dance rituals (113-15).[2]

Both the *hamatsa* ceremony's lasting quality and the echoes of ancient religious beliefs that continued to resonate showed how important a role it played in Kwakiutl culture. The themes of ritual death and rebirth, of continuity with the past in the face of social devastation, of ultimate reliance on the power of transformation and resurrection — all endured.

According to anthropologist Pliny Goddard (1924, 86), the Kwakiutl gave specific accounts of killing slaves to provide "food" (i.e. spiritual sustenance) for members of the elite cannibal society. Among the houses that the Kwakiutl believed were occupied by supernatural spirits, none was more important than the home of *Baxbakwalanuxsiwae*. The wild, terrifying Man-Eater not only gave the band its most prized ceremony, he "is believed to still initiate all the candidates received into the cannibal society," wrote Goddard in 1924, confirming Boas' observations. Anthropologist Philip Drucker expressed similar views in the 1950s and 1960s (Drucker 1955, 148-53; 1965, 161-67).

Among the Kwakiutl, each spectacular winter ceremony began with at least one man announcing that his son was ready to assume membership in a secret society, the highest of which was the cannibal society. Over time, these societies had taken the place of *numayms* — lineage groups that formed the primary units of the social structure. Similar to clans, each *numaym* had its own guardian spirit, mythical ancestor, or totem which was represented by a crest. The crest and the privileges that went with it were the property of the *numaym's* highest ranking member.

These elite groups, which were limited to select families, gathered at specific, separate locations. They formed a strictly ranked nobility (Boas 1895, 338-39; Mead [1937] 1976, 184-88; Spradley 1963, 21-24). Ownership and elitism were the secular motives for displaying crests, but these representations always conveyed an older, simpler, more basic content of spirit power (Carlson 1992, 16).

Hamatsa dancer, *sketched by Franz Boas' artist in 1895.*

A son's right to initiation in a society was won through marriage. As part of the marriage bargain, the prospective father-in-law promised to give the groom a place in a secret society. He also held the membership in trust for his son-in-law's male children. When a grandson came of age, his father asked the father-in-law to complete the deal. The father-in-law returned the dowry plus interest — often as much as five times the wealth originally delivered (Drucker 1955, 122).

Only rich men's sons could join the secret society, which was limited to a few members of a clan. The dues paid to the society were steep and the cost of a huge feast could be enormous. But admission brought prestige and influence. Society members were viewed with awe. Everyone took care not to offend them.

The entire band was called together and notified of the pending dramatic ceremony, which always revolved around a single theme: the young hero's encounter with a spirit who kidnapped him, gave him supernatural powers, and returned him transformed to the village. The people were told to purify themselves and abstain from all sexual relations during the four days that the youth was taken by the cannibal spirit to his home in the north for initiation by the mythological beings that lived there.

When four days had passed, the band members were instructed to reassemble for the boy's anticipated return. During the winter ceremony, the people were grouped according to the societies in which they held membership. The *hamatsa* or cannibal society held the seat of honour, with the others ranked according to animal names. Each individual was given a special name during the ceremony, which consisted of three days of dancing and celebration (Drucker 1955, 123-25).

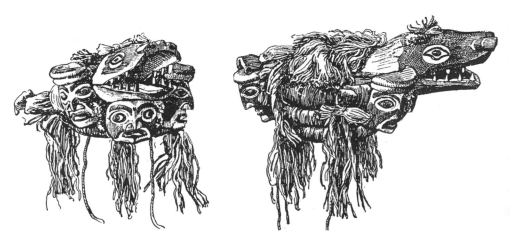

Hamatsa head ring *(front and side view),*
collected by Johan Adrian Jacobsen in 1881.

Early in the morning on the ceremony's climactic fourth day, the Ghost Dancer announced the novice's return. Older members of the *hamatsa* society ran in from both ends of the long house and dropped from the rafters crying "Hap, hap, hap (eat, eat, eat)." Attracted by the cries, the novice jumped down from a hole in the roof (the Mouth of Heaven) and ran around the fire wearing a skirt of hemlock branches. He had returned from the spirit world. He wore a head band but no mask. His face was grotesquely distorted by his craving for human flesh. He trembled with excitement, gnashed his teeth, and moaned. He attacked everyone, biting flesh whenever he could. Chased by the *hamatsas,* he escaped through a secret door at the rear of the building, leaving his hemlock skirt behind. After it was burned, the assembly was dismissed.

The band waited on the beach for the novice *hamatsa* to reappear, so they could catch and tame him. They used a naked man as bait. When the novice rushed up and bit the volunteer, he was surrounded by the people. The novice's *kinqalalala* (female guide) appeared. Naked, she danced lasciviously backward into the long house, trying to lure him inside. But the *hamatsa's* desire could not be satisfied by sexuality.

By raising a cannibal pole and setting up the screen that portrayed the front of Man-Eater's sacred house, the people finally convinced the *hamatsa* to come inside. The cannibal pole was a series of faces with wide mouths, through which the *hamatsa* climbed up and down. His passages between heaven and earth represented a series of swallowings and vomitings — necessary steps in the process of transformation. Each time the *hamatsa* came out of a mouth he uttered the cannibal cry: "Hap, hap, hap." At the bottom of the pole was the frightening figure of a *tsonoqua.*

The *tsonoquas* were giant, wide-eyed, hairy, black-bodied women who lived deep in the woods. Strong enough to tear down large trees, these big-breasted creatures could travel underground and shout so loudly that lightning flashed from their canoes. They lured children away from their homes, roasted them alive and ate their flesh. But a *tsonoqua* had two fatal flaws: vanity and stupidity. Clever warriors could trick her into making herself vulnerable enough to be killed. When her skull was used as a wash basin, the child bathed with its water became unusually strong (Boas 1935, 144–46).

After slipping up and down the pole three times, the frenzied *hamatsa* ran around biting people's arms. He nibbled on a corpse offered by his *kinqalalala*. He fled repeatedly to the secret inner room through Man-Eater's mouth. In this symbolic womb, he regurgitated all the flesh he had consumed. His helpers made a careful accounting of the token payments given to the spirits by all those who had agreed to be bitten by the *hamatsa*. As Man-Eater's agent, he knew how to transform that flesh into creative substance and reaffirm humanity's ultimate destiny.

Typical cannibal pole.
After climbing to the top of the pole, the initiate faced downward, uttered the cannibal cry, and entered the mouth of the man on top. Next, the initiate came out of Raven's mouth, gave the cannibal cry, and slipped into the man's mouth below. Then the initiate emerged from Tsonoqua's mouth at the bottom of the pole and voiced the cannibal cry again.

Through all these acts, the *hamatsa* demonstrated the powers with which the spirits had endowed him. It took considerable dancing and singing to calm him down (Boas 1935, 127; Underhill 1945, 189-90; Walens 1981, 16, 141-48).

"In theory, the cannibal novice, while he has been absent, has become accustomed to eating corpses," wrote Goddard. "In the accounts of former ceremonies his woman attendant entices him into the assembly house by holding in front of him a corpse secured from the nearby village burial place. The candidate is said to have eaten the dried skin from the body and to have been joined in his feasting by the older members of the society. Often there would be contests to see which 'tribe' had a cannibal society member that could outdo the others in corpse eating. There are also accounts of slaves being killed to supply fresh food for the cannibals" (Goddard 1924, 128).[3] Anthropologist Margaret Mead ([1937] 1976, 201) noted that the *kinqalalala* was naked.

According to Goddard, Drucker and others, the winter ceremony's religious significance was grounded in the Kwakiutl belief that, during this period, invisible supernatural beings, who usually remained remote, made social contact with men. Similar rituals were practised by other bands. Drucker said the Kwakiutl ceremonials were "primarily theatrical productions" for "displaying hereditary privileges rather than predominantly religious rites" (Drucker and Heizer 1967, 82).

In 1944, two decades after the Canadian government had outlawed the key ritual, anthropologist Ruth Underhill noted: "The [cannibal] societies have long disappeared from the Northwest and perhaps they were fading away even before the white men came. The spirit dance, however, was too deeply connected with men's interpretation of life to completely disappear, and we have seen how some people carry it on to the present day" (Underhill 1945, 190). Despite the impact of Christianization, the natives' whole pattern of living, which evolved around the vision quest, would not die. Winter ceremonies continued. Spirit dancing, though suppressed by the church for decades, was secretly sustained and eventually revived in the 1950s and 1960s.

Winter ceremony at Gilford Island in 1946. Photo said to be taken by a provincial policeman. (Courtesy: Royal British Columbia Museum PN 15250-41)

In 1953, anthropologist James Spradley analyzed the guardian spirit quest as it was practised by the Kwakiutl. He found that it involved both ideological and ritualistic components, the underlying theme being self-purification. From early childhood until late in life, every member of the society was expected to engage in the quest. Down through the ages, the emphasis in these spiritual experiences had shifted from the individual to the group, from the spontaneous to the formal, from induced psychological states to simulated experiences, from personal acquistion of power and privileges to ritual transmission of inherited rights (Spradley 1963, 7, 14-15, 18, 51-54).

According to Spradley, this historical development saw the "ritual constellation" of the guardian spirit quest become the basis for 18 secret societies among the Kwakiutl. It was the key feature of initiation ceremonies that involved six stages: preparation, abduction, isolation, return to normality, validation through public display, and purification. The ceremony reaffirmed basic cultural values and transmitted them from one generation to the next, giving continuity to the social order. The principal norms included dependence, collective cooperation, individual competition, emotional expression, and acceptance of inequality in rank and wealth (35, 26, 81, 75-80).

In 1972, Spradley edited the autobiography of James Sewid, an influential Kwakiutl who helped preserve the cannibal dance ceremony during the entire period that it was illegal. Sewid, who was first initiated into the cannibal society at age five, gave a detailed description of his re-initiation as the secret society's top dancer at Alert Bay in 1932, even though it was against the law. Sewid played a key role in deceiving an investigating Mountie from Ottawa about the true nature of the ceremony and in convincing the sergeant to turn in a favourable report. He also described another ceremony held in 1965 (Spradley 1969, 81-94, 245). By 1974, the guardian spirit ceremonial practised by Coast Salish, a variation on the Kwakiutl theme, was being hailed by white academics as a highly effective therapeutic treatment program (Jilek 1974, iii).

Present day Indian leaders have struggled to keep the ancient legends, songs, and dances alive. Quietly and persistently, native elders have urged young people trying to adapt to life in big cities not to lose touch with their heritage. The impact of spirit dancing has been contradictory: it has helped restore ancient traditions for the group but it has not always benefited individuals. For example, the sacred ritual is often used as a type of native therapy for people suffering problems with drug and alcohol abuse. After four days of rigorous initiation, a person is supposed to have visions of his powers, hear his "spirit song" and emerge with a new, positive outlook on life. But since 1972, at least seven coastal Indians in British Columbia have died during the spirit dance ceremony. Inquests into some of the deaths concluded that they were accidents or "due to natural causes." In defending the practice, natives say the people who died were in poor health. They say it is an honour to be allowed to dance, and many people volunteer.

But David "Rocky" Thomas of Duncan, British Columbia, had a contrary experience. In February 1988, eight men from the Cowichan band grabbed the 35-year-old longshoreman and took him to the Somenos long house where they forced him to endure the grueling four-day ritual. Unknown to Thomas, born the son of the hereditary chief of another band, his common-law wife had asked the elders to initiate her husband.

"They held me horizontally in the air and took turns, two at a time, biting me and digging their fingers into my stomach," said Thomas. "They did it four times each morning and four times each night for four days. During that time they never gave me any food, except for two cups of water a day." As part of the spiritual awakening, he was also hit with a ceremonial pole-rattle of heated deer hooves and whipped with cedar branches. The torture put Thomas in hospital, suffering from dehydration and ulcer problems. He sued seven members of the band. In February 1992, B.C. Supreme Court Justice Sherman Hood awarded him $12,000 in damages.

The defendants claimed they had an aboriginal right to initiate spirit dancers. "We treated Rocky the same way we have done it for many years," said Leonard Peters, the Cowichan band elder and spirit dancer who supervised the ritual. "One of our elders told us 'no roughing up, no biting.' So I saw that nothing like that happened. If this decision stands, it could dismember part of our culture."

But Justice Hood noted that another man had died during the ceremony two days before Thomas was abducted. "If spirit dancing includes criminal conduct as an integral part of it," said Justice Hood "it could not be said to be an aboriginal right." He suggested the ceremony be restricted to willing subjects.

Thomas's legal action was the first time in Canada that a native has sued for being subjected to ritual cannibalism. In the wake of his court victory, Freda Cooper, a 59-year-old Salish woman who is a member of the Native Women's Association of Canada, said she knows several women who have been abducted for spirit dance rituals but are too fearful to seek recourse in the courts (*Vancouver Sun*, March 16, 1992).

Despite the publicity surrounding the Thomas case, the number of willing spirit dance participants may be increasing, if Henry Seaweed is an example. He is one of many native people who are returning to "the old ways" to regain their spiritual bearings. The 55-year-old Vancouver postal worker is the grandson of Willie Seaweed, great chief of the Nakwaxda'xw, a southern Kwakiutl tribe from Blunden Harbour in Nugent Sound. When he was six, Henry received the grizzly bear dance from his grandfather. At age eight, he heard stories about Man-Eater, spent two months in seclusion at home and returned from the spirit world to perform the cannibal dance in the big house. Without fully understanding the ritual's significance, the youngster became a man and a member of the prestigious society of *hamatsa*.

As a young man, Henry went against his grandfather's wishes, married a white woman and took a job in Vancouver. He did not dance again for almost 20 years and became a heavy drinker. In 1974, he travelled to Campbell River for a pole-raising to hear his father, Joe Seaweed, sing. But Joe got drunk instead. Henry went to the ceremony alone, and accepted the elders' invitation to dance. He danced again in 1977 at a huge potlatch in Alert Bay. In January 1992, Seaweed returned to Alert Bay for another Kwakiutl potlatch. He taught three young men the *hamatsa* dance and performed it during the 16-hour ceremony.

Henry Seaweed does not pretend to understand some of the issues that face native people today, but he does know they need to keep their culture alive. He helps by teaching them to dance. "I'll keep dancing until I'm too fat to get up and do it," he says (Kines 1992).

The comparative study of modern spiritualism, mysticism, and religious ecstasy by people of all shades of opinion brought a new appreciation of the transcendental experiences achieved by Northwest Coast Indians during their winter ceremonies. With their cannibalistic overtones placed in proper perspective, and viewed as a fundamental part of a highly developed religious system, these rituals were finally seen as profound spiritual dramas involving the seizure of a human being by a divinity. Psychiatrists, theologians and social workers began to develop what one social anthropologist called a "sociology of ecstasy" (Lewis 1971, 18ff).

Central to this state of possession by a spiritual force was the shaman, who conquered and domesticated malign power and transformed it into benign spiritual energy. Professor Ioan Lewis' description echoes the experiences of the *hamatsa*.

> The shaman's initiatory experience is represented as an involuntary surrender to disorder, as he is thrust protesting into the chaos which the ordered and controlled life of society strives so hard to deny, or at least to keep at bay. No matter how valiantly he struggles, disorder eventually claims him and marks him with the brand of a transcendental encounter. At its worst . . . this is seen as a baneful intrusion of malign power. At its best . . . it represents a danger-laden exposure to the powers of the cosmos. In both cases, the initial experience withdraws the victim from the secure world of society and of ordered existence, and exposes him directly to those forces which, though they may be held to uphold the social order, also ultimately threaten it.
>
> This symbolic wound, which asserts the supremacy of the

gods as the arbiters of both disorder and of order, is a necessary but not a sufficient condition for the assumption of the shamanistic calling. . . . Out of the agony of affliction and the dark night of the soul comes literally the ecstasy of spiritual victory. In rising to the challenge of the powers which rule his life and by valiantly overcoming them in this crucial initiatory rite which reimposes order on chaos and despair, man reasserts his mastery of the universe and affirms his control of destiny and fate.

The shaman is thus the symbol . . . of independence and hope. Through him the otherwise unfettered power of the world beyond human society is harnessed purposefully and applied to minister to the needs of the community. If by incarnating spirits he embodies the most profound intrusion of the gods into the realm of human society, his mastering of these powers dramatically asserts man's claim to control his spiritual environment and to treat with the gods on terms of equality. In the person of the shaman, man triumphantly proclaims his supremacy over elemental power which he has mastered and transformed into a socially beneficent force. (188-89)

This transcendental experience "is not to be understood in terms of individual psychopathology," said Lewis. On the contrary, it is a "culturally defined initiation ritual" that binds shaman and divinity together, each possessing the other. Spirit possession and shamanism are a type of "pre-scientific psychotherapy," Lewis concluded. Through his heroic role, the shaman transmutes the negative aura of witchcraft and cannibalism into positive charisma. The "patients" construct a social myth that is relived by the shaman, who describes the experience for those he serves (192-94).

Some of the most profound descriptions of the world view that was shaped by this powerful, enduring purification process have come from those contemporary interpreters of native ways known as anthropologists.

12

The Natives' World View

The cannibal spirit made me a winter dancer.
The cannibal spirit made me pure.
I do not destroy life; I am a life maker.
SONG THAT PRECEDES CANNIBAL DANCE
(BOAS 1966, 253)

IT IS IMPOSSIBLE for any of us to liberate ourselves completely from the way of life in which we were raised, yet anthropologists — committed to a global view of human life — have shown that partial liberation is possible, if one is prepared to become sufficiently absorbed in another way of living and recognize the contingency and relativity of one's own value system. Franz Boas believed that by articulating cultural differences and diversity, responsible "Other-knowing" is not only possible, but it can involve discovery of "fundamental tendencies common to humanity" (Boas 1940, 341).

"We think, feel and act faithfully to the traditions in which we live," wrote Boas. "The only means by which we might be freed is the immersion in a new life and understanding for a thinking, a feeling, and an acting that has not grown up on the soil of our own civilization, but that has its sources in another cultural stream."[1] Convinced that anthropology provides the means for liberating the human mind, Boas strove to depict native culture on its own terms, not on ours. He actively campaigned against ethnocentrism. The extent to which he achieved that objective is a

225

matter of debate among contemporary anthropologists. But the magnitude of his findings remains impressive.[2] From 1888 to 1931, Boas and his native assistant George Hunt collected almost 10,000 pages of published details about traditional values and ideas among the Northwest Coast Indians. More than two-thirds of it concentrated on the Kwakiutl.

Boas developed a type of "salvage ethnography" that culled ethnographic facts from the ruins of contemporary native cultures. The aim was to reconstruct traditional cultures, using information obtained from the memories of elders about the fading vestiges of a rapidly receding past. Despite the mass of details that he accumulated about the Kwakiutl, Boas was never able to create a unified picture of that complex, but representative native culture. His numerous followers, many of whom produced excellent studies, paid little attention to the intellectual, philosophical, and psychological content of Northwest Coast society.[3] Few of them avoided the trap of translating the outward forms of native culture into the limited set of concepts that make up our own world view. Most of these studies were based on fieldwork after 1935, which would soon shift from salvage ethnology to studying native adaptations to changing conditions. Demographic and economic collapse had already drastically altered traditional beliefs. Where outward ritual forms did remain, their full inner meaning had been lost. With few potlatches to observe, ethnographers relied almost entirely on informants who remembered "the old ways." But none of them was able to explain fully — to their own people, let alone researchers from another culture — the thinking behind the legends they recounted and the ceremonies they recalled.

Ironically, that role has fallen to a new breed of shamans — anthropologists who often enjoy unusual and privileged positions as professional intermediaries between cultures. As noted earlier, one of the first was Ruth Benedict who advanced the theory that Northwest Coast Indians held a Dionysian world view, which stressed the importance of seeking transcendental feelings of ecstasy through excess. Her rich, imaginative interpretations of native myths offered new insights into the way these people may have looked at life.

Benedict found that the *guardian-spirit* experience, which involved a select individual being *possessed* by a supernatural power and having a *vision,* was the "largest and most basic concept of Indian religion" in North America (Benedict 1974, 43). She said it was reflected in tribal mythology across the continent. But no native society had integrated the complex into the fabric of their culture as thoroughly as the Northwest Coast Indians. Their mythology was dominated by stories about a large number of guardian spirits with personal names, particular superhuman powers, unique personalities, and legendary life histories. None was more powerful than *Baxbakwalanuxsiwae* — the most fearsome supernatural god. No intermediary was more important than the *hamatsa.* As the incarnation of a god, he played the role of *avatar* in Hindu mythology.[4] Northwest Coast society was protected, preserved and held together by ritualized practices aimed at keeping the guardian-spirit relationship active and viable. It was a concept that unified the culture for ages (81, 44, 25-26).

For example, the Kwakiutl integrated the guardian-spirit concept into the organization of their clans and secret societies. Once an individual member was initiated into a secret society and recognized as a guardian spirit to whom a supernatural patron had appeared, this badge of rank, authority, power and wealth in the clan was passed on from one generation to another by inheritance. Elaborate winter ceremonials maintained the tradition of celebrating the guardian-spirit experience and recognizing the limited number of those who held this special title. The powerful belief was sustained. But the more a *vision* could be inherited, the less important its authenticity became, compared with simply maintaining social organization. According to Benedict, the experience of repeated spiritual revelations which had unified Northwest Coast society for thousands of years became largely a "social fiction" (Benedict 1974, 55, 12-13, 26, 67). In the 1990s, that way of life is struggling to renew itself.

Koskimo *Hamatsa* emerging from the woods.
Photograph by Edward S. Curtis, 1914.
(Courtesy: Native American Trading Company, Denver)

When it comes to explaining Kwakiutl culture as it was lived and envisioned by the natives in the distant past, Stanley Walens, professor of Anthropology at the University of Virginia, is probably the scientist who has addressed the task most successfully and eloquently (Walens 1981). Starting with a different premise from Benedict, Walens added a significantly new slant to the interpretation. He characterized the Kwakiutl pursuit of transcendental feelings in their religious actions as Apollonian, not Dionysian. In his view, they sought order, not excess. He said the Kwakiutl vision quest, sacred dances, potlatches, and ceremonials were all aimed at seeking sacred states of superhuman self-control and purity, not ecstasy (41). During the search, an initiate realized that the guardian spirit provided essential assistance. At the same time, the person believed the supernatural was dangerous; it could only be overcome by careful performance of rituals and alertness at the time of encounter.

Walens set out to examine three aspects of the Kwakiutl world view: its fundamental structure, the rules of morality that sustain it, and the way these operate "throughout the entire intellectual universe of the Kwakiutl" (5). He asserted that the Kwakiutl defined their identities, their ideal society, and their place in the natural universe through a basic set of metaphors — all related to assimilation, eating, and cannibalism. As a universal activity, eating formed the basis for morality in a totally interrelated and sympathetic system of causality that was significantly different from our self-centered linear concept. "The Kwakiutl universe is predicated on a single, fundamental assumption," said Walens. "Some beings are eaten by other beings and . . . it is the role of some beings to die so that other beings may feed on them and live" (12). Food was the metaphor of social relationships. Morality stemmed from renunciation of self-interested desire, from overcoming — not ignoring — evil thoughts and desires (137).

Visually, the Kwakiutl world was filled with mouths belonging to a variety of fearsome, voracious creatures. Oral imagery played important roles in myths, rituals, social organization, and healing. For example, by chewing, sucking, moaning, spitting blood, and vomiting, shamans used their oral power to counteract destructive supernatural forces that brought illness and death. Animals used for major crests — beaver, bear, eagle, wolf, raven, and killer whale — possessed three similar traits: they were social, noisy, and ravenous.

Creation, birth, and child-rearing were also seen as oral processes. For the Kwakiutl, the source of human life did not reside in semen but in vomit (Walens 1981, 15). The infant's primal hunger for food was related to the adolescent's craving for status and power. To counteract this destructive voracity, parents employed a long series of repressive practices throughout their offsprings' childhood. Walens noted that, in pre-adolesence, these climaxed in formal rituals:

> The ultimate projection of the power of primal hunger comes in the Cannibal Dance of the sacred winter ceremonials. The *hamatsa's* desire to eat human flesh is a manifestation of all the forces that can destroy society, and the ritual of taming the 'cannibal' is a metaphorical extension of child socialization. The Cannibal Dance is a sacred dance, not just an expression of secular relations and secular powers. It is the keystone to the entire interaction between mankind and the supernatural, between the bestial and humane facets of human nature, and between the cosmic forces of creation and those of destruction. It both represents and is the moment of the utter taming of those forces that would send the world into the chaos of uncontrollable rapaciousness. (15-16).

The winter potlatch, featuring the cannibal dance, unites all creatures within a unitary, coherent system of behaviour that reflects a basic morality. This makes its religious significance far more important than its economic overtones.

The Kwakiutl believed that humans survive only because the spirits gave them food. In return, people were obligated to give lives, in the form of human souls, to the spirits. The transformation of rebirth occurred through two processes: vomit and fire. "Through cyclic reincarnations, the original ancestors of the

Two masked performers in the Kwakiutl winter dance represent Cannibal Raven and *Hoxhok* — huge mythical birds serving in the house of the supernatural man-eating being, Baxbakwalanuxsiwae. *The mandibles of these large wooden masks are controlled by strings. Photo by Edward S. Curtis, 1914. (Courtesy: Garfinkel Publications)*

Kwakiutl remain alive throughout all time," said Walens. "Animals, spirits and humans form a ritual community — a cooperative mutual-assistance group" (17-24). The anthropologist Irving Goldman designated them "ritual congregations":

> No part, no person, no tribe, no species, no body of supernatural beings is self-sufficient. Each possesses a portion of the sum of all the powers and properties of the cosmos; each must share with all or the entire system of nature would die. . . . Kwakiutl religion represents the concern of the people to occupy their proper place within the total system of life, and to act responsibly within it, so as to acquire and control the powers that sustain life. (Goldman 1975, 177)

Reciprocation and transformation provided another way of being in the world.

Myths are created to tell us what transpires in the soul. The repetition of creation myths by the Kwakiutl ceremonies represents the equivalent of prayers. These are followed by ritualized sacred actions that have magical consequences. This state of sacredness is so powerful that it can engender fear and trembling in the depths of the soul. It stems from awe at the spirit-world's power, from awareness of personal insignificance, and from the act of transcending everyday reality. The impact of this sacred state is seen in the frenzied trembling displayed by the dancer.

Initiation into the cannibal society involves the expression in human life of the vast powers that originate in and emanate from the home of Man-Eater — the personification of insatiable hunger and its destructive force. All *hamatsa* are related by their communion with the cannibal spirits, especially *Baxbakwalanuxsiwae*. Although membership in the society may be inherited, the heir cannot dance in a sacred ceremony until he has had a vision that confirms his transcendence (Walens 1981, 43-44).

Among the Kwakiutl, as in all Northwest Coast societies, the collection and distribution of food was tightly organized into subordinate, but cooperative and interdependent roles. Through special rites, chiefs convinced food-animals to give up their bodies to humans. Designated commoners collected the food, which was owned communally and always retained the essence of the animal from which it was taken. One group of people controlled the food itself; another group controlled the process by which it was transformed. Similarly, through ritual cannibalism, the tribe controlled the people's flesh; the *hamatsa,* through his relationship with Man-Eater, controlled the process of purification and renewal. New life could be created only when both groups cooperated. Behind the entire process was the power of *Q!aneqelaku,* the Transformer — the spirit who creates the cycle of reincarnation that transforms an amoral, hunger-driven existence into a state that is moral and hunger-controlled. The Transformer myth expresses the charter of Kwakiutl society. It also establishes the basis for morality (Walens 1981, 83, 137).

"Hunger is the force that motivates the world," said Walens "and the control of hunger gives man and spirit the ability to control the world's motion." The cannibal dance ceremony reenacts this primal conflict between hunger and its submission to collective ritual, between narcissistic desire and socialization. All the rituals involve the concept of taming the initiate and returning him to live in society.

As a ceremony about symbolic rebirth, the cannibal dance shares a common metaphorical structure with other Kwakiutl ceremonies of initiation. The taming of *hamatsas* resembles the socialization of children. The initiates came from the spirit realm to which Man-Eater had taken them. Like the first *hamatsa,* they come into the world naked, they are reared by a female assistant, they dance in the womb and live off their mother's flesh, their hunger cannot be denied, they are ignorant of proper behaviour, and they will eventually devour their parents' wealth (Walens 1981, 157).

The Kwakiutl believed all humans were cannibals, who came into the world from the animal realm. As all humans carried vestiges of their previous cannibalistic identity, each one had to be socialized. "The *hamatsa* ceremony recapitulates the entire process of birth," said Walens. "The actions by which the *hamatsa* is captured and tamed recapitulate the rituals by which a soul is captured, tamed, and reborn. Once humans have reaffirmed their willingness to allow this spirit to live among them, the *hamatsa* retires to the sacred inner room and vomits up the transformed flesh, an act symbolic of his transformation from a destructive to a creative being. . . . The *hamatsa* is finally tamed when he is made to inhale the smoke of a burning blood-soaked menstrual napkin, the transformed substance of the womb" (158). Once the sacred smoke enters his body, he is satiated, because his primal desire for food has been satisfied. Further purification, fulfillment of certain obligations, and observation of taboos for four months confirmed the *hamatsa's* separation from his supernatural associates and his reintegration into society.

Kwakiutl cannibalism did not represent the type of gastronomic custom that may have existed among certain aboriginal societies in Africa or the South Sea Islands. On the contrary, the eating of human flesh was abhorrent to all Northwest Coast Indians. It was precisely this loathing that made the gruesome rite all the more powerful (Mead [1937] 1976, 201). According to Walens, ritual cannibalism reenacted the concept that is the keystone of Kwakiutl thought:

"Hunger is power, but the knowledge of how to control hunger is an even greater power." Even the *hamatsa's* ferocious hunger can be conquered by the force of organized social action. The strength of ritual can transform the cannibal's destructive craving into self-control and creative power. Despite hunger's terrifying power, despite its fearsome masks, morality can prevail (Mead [1937] 1976, 162).

The Kwakiutl winter ceremonials teach a basic survival principle: if humans have the knowledge to use food properly, they never need to fear starvation and death. A wise hunter does not kill merely for food or because he is hungry. He has a responsibility to kill, to eat, and to sustain those human and supernatural beings with whom he shares a covenant. That social charter is focused on controlling hunger — the force that motivates the world. Only by conquering it can both human beings and spirits find the ability to control the universe jointly (Mead [1937] 1976, 162-63, 137).

"Today," said Robert Ardrey "we have small hope of comprehending our world unless we understand that man still, in his inmost being, remains a hunter. . . . Ritual guided our hands — the rituals of a hunting people that would lend hope to the hunt and protection for the hunter. . . . The central concept that we brought to evolving man was the concept of death. . . ." According to Ardrey, our hunting days left two "ineradicable legacies" imbedded in our psyches: "an inner need to believe in forces larger and more enduring than oneself" and the illusion that humanity holds a central position in the universe (Ardrey 1976, 9, 177, 202).

The next chapter suggests a way to extricate ourselves from that dilemma.

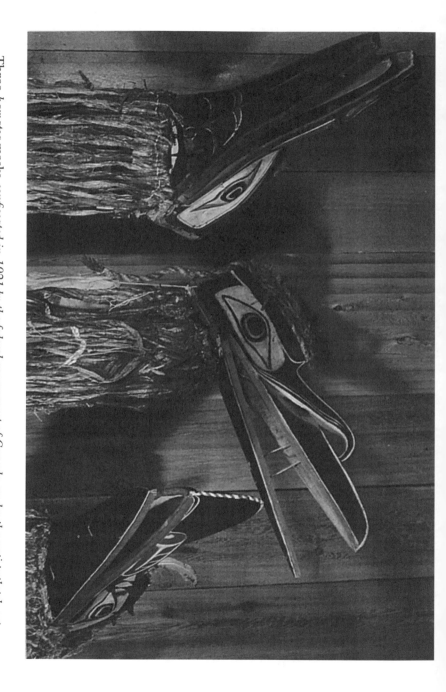

Three *hamatsa* masks confiscated in 1921 by the federal government of Canada under the anti-potlatch act. In 1979, the National Museum of Man in Ottawa repatriated these masks and others and returned them to the Kwakwaka-wakw. Now, the masks are on display in the Kwagiulth Museum and Cultural Centre on Quadra Island and the Umista Cultural Centre in Alert Bay. Photo by V. Jensen, 1980. (Courtesy: Umista Cultural Centre)

13

Conjuring a New Morality

*Man feels himself lost in the cosmos because he is
no longer involved in nature. He has freed himself
from superstition but, in the process, has lost his
spiritual values to a positively dangerous degree.*

CARL JUNG

IF IT IS TRUE THAT we find ourselves today caught in a dou-
ble-bind between yearning to believe in a power greater than our-
selves and foolishly thinking we are masters of the universe, what
can be gained from studying the *hamatsa's* vision quest? First, psy-
chiatrists and religious thinkers tell us that the only way out of a
double-bind is to catch one's seemingly demonic tormentors (in
this case, conflicting attitudes) off guard, to start playing unilater-
ally by a new set of rules, and to take an imaginative, daring leap
into unfamiliar territory. Surprisingly, creative solutions often
result. Secondly, as a metaphor for spiritual renewal, the *hamatsa*
model is novel enough to be intriguing, sufficiently challenging
to stimulate the mind and the imagination, and flexible enough
to provide plenty of room for innovation and adaptation.

The aspect of the history of white-native relations on the
Pacific Northwest Coast which has been the subject of this book
indicates that now is the time to seek new sources of spirituality.
During the modern period, formal religion has seen steadily
diminishing participation in communal ritual. Simultaneously,

Europeans and their descendants have systematically destroyed, and nearly obliterated native cultures. In the process, both sides have lost touch with rich spiritual traditions. All of us need to go back and retrieve what we lost.

About four hundred years ago, Western civilization started turning away from the sacred as a viable, powerful mode of thought and behaviour. Post-Renaissance European society shifted its focus to a new, risky secular faith. Dudley Young, author of *Origins of the Sacred,* and others have called it "scientism" — science as religion (Young 1991, 23).[1] Industrialized people have increasingly severed their spiritual connections with the natural world and sacrificed their primal souls in favour of mathematics, machinery, and manipulation. By committing ourselves to science and technology, we have made remarkable progress, but we have also lost touch with our instincts for myth, magic, and mysticism. We have forgotten the ancient meaning of ritual, which often reflects the human subconscious. Alienation, despair, numbness, and dread are pervasive.

Religious forms persist, but the sacred structure of the higher moral order that was grounded in the will of God and a hierarchical chain of life has been discredited and swept away. Religion, ritual, magic, heroism, the sense of a higher purpose, and a broad vision no longer have the power to organize our world. Instead we value individualism and the primacy of what Charles Taylor, professor of Political Science and Philosophy at McGill University, and others have called "instrumental reason" (Taylor 1989 and 1991)[2] — the kind of rationality used to calculate the most efficient means to a given end. Both human characteristics are proving to be two-edged swords.

Individualism has given us more personal freedom and self-fulfilment, but it has also spawned narcissism and nihilism. Instrumental reason has enabled us to develop powerful, liberating technologies, which at the same time threaten to control and possibly destroy our lives.

"What we call man's power over nature turns out to be a power exercised by some men over other men with nature as its instrument," said Clive Staples Lewis in 1943, when he delivered a modest, but remarkably prophetic lecture titled "The Abolition of Man" (Lewis 1947, 35). He argued that our headlong use of applied science to conquer nature has ominous implications for humanity, particularly in the arena of eugenics — the improvement of the human species through the control and manipulation of hereditary factors.

"All long-term exercises of power, especially in breeding, must bear the powers of earlier generations over later ones," said Lewis. "The later a generation comes — the nearer it lives to that date at which the species becomes extinct — the less power it will have in the forward direction. . . . The final stages come when man — by eugenics, by pre-natal conditioning and by an education of propaganda based on a perfect applied psychology — has obtained full control over himself. Human nature will be the last part of nature to surrender to man. The battle will then be won. . . . But who, precisely, will have won it?" (36-37)

Lewis predicted it would be "the conditioners" — those who reduce values to mere natural phenomena and train us how to think. "The conditioners choose what kind of artificial *Tao* [defined by Lewis as "natural law, traditional morality, or first principles of practical reason"] they will, for their own good reasons, produce in the human race. They are the motivators. . . . It is not that they are bad men. They are not men at all. Stepping outside the *Tao*, they have stepped into the void. Nor are their subjects necessarily unhappy men . . . they are artifacts. Man's final conquest has proved to be the abolition of man" (39-41).

In 1977, the Iroquois Indians issued a wake-up call to the Western world at a United Nations Conference on Indigenous Peoples. They said: "Today the species of Man is facing a question of [its] very survival. . . . The way of life known as Western Civilization is on a death path on which their own culture has no viable answers. When faced with the reality of their own destructiveness, they can only go forward into areas of more efficient destruction" (Mohawk Nation 1978).

Many people in our culture share that desperate outlook.

They view technological civilization as an unmitigated decline, because modern reason has triply divided human beings within themselves, among themselves, and from the natural world. They claim we have lost contact with our own natural being, with natural relationships, and with the earth and its rhythms — fundamental qualities that our aboriginal ancestors possessed. Driven by an imperative to dominate our surroundings, we are condemned to unending battle against nature.

This kind of despair has been articulated repeatedly since the Romantic period. But some modern thinkers, both conservative and liberal, reject such fatalism and call for a complex, multi-level intellectual, spiritual, and political struggle to create a moral renewal.

On October 5, 1993, Pope John Paul II issued a 179-page encyclical called *Veritatis Splendor.* It is a remarkable and controversial document that raises fundamental questions about the role of conscience in a technologized world.

Earlier that summer, the Pope spoke to the same issue when he addressed a huge World Youth Day crowd in Denver, Colorado on August 12. He said that moral evil flows from unprincipled personal choice, "because conscience itself is losing the ability to distinguish good from evil. . . . In a culture which holds that no universally valid truths are possible . . . good comes to mean what is pleasing or useful at a particular moment. Evil means what contradicts our subjective wishes. Each person can build a private system of values." According to the Pope, this kind of relativism leads to chaos and self-destruction. He called for a return to an absolute moral code. By implication, he demoted the role of conscience.

Pope John Paul was reaffirming the Catholic Church's traditional concept of natural law, which is at the heart of *Veritatis Splendor.* Natural law has been defined as humanity's innate morality — that which we feel instinctively or intuitively to be right and fair even though it is not prescribed by any legislation, code, or document. As we have seen, Lewis called it *Tao.* To the extent that human beings act on these "first principles of practical reason," they unleash a force that tends to keep human beings human. It is the objective truth that is etched on every human heart. Each of us has the capability of obscuring the etching by making fundamental errors — choosing to violate a higher moral code. But because natural law is a matter of potential, not opinion, it is everlasting. Truth and morality are inseparable. Human reason cannot create values out of thin air and expect nature to conform; humans must rediscover inherent, universal values that are engraved in the human heart.

From the liberal perspective, Charles Taylor voiced a similar challenge when he called for a "retrieval" of the rich moral background and higher ideals that powered the development of Western civilization for centuries, but now have devolved into "the malaise of modernity": debased forms of individualism ("me-ism" and anarchy), instrumental reason (relativism and power-lessness), and political liberty (fragmentation and political apathy). To strengthen the positive aspects of these three modern themes, Taylor said we need to retrieve the "moral force" behind the respective ideals of "authenticity," "self-determining freedom," and "democratic empowerment." Taylor argued that we should not give up personal values. But he pointed out that it is futile and foolish to try to adopt at random any values that attract our attention, regardless of where they come from or how inconsistent they may be. A functional morality is grounded in wisdom that has accrued from life experience, one's cultural history, and an educated conscience.

Our future is in peril unless we can find direct ways to influence human behaviour, individually and collectively. For that to happen, we need to transform our world view. For centuries our behaviour has been sanctioned by a cosmology that tells us it makes sense to organize our lives in terms of consumption and self-fulfilment. The positive results include remarkable technological development, economic growth, and creativity. But on the negative side, we act as if the world were made for us to exploit and control. We have spent the earth's resources in a vain attempt to buy immortality, only to realize that our continued presence inevitably depends on what is left untouched. We strive for self-sufficiency, independence, and autonomy. Seldom in the history of Western civilization have we placed reverence for life above the need to secure our survival. As long as we remain preoccupied with this drive for unfettered freedom, our long journey of self-deception will continue to propel us toward oblivion.

To stave off ecological disaster, we need a new cosmology — one that is more adequate for meeting the challenge of runaway scientism, which threatens either to blow us up with nuclear technology or to erode our humanity with the equally risky instruments of biotechnology — reproductive and genetic engineering. In the last fifty years, nuclear proliferation has escalated beyond our control. Now reproductive intervention is revolutionizing fundamental ideas about what it means to be human, and genetic manipulation is threatening to consume our identity one cell at a time. We seem bent on a perverse process of cannibalizing ourselves — sacrificing one unit of life for the sake of another of the same kind. It is a perilous path.

It takes time for a sea change to occur in the way we view the world, and the tide will turn only when we find the will to cast off the technological determinism that has gripped our consciousness for centuries. Nuclear bombs, reproductive intervention, and genetic manipulation are disturbing realities of modern life. They are also human inventions that can be removed from our culture or at least brought under control. First, we must find the courage to open our minds and the determination to form a fresh vision of a new moral order.

A movement may be emerging composed of young "warriors" who are prepared to take on a formidable enemy — the consciousness of contemporary Western society. These intellectual and spiritual pioneers are today's *hamatsa* — avatars who have walked the line between the shallow and dangerous swamps of modern culture and its grand and promising frontier, between the world of the living and the realm of the spirits. From these states of lucid dread, these men and women have returned cleansed, transformed, and inspired by a new sense of purpose. As guides to the

future, their task is to shatter the old world view and lead human-
ity to a land of promise by way of a different, largely unexplored
route. Their goal is to replace our blind, exploitative compulsions
with a clear vision of self-determination. We can free ourselves by
altering the conditions of our existence, by harnessing the sub-
conscious forces that dominate us.

The bridle for our sacrificial instincts is to be found within
those subconscious drives, which spring from our prehistoric past.
What keeps us from re-exploring that primitive inheritance and
satisfying our undeniable religious hunger is the fear that dragons
lie in wait for the unwary searcher. Primitive fears that made can-
nibalism taboo have been transformed into a modern taboo on
thinking about cannibalism. But the *hamatsa* have charted the
way.

Some of them are psychohistorians and psychoanalytic sociol-
ogists such as Eli Sagan. Asserting that "cannibalism is the ele-
mentary form of institutionalized aggression," Sagan argued in
1974 that "there is something of cannibalism in all subsequent,
sublimated forms of institutionalized aggression." For example, a
person who practises racism is not a cannibal *per se,* but there are
remnants of cannibalism incorporated and sublimated in his
behavior (Sagan 1974, 109).

"War, slavery, racism, imperial domination, destruction of infi-
dels, fascism, the tyranny of men over women, and capitalism are
all the descendants of cannibalism," claimed Sagan. He said the
history of sublimated social aggression began with killing and eat-
ing, which gave way to only killing, which turns into dominance
and tyranny, which are channeled into competition — "a form of
aggression that takes its satisfaction from winning because there is
always someone who loses" (110).

"When it becomes an institutionalized social form and the
losers are left to live in intolerable conditions, without adequate
food, clothing, housing, medical care, education, or expectation
of life, then such a system of winners and losers is an institutional-
ized form of aggression," argued Sagan. "It is a hypocritical
tyranny" (110). The cannibalization of society unleashed in the

inner cities of North America is a glaring example. The cannibalizing of ethnic groups in Bosnia is another.

According to Sagan, 99 percent of all cultures have practised some form of institutionalized aggression (xix). Sagan and others argue that a society undergoing great cultural stress causes some of its members to regress to primitive forms of expressing aggression. "Such regression is pathological," said Sagan. "The sign of a sick society" (140). A healthy society gradually sublimates social aggression into religious ritual, common spiritual values, moral imperatives, and the functioning of conscience.

Today, many intellectual *hamatsa* are turning to non-Western moral resources for their ideas. A few of them are cultural or psychoanalytic anthropologists, who are not only delving into the religion, mythology, literature, and folklore of other cultures but are also aware of the latest developments in molecular genetics. These warriors of the mind started from a single premise: if we want to understand what it is to be human, we will have to explore our earliest beginnings — mysterious, timeless, mythic, archetypal sources. They have found that myths contain universal themes that have nourished creativity, cohesiveness, and moral order in human societies throughout history. They are sifting through mounds of cross-cultural information for fragments of wisdom that will at least guide our journey and possibly give us a parable for reducing the friction that exists between human values and scientism.

More and more, this discord stems from the tendency to cannibalize ourselves with modern technology. To counter that trend, the mythology of the early Northwest Coast Indians — elaborately represented by the Kwakiutl — offers the most provocative, thoroughly documented metaphor that we could ask for. As the anthropologist Peggy Reeves Sanday noted, "Cannibalism is never just about eating but is primarily a medium for messages having to do with the maintenance, regeneration, and, in some cases, the foundation of the cultural order." These metaphysical messages are universal and timeless. "Underlying the specific performance of cannibal ritual is a generic human concern for perpetuating life beyond the limits of individual life histories," said Sanday (Sanday 1986, 3, 54). In ritual cannibalism she found a rich source of myths, symbols, and ceremonies by which tribal people explored their relationship to the world, to other beings, and to life itself (31).

It would be naive to suggest that cosmological perspectives are easily portable from one society to another, and it is not being advocated here that any aboriginal rituals or ceremonies be appropriated or copied by Westerners. It would also be presumptuous to pretend that the Kwakiutl analogy offers Western civilization a comprehensive set of moral guidelines, but it does provide at least three over-arching concepts that could form the foundation of a powerful ecology. These ideas are outlined in the balance of this chapter. Taken together, they could make up a serious package of reform measures — a more authentic form of realism, not fuzzy, liberal idealism. The final chapter of this book will examine ways to achieve these objectives.

Social Integration — The world view of the Northwest Coast Indians included the sophisticated belief that power and prestige flowed directly from one's human and supernatural ancestors, showing that they recognized the importance of biological (i.e. genetic) inheritance. Unable to rely on science for genetic improvement, these indigenous societies turned to mythology and ceremony, often featuring ritual cannibalism, to influence supernatural forces. But each person knew that the essence of who he or she was came from thousands of years of being part of a distinctive family and a rich culture.

Through ritual, they continually acknowledged that their first ancestors had transformed from specific supernatural beings. When a native dancer placed a raven mask on his head, he was not pretending to be a mythical bird. Through a transcendental process, he became Raven. Through a spiritual awakening, he made contact with a larger life force, a greater energy than his own. In dancing the emotion of Raven, he acknowledged the power of the creature he had absorbed — the Raven soul inside himself. He also reaffirmed a spiritual connection with his ancestors. It was this relationship, more than any other, that made him fully integrated with his natural and social world. Nothing reaffirmed this sense of unity more than the cannibal dance ceremony, because the *hamatsa* was acting as a spiritual go-between for the entire community.

The need for this vision of social integration has never been greater than it is today. Many of us tend to think of ourselves primarily as isolated, separated individuals who are often alienated from society. As noted above, individualism has contributed positively to self-fulfilment, self-determination, and originality. But individualism has also led to a misdirected quest for self-containment, which tends to reject the past as irrelevant, deny the responsibilities of solidarity, shun the demands of citizenship, and ignore the needs of the natural environment.

To rekindle a sense of cohesiveness, we need to act collectively to restore our connections with the natural world, to find new ways of celebrating successes and commemorating setbacks, to participate in innovative ceremonies that pay tribute to those who have led the way, and to create vital forms of ritual that remind us of the rules and expectations of spirituality.

A Threatening World — One of the most provocative concepts of the natives' ecology was the belief that they lived in a spontaneous, unpredictable, sometimes menacing environment — one that commanded respect and had to be appeased, i.e. "fed" through acts of ritual cannibalism. Because this idea challenges the scientific notion that nature is morally neutral, it offers the kind of analogy that might enable us to look at our present dilemma in new ways.

Another culture's songs, dances, masks, and rituals are difficult to understand because they express a radically different world view. But their power invites us to make imaginative leaps. To penetrate these symbols of an earlier time, we have to revisit an age when supernatural creatures stalked the forests and heroic young men went searching for cannibal spirits — hostile demons who ruled the world. The ceremonies that commemorated the mythical encounter with these fearsome beings helped the people cope with the mysterious forces in their lives — nature's destructive power, spirits of the sea and forest, and the dark side of their own minds. As legendary medieval knights undertook mythical journeys to slay dragons, the *hamatsa* were sent into the wilderness to confront the embodiments of darkness — those forces that we fear most.

The Kwakiutl mind was preoccupied with hunting, and one of its key elements was the notion that animals might hunt and eat men (Reid 1979, 251). "Since animals are the source of life for humans, animals represent a powerful force that must be assuaged in ritual practice at the same time that the force is incorporated for social ends," wrote Peggy Reeves Sanday in probing the origins of ritual cannibalism among the Kwakiutl. "If humans do not respect the other-than-human power of their compatriots, the latter are in danger of being dominated by their animal-spirit power and cannibalizing humans" (Sanday 1986, 39).

Today, some of our greatest fears are linked to nuclear power and molecular genetics — the very elements of our temporal existence. If these forces are violated, upset, or unleashed in the wrong way, the reaction will be anything but neutral. We are well on the way to consuming our world. The void beckons. It is our ultimate terror.

As a metaphor for our condition, the ritual cannibalism practised on the Pacific Northwest Coast gives us a rich perspective from which we may be able to forge new respect for our environment.

Haida transformation (or double) mask:
closed, raven as a bird; open, raven as a man.

Indebtedness — The Northwest Coast Indians acknowledged that, from the beginning of human life, their world was unified by endless acts of transformation. Ritual ceremonies linked individuals to both the spirit and animal realms, aligned them to the community, and tied it to the world at large. The moment when all these integrating forces came together and indebtedness reached a crescendo was the potlatch, which gave the natives a broad definition of who they were. As the ritual equivalent of a constitution, it determined all the fundamental relationships: politics, government, medicine, education, territory, jurisdiction, and, most importantly, religion.

Many of these aspects of the potlatch, especially remnants of ritual cannibalism, disappeared during the decades of white repression. But the spiritual traditions survived. They remain a vital part of several Northwest Coast Indian communities. The potlatch continues to give these people a way to celebrate publicly the passages of life, to reaffirm their commitment to a community, and to experience the universal power of transformation. Significantly, the gesture that binds potlatch participants together and fixes this extraordinary event in their memory is the act of giving one's wealth to others. Indebtedness is the central feature.

The fatal flaw in the cosmology of Westerners is our narrow, self-centered attitude toward our surroundings. It has turned us primarily into takers, not givers. To act responsibly, one has to feel an obligation, an indebtedness. That can only come from recognizing one's relationship to others and the interdependence of all living things. As long as a large segment of humanity clings to the illusion that it is self-contained and continues organizing the world exclusively for its own benefit, it cannot open its consciousness to being indebted. If we are self-sufficient, then we are free to do as we please. But if we need things outside ourselves, then we must take more than our own desires into account when we act.

In reality, the great void that separates modern people from both their primal souls and the natural world should be filled with indebtedness. We are enmeshed in a complex network of relationships, all of which have contributed to our creation and prolonged our existence. The universe owes us nothing; we owe everything to the cosmos. To acknowledge that debt, we must learn how to act in ways that not only serve our self-interest but also respect universal interests. Responsibility means balancing the ledger — continually repaying what we have received; keeping the environment "fed" or nourished through active conservation, protection, and resource renewal. We need to return to the essence of liberalism: maintaining a balance between the outside forces that affect our lives and a personal sense of responsibility.

Among the early Northwest Coast Indians, all of these ideological or spiritual concepts were embedded in the mythology and ceremonies that involved ritual cannibalism. In the next chapter, we will examine four patterns of aboriginal behaviour that flowed from these ethical principles. Each offers practical, challenging means for transforming our world view.

14

Seeking a New Journey of Purpose

*According to the genetic apocalypse, there
shall come a time when there will be none like
us to come after us.*

PAUL RAMSEY (1970, 25)

WE HUMAN BEINGS are the only creatures who can peer into
the future, contemplate our deaths, and consider what we will
leave our children. Now a terrifying new dimension has been
added to our foresight: the real possibility that humanity will
destroy life itself. History challenges us to seek a new journey of
purpose. Anthropology, psychology, philosophy, and ecology
point the way, if we can give up our ethnocentrism and look for
sources of spiritual renewal in other cultures. We must find a
deeply felt, shared vision that is rich enough to inspire the sense
of collective obligation required to save our planet from catastro-
phe. We also need ritual guidelines that are strong and supple
enough to harness the dangerous ecstasies that lead us to aggres-
sion and violence. To reach these goals, we need to adopt some
time-tested patterns of behaviour. Four such concepts — all linked
directly to ritual cannibalism — were integral to Northwest Coast
Indian life and sustained their ecological outlook.

Sacrifice — Without sacrifice, social order collapses and vio-
lence reigns supreme. For the last 10,000 years humanity has

striven to control violence in three ways: religious beliefs, economic power, and politics backed by military force. Each method has led to different forms of social order. By relying almost exclusively on the latter two forms, contemporary society lurches toward the brink of crisis. It is time to revisit an era when both personal and divine sacrifice were an integral part of a religious worldview.

Through elaborate forms of ritual cannibalism, the Northwest Coast Indians acknowledged that humanity survives by the grace of nature's sacrifice. By the *hamatsa's* rigorous initiation, he learned that becoming an intermediary between the human world and the spiritual realm required several acts of sacrifice: purification, isolation and solitude, surrender to frightening supernatural forces, possession by wild spirits, and lifelong service to the community. All the cannibalistic rituals were designed to drive home the concept that sacrifice is the key to securing human existence, survival, and social order. The ethic of balance, for which humans alone are responsible, entails returning to the cosmos some measure of the sacrifices the universe has made for humanity.

More than any other known culture or set of cultures, the Northwest Coast Indians institutionalized the practice of sacrifice, expressed it collectively, and sustained it generation after generation. Such groups as the Kwakiutl did not indulge in token sacrifices to expiate guilt. They engaged in truly significant, often painful, sometimes actual sacrifice.

Two ideas were central in Kwakiutl thought: metamorphosis and reciprocation. They characterized themselves collectively as "Smoke of the World" (Goldman 1976, 19). Smoke and fire were the most important metaphors of their cannibalistic rituals. To light a fire, was to communicate with the spirits. Shamans said that The-One-Sitting-on-the-Fire and his wife, Heat-Under-the-Fire-Woman, were the life or the soul of the fire in the house. He was the fire and she was the heat. Without both of these "helping spirits" — who many Indians believed were a real man and woman — no firewood could burn (Boas 1921, 1331-33).

The fire's smoke was the visible transfer of material from the human world to the realm of the spirits, who depended on this sustenance and reciprocated by providing food for human survival. By calling themselves "Smoke of the World," the Kwakiutl highlighted their self-image as central actors in the perpetuation of the cosmic cycle (Walens 1981, 9).

The origin of ritual cannibalism among the Kwakiutl was based on the dialectic of reciprocity between animals and humans. They conceived of a reciprocal relationship between the eater and the eaten. Just as animals were hunted, so were humans. Whoever wanted to get food had to become food. Since animals such as salmon gave their flesh to humans, the Kwakiutl believed they should be prepared to reciprocate in kind to maintain a critical web of spiritual communion.

As a people who relied on anadromous (upward running) fish for about 5,000 years, the Kwakiutl formed a special reciprocal relationship with salmon. Like the complementary forces of *yin* and *yang* in Taoism, humans and salmon were interdependent. As mirror images, humans and salmon were united by complex resurrection rituals, which also involved the other animals that eat salmon. The anthropologist Stanley Walens explained the logic of these relationships as follows:

> Since salmon are humans [and vice versa], and humans eat salmon, by analogy humans eat humans and are thus cannibals. Furthermore, crest animals that eat salmon are themselves *de facto* man eaters. . . . Most crest animals actually do eat humans, either live (killer whales, wolves, and bears) or dead (eagles and ravens). Thus, because these animals are all direct links in the cycle of resurrection for both humans and salmon, they are themselves by definition humans. All those animals whose food is in some way related to that of humans . . . must be dealt with in a manner consistent with the highly sacred character of man's role in the chain of being. (Walens 1981, 101)

Many Westerners are losing touch with the concept of sacrifice. In contemporary society it is often seen as an alien idea because it means giving up a degree of control over one's destiny. We are accustomed to maintaining our security at nature's expense. Over the centuries, we have concentrated on acquiring knowledge that we can use to control, harness, and exploit natural resources. Nature has sacrificed more and more so we can become increasingly secure. In the process, we turned nature's bounty into objects for us to manipulate and consume. Throughout our long history of exploitation, we have seldom tilted the scale the other way. Now, the planet faces disharmony and an uncertain future. Our predicament leaves us with much to learn from the traditions of native people.

Deciding to sacrifice short-term security for long-term survival requires a total transformation of the way we view the future. It begins with a new approach to acquiring knowledge. Instead of seeking it primarily to dominate and control nature, we need to learn how to cooperate with the environment. Our access to technological knowledge has been impressive. It has given us remarkable power over our world, enabling us to appropriate natural resources and usurp nature. But in the process, this technological power has polluted the planet and exhausted much of the earth's bounty. Meanwhile, we remain pathetically ignorant when it comes to "empathetic" knowledge — awareness of fundamental relationships, reverence for the living community, and recognition of our special responsibility as its guardians.

Consecration — To transcend the current triumph of secular ideals and create an enduring civilization, we need a new definition of sanctity and a political culture that is infused with a profound sense of the sacred — that which is at the centre of our being. To forge a program for global survival, we must restore the twin concepts of sanctity and evil at the centre of political life. Without a sense that each of us is capable of evil, no one is responsible, everything is a symptom, and we are all victims. Where there is no evil, there is no god.

Through ritual cannibalism, the Northwest Coast Indians acknowledged the sacredness of all life forms — their distinctive life cycles, marvellous transformations, and mysterious connections. Again, the metaphors of fire and smoke capture the essence of this reverence. To us, the sacrifice of enemies or slaves contradicts such a reverential attitude. But Freud pointed out that, in totemistic societies around the world, even the killing of such persons was governed by strict observances. These included appeasement of the slain enemy, restrictions on the slayer, acts of expiation and purification by the slayer, and certain ceremonial rites. "The conclusion that we must draw from all these observances is that the impulses which they express towards an enemy are not solely hostile ones," said Freud. "They are also manifestations of remorse, of admiration for the enemy, and of a bad conscience for having killed him" (Freud 1946, 36, 39).

The Kwakiutl called themselves not only "Smoke of the World," but also "Smoke from their Fires" (Ford [c1941] 1961), which suggests they viewed humans as consumers of energy, who are transitory and in transformation. Both the fire's wood and the human being are dynamic points in the continuum of time and space. But smoke and the individual's life are both impermanent and insubstantial. As smoke is produced by the consuming fire, a human's life history consists of consuming natural wealth by fire. When the fire burns out, both smoke and humans vanish forever (Walens 1981, 10). The intimate relationships among humanity, the natural world, and the spiritual realm were pivotal in the Kwakiutl's self-concept.

During the last few hundred years, we have alienated ourselves from the natural world. Our journey has brought us to a fateful crossroad: we can choose to go on recklessly engineering life or become cooperative participants. Any search for a middle way means turning toward cooperation and participation. There are only two approaches to the age of biotechnology: engineering and ecology — technological mastery or ecological participation. We must choose one way or the other. The choice means committing ourselves to a distinctive set of values. We must decide which we value most: short-term physical security for a certain portion of one species or long-term survival of a delicate global ecosystem; temporal perpetuation at any price or an immortality grounded in spiritual renewal; the power of being architects of illusion or the responsibility of shared stewardship.

To end our exile and rejoin the community of life, we must protect ourselves from ourselves. We will have to overcome our compulsion to dominate the earth. Recognizing that we are only tenants, we will have to abdicate our sovereignty and pursue a cooperative type of management. The challenge of our age is to reconsecrate nature, to respect its sanctity by restoring proper relationships between ourselves and the rest of creation.

Companionship — The primary function of ritual cannibalism among the Northwest Coast Indians was spiritual instruction. Through these ceremonies, the elders and the wisest members of the tribe initiated young *hamatsa* into ancient traditions and taught them what they needed to know to play their role in perpetuating the culture. Above all, a *hamatsa* learned how to experience his spiritual centre, find his sense of poise, and honour all living things. The mark of a successful quest was the recognition that the entire community of life is connected and kept in balance by the mediation of empathetic, respectful individuals. This ecological vision of the human's place in a dynamic world teeming with life was nourished by a deep sense of companionship and belonging. It acknowledged the necessity of participation, sharing, vulnerability, and sacrifice — the willingness to risk one's immediate physical security and to suffer a bit to make things good for the community.

Today, both reproductive and genetic engineering are stripping one organism after another of its identity. We are stocking the planet with artificial people, fabricated creatures, and living gadgets loaded with synthetic devices. Our technologically designed world appears to run smoothly, but it is being drained of the passion that springs from companionship. Without this spiritual nourishment, human existence becomes lonely and loses its purpose.

By reducing life to technical manipulations, bioengineering has the potential to purge the possibilities of psychological transformation that humanity requires to stretch its spiritual boundaries and merge with a community of life. Our dreams have few outlets, our myths are bereft of wisdom. Our increasingly computerized and mechanized culture has forgotten the power that ritual and ceremony can have in bonding a community. We have become isolated and separated individuals.

Yet there is a growing yearning for the security that ritual once provided, for the stability that came from a closer association between humans and nature. It is a testament to the strength of the Northwest Coast Indian culture that the *hamatsa* tradition remains an important part of their lives. But the rest of us face a difficult question: Can we create meaningful and authentic rituals of our own that will help us cope with the threat of runaway technology?

To counterbalance the destructive technological transformations flowing from biological engineering, we need to come together as ancient people did. We, too, can unite in a cooperative partnership to retrieve our natural heritage through active participation in convincing rituals, powerful spiritual instruction, and collective action.

Discipline — All of the *hamatsa's* preparation, training and initiation focused on the need for self-discipline in a world filled with fear, dread, and potential anarchy. He had to purge himself of desire, endure solitude and starvation, control his appetite, and make himself vulnerable to fearsome supernatural spirits. His quest was lonely and dangerous, but it was essential to his community. To prove himself worthy, he had to overcome inhibitions, eat human flesh, and demonstrate that he was overcome by spiritual ecstasy. To feed his ancestral spirits, he had to regurgitate what he had consumed. As a mediator, the *hamatsa's* sacrifices played a crucial role in ensuring his people's immortality. By his rigorously disciplined acts, he showed that people can hope to live on only if they go without, give something back, and leave something unspent. This is what stewardship means. This is what is required to be a guardian of humanity's true legacy: the gift of life for future generations.

The lessons for today's world are clear. We must ask ourselves:

How much is enough? We must find the will to control our appetites. We must discipline our extraction and consumption of natural resources so that the environment has the time and the capacity to reproduce. Our actions must respect the integrity and sanctity of all living things. We must summon the courage to make ourselves vulnerable. We must have the wisdom, willingness, and determination to live more simply and frugally, and to share our wealth.

Above all, these ecological imperatives, which are based on the principle of restoring a balance between humanity and the environment, require rigorous intellectual discipline. Difficult choices will have to be made between activities that contribute to human development at considerable cost to the environment and those that help protect and restore natural resources but restrict human freedom and drain our treasury. In many ways, we will have to learn to say "no" — even to our cherished idea that unlimited, unrestrained freedom of inquiry is sacrosanct. Pushed far enough, all human activity, including the right of intellectual discovery, involves questions of ends and means. Instead of pursuing knowledge almost exclusively to exploit our surroundings and manufacture more efficient, commercially viable products, we must seek new, more empathetic forms of knowledge that enable us to become effective mediators in preserving our biological heritage. We must strive to reach out as participants in the environment, find the hidden connections that unite existence, maintain those subtle relationships, and balance social and economic needs with biological rhythms.

Formulating a world view that places survival of the ecosystem above unrestrained technological development is bound to prove unwelcome and unpopular. It is unlikely to win converts easily. But it is the absolute prerequisite for conjuring a morality that will save the planet — a challenge that is gaining encouraging recognition from increasing numbers of prominent scientists. More and more of them are calling for a new sacred covenant between humans and nature.

"The attempt to control and dominate is at the heart of our

global eco-crisis," says geneticist David Suzuki. "What drives us down this path is the belief that we are gifted with the power and the mandate to conquer nature. The more we live in a human-created environment and the more we are separated from our biological roots, the easier it is to see the imposition of the human will as *natural*. To restore a balance with the natural world, we need a shift in attitude that recognizes our biological roots and our interdependence with nature" (Suzuki 1992).

Stanford University ecologist Paul Ehrlich argued that "a quasi-religious movement — one concerned with the need to change the values that now govern much of human activity — is essential to the persistence of our civilization" (Ehrlich 1986, 17-18). The same sentiment was conveyed in a statement for Preserving and Cherishing the Earth, signed recently by dozens of renowned scientists: "As scientists, many of us have had profound experiences of awe and reverence before the universe. We understand that what is regarded as sacred is more likely to be treated with care and respect. Our planetary home should be so regarded. Efforts to safeguard and cherish the environment need to be infused with a vision of the sacred."[1]

Reaching for that vision will require determination and a willingness to entertain unfamiliar, even strange ways of looking at humanity's relationship with the earth. The deeper significance of ritual cannibalism, as it was practised by the early Northwest Coast Indians, offers an especially provocative perspective. It provides us with a metaphorically rich analogy for stretching our imagination, reaching for new moral principles, and transforming our way of life.

Will our relationship to nature remain obscured by contempt, desecration, heartless individualism and pride? Or will we pursue an ecological vision that is grounded in reverence, awe, gratitude, and humility?

The answer must come from several directions and from all levels of society, until a groundswell of opinion forges a mass movement capable of shaping a humane destiny. A new journey of purpose is needed to save our world from technological peril and ecological disharmony. Our survival as a species must compel us to seek a new path. Because it involves widespread sacrifice and sharing, it will be steeper and more arduous, but it will be more challenging and nobler. It is the path of our generational responsibility. We owe it to our youth to make difficult choices. Their future will be shaped by our resolve. If we turn away from that sacred responsibility, we will violate the legacy that the First People have left us.

Only such a deeply-shared spirit can spark the sense of collective obligation, commitment, and dedication needed to meet humanity's awesome spiritual challenge: to achieve the character and acquire the skills to live much more frugally than we do, to waste less, to care more for ourselves and each other. We have only two choices: return to traditional values that stressed conservation, preservation, and the integrity of living things or continue to accept blindly the potentially devastating changes spawned by technology.

If we choose to renew the Tao (norms) of the past, we might benefit by turning in part to the wisdom that aboriginal people conveyed in their myths, legends, and stories. For that broader perspective we need to shift from epic legends recounting the *hamatsa's* elite, crucial role to the short folk tales that reflect how native people in general conceived their relationship to the web of life this spiritual intermediary maintained. As these stories did not belong to influential individuals or families, they are more widely known than the *hamatsa* legends, which are the personal property of select social groups. During long winter evenings, it is common to see an old man or woman surrounded by youngsters listening attentively to one of these tales. No matter how many times the story has been heard, it is always punctuated by laughter at the humorous incidents that were anticipated by the listeners. One of the most popular fables among Northwest Coast Indians was "Raven's War on the South Wind."[2] Raven is the natives' mythological culture hero. The South Wind often blows in heavy rains from the ocean.

According to the tale, the South Wind blew so incessantly that all the wild creatures were forced to stay in their huts. Unable to hunt, they grew hungry. Smoke rolled back down their smoke vents, irritating their eyes. Exasperated, Raven called a war council to plan an attack on the South Wind's Master (*Metalanuk*) who lived in a house on an island.

Raven obtained a special canoe and the war party paddled to the South Wind's home. But a stiff gale made it difficult for them to land. It was caused by the South Wind's Master, whose farts were so strong that the war party was nearly overcome.

But the raiders finally made it ashore. Following Raven's orders, Halibut and Flounder, being flat, slippery fish, lined up outside South Wind's doorstep. Either Red Cod or Wren slipped into the house and started a smudge.

As the South Wind's Master staggered out of the smoke-filled hut, he slipped on the fish and slithered down the beach. Waiting for this moment, the other animals whacked him on the head with clubs that were as hard as a deer hooves. They tried to beat his brains out.

Faced with death, South Wind's Master cut a deal. Promising not to break wind all the time, he agreed to alternate the weather between four foul days and four pleasant ones.

The moral is simple and profound. By combining their natural aptitudes, the annoyed but individually helpless animals managed to overcome a masterful spirit in his own house. The story appealed to a wide audience because it met a common need: vicarious release of suppressed resentments. This is how small people could triumph over the great ones who oppressed them. The event was so ludicrous it gave the listener a belly laugh. It was a tale that was too good to keep to oneself. In different variations, it spread throughout the realm of Northwest Coast Indians, and it travelled around the earth.[3]

Today, the ancient myth of *Metalanuk* offers a provocative metaphor for overcoming and transforming the supernatural forces we have unleashed in the world. According to Dudley Young, literature instructor at the University of Essex, England, the word for wind or breath in every culture means soul or spirit, and the word for pollution means the bad breath of divinity — parodied perfectly by the fart (Young 1991, 180, 204). We have allowed our divine technology to defile the planet. To cleanse it, we must first call for a quarantine, if not a moratorium, on *Metalanuk's* unbridled behavior. Then we must heal those divisions in the human soul that brought us to this precipice.

Instead of passively allowing runaway technologies of nuclear, reproductive, and genetic engineering to consume and cannibalize humanity, ordinary people need to exercise their independence, assert their rights to have technology limited by a common ethic of care and concern, and engage in the crucial grass-roots psychological, religious, and political struggle required to avoid catastrophe. We must return to the mythic voice of primitive experience, to the ways in which magic, legend, and ritual were used to talk to the gods without being overwhelmed or swallowed by them. The challenge is to negotiate a covenant among ourselves that allows common principles and reason to prevail. The divine power humanity encounters in violence is better met in renunciation of the potential for violence that is inherent in uncontrolled technology. Let us return to the gods the power to mutilate and destroy.

*

"Of course," I said to myself, "I do not believe in supernatural beings. Still — who understands the mysteries behind the forest? What would one do if one did meet a supernatural being?" Half of me wished that I could meet her, and half of me hoped I would not.
EMILY CARR (1941, 36)
after encountering a *tsonoqua* pole

Bella Coola *tsonoqua* mask.

AFTERWORD

Venture of Renewal

*Superiority? Inferiority? Why not the quite
simple attempt to touch the other, to feel the
other, to explain the other to myself?*
                    FRANTZ FANON (1967, 231)

IN THIS BOOK I have aimed at far more than recounting the historical record of cannibalism among the Northwest Coast Indians. Had the study stopped there, it might have perpetuated a Euroamerican concept of history that, too often, has been expressed in the paralyzing terms of cultural dispossession, distortion, and destruction. The psychiatrist Frantz Fanon summed up the process as follows: "Every colonized people — in other words, every people in whose soul an inferiority complex has been created by the death and burial of its local cultural originality — finds itself face to face with the language of the civilizing nation" (1967, 18). During the colonial period, few terms caused more havoc than *cannibalism*. Several writers have observed that, regardless of the anthropological "facts" behind various practices of anthropophagy, the cannibal appelation occurred within a discourse of "othering" (Hulme, 1986; Fabian, 1983; Slemon, 1992). It attempted to regulate and control cultural differences by delineating an imaginary boundary between communities, opposing civilization with savagery, and placing the "other" (the practising cannibal) outside historical time.

To broaden the perspective and create cross-cultural opportunities for reconciliation, I have gone beyond recapitulating the historical record to probe the ideological, psychological, and spiritual sources of the cannibalistic rituals that still form a central aspect of some remarkable cultures on the Pacific Northwest Coast. I have also sought to expose Euroamerican readers to anxieties derived from centuries of colonial domination.

We have seen how the Euroamerican view of the Amerindian world began in hypocrisy, exploitation, and genocide. Those early encounters left a persistent legacy of resentment, ambivalence, and confusion. The cannibal became an alibi for a history of oppression. Now, post-colonial Amerindians have a past to reclaim, a reprisal to exact. Euroamericans have an obligation to reexamine the notion of cannibalism, a reparation to make.

Coming from markedly different perspectives, contemporary North Americans must confront the cannibal concept that has clouded the past, come to terms with it, liberate themselves from the lies of history, respond to each other in radically new ways, and work together to reorganize society. As the smoke of misunderstanding clears, we may be able to shift from defining and justifying differences between "us" and "them" to striving for renewal. The dialogue of liberation expresses a universal hunger to transform and begin again.

I have tried to contribute to that conversation.

Haida painting of a shark, cut apart and spread open,
symbolizes the author's effort to increase intercultural understanding.

NOTES

AUTHOR'S NOTE (pages xi–xiv)

1 Yet recent research suggests that Basque fishermen and whalers regularly visited Labrador and Iceland at least a century before Columbus arrived in the West Indies. See Hadingham (1992, 34-42).

CHAPTER 1 (pages 31–54)

1 According to Marlene Goldman, assistant professor of English at the University of Toronto, the damage done by Bishop Douglas went much further. "In tampering with Cook's views, Douglas not only manipulates the facts, he also sets the 'creative' literary parameters for future explorers . . . such as Samuel Hearne and David Thompson, the two authors whose well-known works of Canadian exploration literature . . . impute a relationship between Natives and cannibalism" (Goldman 1996, 44).

2 Cook's two vessels actually anchored in Ship Cove (now called Resolution Cove) for four weeks. His observations, and those of his officers, about the Mowachaht were based on dealings with those natives who came to his vessels by canoe and some brief visits to their villages.

3 Based on evidence recently uncovered by archaeologists, it is also possible that a separate cultural group of so-called Paleoindians were already living in the Western Hemisphere hundreds of years before Siberians crossed the Bering Strait. In 1978, Dr. Michael Kuns, an archaeologist with the U.S. bureau of land management, found a human campsite on a flat-topped mountain about 550 kilometres

north of Fairbanks, Alaska. In March 1993, Kuns said arrowheads and charcoal found there were 11,700 years old. Other scientists have theorized that the first Paleoindians to reach the Pacific northwest coast were Siberians who travelled by boat. Another theory suggests the earliest inhabitants of North America came from European stock, perhaps migrating across northern Asia and then over the Bering Sea land bridge.

4 Extrapolation from Meares's estimates in 1788.

5 In the native tongue, the word *nu-tka* means "circling about," "go around," or "make a circuit." Two investigators (Efrat and Langlois 1978, frontispiece, 15, 55) claim the natives actually were advising Cook to *nutka icim* — "go around the harbour" to a better anchorage.

6 On January 19, 1777, Ledyard had recorded that, during a brief encounter with Hawaiian natives, several of them had offered one "Indian's arm roasted" to the ship's surgeon and "signified to us that it was very good eating." Ledyard said the surgeon refused the offer, showed "the greatest degree of abhorrence," and "we never after saw another instance of it while among them." Subsequent investigators found the Hawaiians were never at any time in their history cannibals.

7 Editor E.F. Howay adds the following footnote: "It was common belief that the Indians of the Northwest Coast were cannibals; but the better opinion is that cannibalism did not exist save as a ceremonial affair or part of a religious rite (Howay 1930, n72).

8 James Hanna had arrived secretly to trade for furs in 1785, but no firsthand account of his stay at Nootka Sound exists.

CHAPTER 2 (pages 55–74)

1 Probably a few miles south of Estevan Point at the northwest tip of the Hesquiat Peninsula. Pérez named the roadstead *San Lorenzo* and the early Spanish navigational charts marked what we now know as Nootka Sound *Surgidero de San Lorenzo*.

2 Since 1513, Spain had viewed the entire region as a "Spanish Lake" that was the exclusive domain of the King of Spain.

3 Also see chapter three.

4 Viceroy Flóres sent four Franciscans on the Martínez expedition to Christianize the natives: Fathers Francisco Miguel Sanchez, Severo Patero, José Espi, and Lorenzo Socies. They were all members of St.

Ferdinand's Royal School for the Propagation of the Faith in Mexico City (Warren Cook 1973, 133, n112). As Sanchez, Patero, and Socies kept journals — Sanchez (1789); Patero (1789); Socies, *"Noticias . . ."*) — the "anonymous Franciscan" quoted here must have been Espi. Some of his observations are found in Sales (1794), published in Valencia. Although Espi is not identified, he was from Valencia.

5 Pilot José Tobar y Tamariz stated (Tamariz 1789) that Martínez shot Callicum. Fray Francisco Miguel Sanchez said (Sanchez 1789) the commander ordered the sailor to shoot.

6 The Mowachaht and other northern Nootkan tribes had frequent contact with their Kwakiutl neighbors in Quatsino Sound and Nimpkish Lake by both overland trails and water routes.

CHAPTER 3 (pages 75–92)

1 Much of the information seems to have come from the English sailors aboard the *Argonaut,* who were imprisoned by Martínez.

2 Many primitive cultures shared the superstition that stepping over a child cast a spell that prevented the child from growing. To undo the spell, one had to step back over the child in the reverse direction (Róheim 1992, 12-13).

3 But Mackay was interviewed in India by Ensign Alexander Walker, who had been strongly convinced that the Mowachaht were cannibals when he visited Nootka Sound in the summer of 1785. Mackay's recollections, unreliable as they must have been, caused Walker to change his mind. See later in this chapter.

4 During the 1770s, sexual abuses by soldiers and the consequent destruction of family structure among the natives fueled uprisings at Mission San Gabriel in California and unrest throughout the new missions (Archer 1992, 4).

CHAPTER 4 (pages 93–116)

1 Historian Wilson Duff estimated the total pre-contact aboriginal population of what is now British Columbia to have been at least 80,000. He said 40 percent of all the native people in what is now Canada lived within the present boundaries of the province. According to Duff's figures, Maquinna could have mobilized a hostile population of at least 7,500 (Duff 1964, 39). But University of

British Columbia geographer Cole Harris says most experts now believe Duff's estimates were too low. Harris puts the province's pre-contact native population at about 200,000.

2 Jewitt published his original report — *A Journal Kept at Nootka Sound, 1807* — a few months after his return. A reprint was published in 1931 by Charles E. Goodspeed & Company of Boston. But only seven copies of this limited edition exist. The slim, 48-page volume is reportedly dull and sketchy. It makes no mention of cannibalism. The accomplished writer Richard Alsop interviewed Jewitt extensively before publishing his ghost-written version in 1815 (reprinted in 1967).

3 More than 100 years later, the renowned but controversial ethnographer Edward S. Curtis took extraordinary, sometimes staged, photographs of Northwest Coast Indians, and obtained information about the wolf dance from native informants. Writing in 1916, Curtis said "the evidence seems to indicate that an ancient wolf ritual possessed by the Nootka tribes has become essentially modified by the influence of the Kwakiutl ceremony, while the wolf dance of the Kwakiutl was borrowed from the Nootka and made a part of their winter ceremony." He said the wolf dance became the featured dramatic performance of the elaborate ceremony. Masked dancers portrayed a legend about the capture of a youth by Wolf people, his recovery, and his "taming" by friends. The initiation ritual belonged to a secret order (Curtis [1915-16] 1978, 11:92, 179; Drucker 1965, 158-60).

4 Anapa Maquinna, who died in 1778.

CHAPTER 6 (pages 129–153)

1 Kevin McNeilly, assistant professor of English at the University of British Columbia, concedes in a forthcoming article that Boas is a "scholar-hero" who "appears to be responsible for the rescue and continuation of Kwakwaka'wakw [formerly Kwakiutl] language and culture, and has provided the means for cultural security which the Native people could not, at the time, provide for themselves" (McNeilly, 5). But he also accuses Boas, as an author, of "intrusive meddling," becoming "a narrative filter," and moulding "'Native' stories to suit his own tonal and conceptual demands" (27). McNeilly concludes: "In Boasian ethnography, the Native is 'recovered' for the

white cultural dominant, and installed in the position of the valuable Other, but an Other, this time, which cannot escape the determinations of the white dominant, which has been rewritten and overwritten by a narrative of white self-discovery" (29).

2 See Grubb (1977, 1-2), Wallas (1981, 13), Jonaitis (1992, 257), Webster (1992, 248-49, 250).

3 Boas said the term *tseka* meant "to be fraudulent, to cheat" and he related this to the largely theatrical nature of the ceremonies (Boas 1966, 172).

4 Curtis said the Yuquot secret society had nine kinds of dancers: fool, deer, shaman, wolf, grizzly bear, warrior, otter, ghost, and cannibal (Curtis [1915-16] 1978, 11:92).

5 Boas included a mask of *Baxbakwalanuxsiwae* in one of his early works (Boas 1895, Fig. 77), but a recent study (Jonaitis, 1991, 152) claims this supernatural figure "never appears on masks."

6 According to anthropologist Thomas F. McIlwraith, who studied Bella Coola (Nuxalk) culture intensively from 1922-1924, these natives believed that powerful spirits implanted supernatural cannibalistic creatures in the *kukusiut (hamatsa)*, "causing them to devour strange foods." If this "cannibalistic incubus" was driven out, the *kukusiut* was to be restored to sanity (1948, 71, 78-79, 115). Anthropologist Joyce Wike claims this incorporation of a super-natural being "sets Northwest Coast cannibalism apart from other traditions of ceremonial anthropophagy." According to Wike, a supernatural being or animal inhabited the *kukusiut*, causing inhuman yearnings for mummified corpses and raw living flesh. "The cravings were fulfilled . . . to pacify the creature," she said. "It, not the human, is actually the eater" (1984, 244).

7 In 1931, Boas filmed this trembling by the *hamatsa* and the film (Boas 1973) is still available.

8 Presumably Captain Alexander W. Moffat, Hudson's Bay agent at Fort Rupert.

9 About 20 years later, George Hunt would give ethnographer Edward S. Curtis a vivid account of this event, corroborating Qomenakula's testimony in gory detail.

10 Anthropologist Joyce Wike (1984, 250, 254) cites this and other references to lethal flesh in commentaries about Kwakiutl and Tsimshian cannibalistic practices to bolster an intriguing suggestion.

She theorizes that the mischievous Nootka deliberately offered "deadly hands" to eighteenth-century European mariners and traders on more than six occasions, not only to sell useless by-products of ceremonial cannibalism, but also to "attack" the visitors by testing their "vulnerability" and tricking them. Given the perceptual gap that existed between the two groups of people, Wike's speculation may be correct.

11 These rare, vintage photographs, which form part of the collection of Randee and G. Ray Hawkins, are held by the G. Ray Hawkins Gallery in Santa Monica, California.

12 According to Hunt, when Gwakiils was initiated, he emerged from the woods carrying a mummy under each arm. When Gwakiils met his hereditary rival, who was already a *hamatsa*, he handed him one of the corpses. The two men held "a contest of man-eating." Gwakiils won by finishing his mummy first (Curtis [1915-16] 1978, 10:n223).

13 Curtis ([1915-16] 1978, 11:69-84) recorded a detailed description of the wolf dance ceremony, which was told to him by Chief Maquinna's grandson. Curtis noted (n80) that any uninitiated person who saw the *hamatsas* while the wolf spirit was in them was required to be initiated immediately. In earlier times, as Jewitt observed, the offender was punished by having spear-points thrust under the skin of the back. According to Curtis, in ancient times "the penalty was death."

14 Curtis said that those who agreed to be "bitten" had previously raised a blister on their forearm by burning cedar-bark over the skin to simulate a raw wound. He said many older men carried numerous scars from playing this role (Curtis [1915-16] 1978, 11:144).

CHAPTER 7 (pages 157–171)

1 Stanford University anthropologist Clifford Geertz cites Boas, Bronislaw K. Malinowski, and Claude Lévi-Strauss as the "founders of discursivity" in anthropology (Geertz 1988, 19).

2 After Sigmund Freud, Géza Róheim (1891-1953) was the most important contributor to the development of a psychoanalytic approach to anthropology and folklore.

3 For a scathing critique of Theroux's pseudo-ethnology and how it typifies the discourse of cannibalism that "has been central to the dispossession of native peoples," see Paul Lyons (1996).

4 *Time,* Jan. 18, 1993, 26-31; *Newsweek,* Jan. 18, 1993, 38.

CHAPTER 9   (pages 183–196)

1 Despite this evidence, the twentieth-century historian-sociologist Reay Tannahill has suggested that the Caribs, like the Papuans in New Guinea and some other island societies, turned to eating human flesh because they could raise nothing but starchy foods, which caused a craving for meat (Tannahill 1975, 17).

2 Ironically, among the Caribs, the word for "cannibal" meant "valiant man."

CHAPTER 10   (pages 197–208)

1 For an overview of the eleven-year controversy among anthropologists about the topic of cannibalism, see Kidd (1988).

2 Emphasis is the author's.

CHAPTER 11   (pages 209–223)

1 In Kwakiutl mythology, the *tsonoqua* were a race of mountain-dwelling man-eating giants, whose female members stole children and salmon from humans. They symbolized the pervasive, potent, wantonly destructive quality of uncontrolled hunger.

2 The entire potlatch was video-taped and may be viewed by arrangement with the Kwakiutl Museum at Cape Mudge. Harry Assu succeeded his famous father, Billy Assu (1867-1965) — one of the most renowned and respected chiefs on the Northwest Coast. The younger Assu was first elected chief of the We-Wai-Kai band in 1954. His description of the 1984 potlatch is perhaps the most complete record of the order of events that is followed today.

3 According to Irving Goldman (Mead [1937] 1976, 201), "on very great occasions a slave is killed and eaten and substituted for a corpse of one previously dead."

CHAPTER 12   (pages 225–235)

1 As translated by the author from the German in Boas (1966, xii): "Wir denken, fühlen und handeln getreu der überlieferung, in der wir leben. Das einzige Mittel uns zu befreien ist die Versenkung in ein neues Leben und Verständis fur ein Denken, ein Fühlen, ein Handeln das nicht auf dem Boden unserer Zivilisation erwachen ist, sondern das seine Quellen in anderen Kulturschichten hat."

2 University of California anthropologist James Clifford calls Boas the "last virtuoso" of a coherent anthropology (1986, 4).

3 One of the exceptions is Irving Goldman. He points out (Goldman 1975) that Kwakiutl culture unifies all creatures in a single, cohesive system of behaviour, which reflects a moral order. This makes the religious aspect of the potlatch far more significant than its economic function. Goldman also noted the important role of metaphors in Kwakiutl thought — for example the equivalance between the structure of a house and that of the universe.

4 As a spiritual "hero," the *hamatsa* followed the universal rites of passage for renewal: separation — initiation — return. See Joseph Campbell, *The Hero with a Thousand Faces* (1949).

CHAPTER 13 (pages 237–249)

1 The other exponents include Lewis Mumford, *Technics and Civilization* (1934), and Henry Adams, *The Education of Henry Adams* (1918).

2 The term's significance was articulated earlier by two German philosopher-sociologists: Theodor W. Adorno and Max Horkheimer. In the 1950s, both men made significant contributions to studies of prejudice and authoritarianism.

CHAPTER 14 (pages 251–262)

1 "Preserving and Cherishing the Earth: An Appeal for Joint Commitment in Science and Religion," issued at a 1991 international conference on environmental and economic development in Moscow, which was attended by religious, political and scientific leaders from 83 nations. The statement was signed by several of the most respected and articulate contemporary Western scientists (Knudtson and Suzuki 1992, 182).

2 Franz Boas recorded eleven versions in Boas (1916, 79-81; 658-60). A brief summary, noting original sources appears in Boas (1935, 140).

3 A full analysis is given in Hoebel (1941, 1-12).

BIBLIOGRAPHY

Alsop, Richard (ed.). (1967) *Narrative of the Adventures and Sufferings of John R. Jewitt.* Fairfield, Washington: Ye Galleon. [Reprint of same title written after personal interviews with Jewitt and published in 1815]

Archer, Christon I. (1980) "Cannibalism in the Early History of the Northwest Coast: Enduring Myths and Neglected Realities." *The Canadian Historical Review* 56 (December):4, 453-479

———. (1992) "Seduction before Sovereignty: Spanish Efforts to Manipulate the Natives in their Claims to the Northwest Coast." Paper presented at Vancouver Conference, Vancouver, British Columbia, April 1992. [Edited version published in Fisher and Johnston (1993)]

———. (1973) "The Transient Presence: A Re-Appraisal of Spanish Attitudes toward the Northwest Coast in the Eighteenth Century." *B.C. Studies* 18 (Summer)

Ardrey, Robert. (1976) *The Hunting Hypothesis.* New York: Atheneum

———. (1966) *The Territorial Imperative.* New York: Atheneum

Arens, William. (1979) *The Man-Eating Myth: Anthropology & Anthropophagy.* New York: Oxford University Press

———. (1979) "Cannibals of the Imagination." *New York Times.* (April 2)

Arima, Eugene Yuji. (1983) *The West Coast People: The Nootka of Vancouver Island and Cape Flattery.* Victoria, British Columbia

Assu, Harry. (1989) *Assu of Cape Mudge: Recollections of a Coastal Indian Chief.* Vancouver, British Columbia: University of British Columbia Press

Attali, Jacques. (1979) *L'ordre Cannibale: Vie et Morte de la Medecine.* Paris: B. Grasset

273

_____. (1991) *Millennium: Winners and Losers in the Coming World Order.* New York: Times Books

Ayyar, Venkatarama (ed.). (1928) *James Strange's Journal and Narrative of the Commercial Expedition from Bombay to the NorthWest Coast of America.* Madras: Government Press

Barnett, Hosmmer Garner. (1942) "Applied Anthropology in 1860." *Applied Anthropology* 1:19-32

Barreiro-Meiro, Roberto (ed.). (1964) *Colleccion de Diarios y Relaciones para la Historia de los Viajes y Descubrimientos 6.* Madrid. [Translation of: "Diario de la Navegacion que Yo el Alf(ere)z de Navio de la R(ea)l Arm(a)da D(o)n Estevan Josef Martinez boy a executar al P(uer)to de S(a)n Lorenzo de Nuca, mandando la Frag(a)ta *Princessa,* y Paquebot *S(a)n Carlos* . . . 1789." Portions also in: Warren Cook (1973); Wilson (1970).]

Barwick, G. F. (trans.). (1911) *Voyage of* Sutil *and* Mexicana *in 1792.* Vancouver, British Columbia: Vancouver Public Library [Unpublished typescript of official version.]

Beaglehole, James Cawte (ed.). (1967) *The Journals of Captain James Cook on His Voyages of Discovery,* vol. 3: parts 1 and 2 "The Voyage of the *Resolution* and *Discovery* 1776-1780." Cambridge: Cambridge University

_____ (ed.). "Charles Clerke's Journal." [See Beaglehole 3:2:1301-1339 (1967)]

_____ (ed.). "Thomas Edgar's Journal." [See Beaglehole 3:2:1351-1360 (1967)]

_____ (ed.). "James King's Journal." [See Beaglehole 3:2:1361-1454 (1967)]

_____ (ed.). "Some Account of a Voyage to the South Sea's in 1776-1777-1778, Written by David Samwell." [See Beaglehole 3:2:987-1300 (1967)]

Bell, Edward. *A New Vancouver Journal on the Discovery of Puget Sound, By a Member of the Chatham's Crew.* [See Meany (1915)]

Benedict, Ruth. (1974) "The Concept of the Guardian Spirit in North America." *Memoirs of the American Anthropological Association* 29 (Millwood, New York)

_____. (1934) *Patterns of Culture.* Boston and New York: Houghton Mifflin

Boas, Franz. (1932) *Bella Bella Tales.* American Folklore Society Memoir 52. New York: American Folklore Society

_____. (1921) "Ethnology of the Kwakiutl." *Bureau of American Ethnology, 35th Annual Report, 1913-14*. Parts 1, 2 (Washington, D.C.: Government Printing Office)

_____. (1935) "Kwakiutl Culture as Reflected in Mythology." *Memoirs of the American Folk-Lore Society*. 28 (New York)

_____. (1966) *Kwakiutl Ethnography*. Chicago: University of Chicago

_____. (1910) *Kwakiutl Tales*. New York: Columbia University Press

_____. (1940) *Race, Language and Culture*. New York: The Free Press

_____. (1930) *Religion of the Kwakiutl Indians*. Columbia University Contributions to Anthropology, 10, Part 2. New York: Columbia University Press

_____. (1895) "Social Organization and Secret Societies of the Kwakiutl Indians." *United States National Museum Report*. (Washington, D.C.)

_____. (dir.). (1973) "The Kwakiutl of British Columbia." Film made in 1930 and edited by Bill Holm. (Seattle: University of Washington)

_____. (1909) "The Kwakiutl of Vancouver Island." *The Jesup North Pacific Expedition*. Vol. 5, Part II. (New York)

_____. (1930) *The Religion of the Kwakiutl Indians*. New York: Columbia University

_____. (1916) "Tsimshian Mythology." *Bureau of American Ethnology, Annual Report*. 31:393-558

Boit, John. *Log of the Second Voyage of the Columbia*. [See Howay (1941)]

Bracken, Christopher Joseph. (1994) "White Gift: The Potlatch and the Rhetoric of Canadian Cannibalism (1868-1936)." Ph.D. thesis, Department of English. (Vancouver, British Columbia: University of British Columbia)

Brown, Vinson. (1977) *Peoples of the Sea Wind: The Native Americans of the Pacific Coast*. New York: Macmillan

Caamaño, Jacinto. (1938) "Extracto de diario . . . 1792." *British Columbia Historical Quarterly*. 2: 84-85. [Translation of: Caamaño, Jacinto. *"Carácter, vida, y costumbres de los Indios de Nuka, y sus inmediaciones,"* 1791. Archivo General de la Nacion, Mexico City, Mexico.]

Campbell, Joseph. (1949) *The Hero with a Thousand Faces*. New York: Bollingen Foundation

Carlson, Roy L. (1992) "Pre-Contact Native Northwest Coast Culture." Paper presented at Vancouver Conference, Vancouver, British Columbia, April 1992

Carr, Emily. (1941) *Klee Wyck*. Toronto: Clarke, Irwin & Company

Cevallos, Ciriaco. Entry of 27 August [1791] in *Libro de Guardias, Atrevida*. MS 755. Museo Naval, Madrid. [Translated in Cutter's (1991), 101-02]

———. Entry in *Viaje en Limpio de las Corbetas Descubierta y Atrevida*. MS 181. Museo Naval, Madrid. [Translated in Cutter's (1991), 90.]

Chamberlain, J.E. (1975) *The Harrowing of Eden: White Attitudes Toward North American Indians*. Toronto: Fitzhenry & Whiteside

Codere, Helen. (1961) "Kwakiutl." In Spicer, Edward (ed.) *Perspectives in American Indian Culture Change*. Chicago: University of Chicago Press

Cook, James and King, James. (1784) *A Voyage to the Pacific Ocean; Undertaken by Command of His Majesty, for Making Discoveries in the Northern Hemisphere . . . 1776, 1777, 1778, 1779, 1780*. 3 vols. London: G. Nicol and T. Cadell

Cook, Warren L. (1973) *Flood Tide of Empire: Spain and the Pacific Northwest*. New Haven: Yale University

Crosby, Thomas. (1914) *Up and Down the North Pacific Coast by Canoe and Mission Ship*. Toronto: Missionary Society of the Methodist Church

Currie, Noel Elizabeth. (1995) "Creating Exploration Literature: Cannibalism in Cook's Third Voyage." Unpublished paper, University of British Columbia, Vancouver, British Columbia

———. (1994) "Cook and the Cannibals: Nootka Sound, 1778." *Lumen: Selected Proceedings from the Canadian Society for Eighteenth-Century Studies*. 13 (Edmonton: Academic Printing & Publishing):71-78

Curtis, Edward Sheriff. (1915, 1975) *In the Land of the Head Hunters*. Yonkers, New York: World Book Co.

———. (1922, 1972, 1992) "In the Land of War Canoes: Kwakiutl Indian Life on the Northwest Coast." Videorecording. (New York: Milestone Film and Video)

———. (1915-16, 1978) "The Kwakiutl," "The Nootka" and "The Haida." *The North American Indian*. Vols. 10 (1915) and 11 (1916) of 20. (New York: Johnson Reprint Corp.)

Cutter, Donald C. (ed.). (1980) *Journal of Tomas de Suria of His Voyage with Malaspina to the Northwest Coast of America in 1791*. Fairfield, Washington: Ye Galleon. [Translation of: Suría, Tomás de. *Quaderno que contiene el Ramo de Historia Natural y diario de la Expedicion del circulo de Globo . . . 1791*.]

———. (1991) *Malaspina and Galiano; Spanish Voyages to the Northwest Coast, 1791 & 1792*. Seattle: University of Washington. Vancouver: Douglas & McIntyre

Darling, Gillian and Green, Cari (producers). (1994) "The Washing of Tears." Documentary film. (Vancouver: Nootka Sound and Picture Company)

Dawson, George Mercer. (1880) "Report on the Queen Charlotte Islands." *Report of Progess for 1878-79*. (Montreal: Dawson)

Dewhirst, John T. (1978) "Nootka Sound: A 4,000-Year Perspective." [See Efrat and Langlois. nu-tka: The History. . . . 1-30]

_____. (Undated) "Yuquot, British Columbia: The Prehistory and History of a Nootkan Village," Part II. Paper presented at the 22nd Annual Northeast Anthropological Conference

Dickason, Olive Patricia. (1984) *The Myth of the Savage and the Beginning of French Colonialism in the Americas*. Edmonton, Alberta: University of Alberta

Drucker, Philip. (1965) *Cultures of the North Pacific Coast*. San Francisco: Chandler Publishing

_____. (1955) *Indians of the Northwest Coast*. Garden City, New York: Natural History Press

_____. (1940) *Kwakiutl Dancing Societies*. Anthropological Records Vol.2, no. 6 (Berkeley: University of California)

_____. (1951) *The Northern and Central Nootkan Tribes*. Washington, D.C.: Government Printing Office

_____ and Heizer, Robert F. (1967) *To Make My Name Good: A Reexamination of the Southern Kwakiutl Potlatch*. Berkeley: University of California

Duff, Wilson. (1964) "The Impact of the White Man." *The Indian History of British Columbia*. 1 (Victoria: Provincial Museum of Natural History)

_____ and Kew, Michael. (1973) "A Select Bibliography of Anthropology of British Columbia." *B.C. Studies*. 19:73-121

Efrat, Barbara and Langlois, William J. (eds.). (1978) *nut-ka: Captain Cook and the Spanish Explorers on the Coast*. Victoria, British Columbia: Province of British Columbia

_____. (1978) *nut-ka: The History and Survival of Nootkan Culture*. Victoria, British Columbia: Province of British Columbia

Ehrlich, Paul. (1986) *The Machinery of Nature*. New York: Simon and Schuster

Eliza, Francisco. "Costumbres do los Naturales del Puerto de San Lorenzo de Nuca," 20 April, 1791. Archivo General de la Nacion, Mexico, Historia, vol. 69. [Cited in Archer's (1992) and Fisher's (1993).]

_____. "Extracto de la navegacion. . . ." [Translated in Wagner 1971]

Espi, José (Anonymous Franciscan?). *Noticias de Nutka.* Archivio General de la Nacion, Mexico City, Mexico, Sec. Hist. vol. 31, fol. 314v. [Portions cited translated in Warren Cook (1973)]

[Espinosa y Tello?, José]. (1802) *Relacion del Viaje hecho por las goletas Sutil y Mexicana en 1792 para reconocer el Estrecho de Juan de Fuca.* Madrid: Royal Printing Office. (Republished in 1958 with Spanish version edited by Jose Porrua Turanzas.) [Also see translations of this official version by Barwick (1911) and of the orginal version by Kendrick (1990)]

Fabian, Johannes. (1983) *Time and the Other: How Anthropology Makes its Object.* New York: Columbia University Press

Fanon, Frantz. (1967) *Black Skin, White Masks.* Trans. Charles Markmann. New York: Grove Press, Inc.

Fidalgo, Salvador. "Report to Revilla Gigedo, 13 November, 1790." Archivo General de la Nacion, Mexico, Historia, vol. 68 [Cited in Archer's (1992) and Fisher's (1993)]

Fisher, Robin. (1977) *Contact and Conflict: Indian-European Relations in B.C. 1774-1890.* Vancouver: University of British Columbia

_____ and Bumsted, J.M. (eds.). (1982) *An Account of a Voyage to the North West Coast of America in 1785 & 1786 by Alexander Walker.* Seattle: University of Washington. Vancouver, British Columbia: Douglas & McIntyre

_____ and Johnston, Hugh (eds.). (1993) *From Maps to Metaphors: The Pacific World of George Vancouver.* Vancouver, British Columbia: UBC Press

Ford, Clellan Stearns. (c1941, 1961) *Smoke from Their Fires: The Life of a Kwakiutl Chief [Charles James Nowell].* Hamden, Connecticut: Archon Books

Frame, Donald M. (ed.). (1976) *The Complete Essays of Montaigne.* Stanford, California: Stanford University

Francis, Daniel. (1993) *The Imaginary Indian: The Image of the Indian in Canadian Culture.* Vancouver, British Columbia: Arsenal Pulp Press

Freud, Sigmund. (1946) *Totem and Taboo: Resemblances between the Psychic Lives of Savages and Neurotics.* New York: Vintage

Geertz, Clifford. (1995) "Culture War." *The New York Review.* (November 30):4-6

_____. (1988) *Works and Lives: The Anthropologist as Author.* Stanford, California: Stanford University Press

Glass, Aaron. (1995) "Swallowing One's Tribe: Reciprocal Assimilation and the Development of the Kwakwaka'wakw Hamat'sa Dance as a Reaction to Culture Contact." Unpublished paper. Vancouver, British Columbia

Goddard, Pliny Earle. (1924) *Indians of the Northwest Coast*. New York: American Museum Press

Goldman, Irving. "The Kwakiutl Indians of Vancouver Island." [See Mead's (1976)]

_____. (1975) *The Mouth of Heaven*. New York: Wiley

_____. (1976) "Ritual Distribution and Exchange among the Southern Kwakiutl: A Cosmological Perspective." Paper read at the Northwest Coast Studies Conference, Vancouver, British Columbia, May 1976

Goldman, Marlene. (1966) "A Taste of the Wild: A Critique of Representations of Natives as Cannibals in Late-Eighteenth- and Nineteenth-Century Canadian Exploration Literature." *Multiculturalism and Representation*, Vol. 10 of *Literary Studies East and West*. (Honolulu: University of Hawaii): 43-66

Gore, Rick. (1996) "Neandertals." *National Geographic*. (January):2-35

Grene, David (trans.). (1987) *The History by Herodotus*. Chicago: University of Chicago Press

Griffin, George Butler (ed.). (1891) "Diaries 20 and 21, July 1774" [of Juan Crespi and Thomas de la Pena]. *Documents from the Sutro Collection*. 2 (Los Angeles: Historical Society of Southern California): part 1:121-23, 187-94

Grubb, David. (1977) *A Practical Writing System and Short Dictionary of Kwakw'ala (Kwakiutl)*. Ottawa: National Museums of Canada

Hadingham, Evan. (1992) "Europe's Mystery People." *World Monitor*. (September):34-42

Harkin, Michael. (1988) *Dialogues of History: Transformation and Change in Heiltsuk Culture 1790-1920*. Ph.D. dissertation. University of Chicago

Harris, Marvin. (1977) *Cannibals and Kings: The Origins of Cultures*. New York: Random House

Haswell, Robert. "Log of the First Voyage of the Columbia." [See Howay's (1941)]

Henige, David. (1991) *In Search of Columbus: The Sources for the First Voyage*. Tucson: University of Arizona Press

Herodotus. *The History*. [(See Grene's (1987)]

Higueras Rodriguez, Maria Dolores and Martin-Meras, Maria Luisa (eds.). (1991) *Relacion del viaje hecho por las goletas Sutil y Mexicana en el ano 1792 para reconocer el estrecho de Juan de Fuca.* Madrid: Museo Naval

Hilton, Susan and Rath, John. (1982) "Objections to Franz Boas' Referring to Eating People in the Translation of the Kwakwala Terms of Baxbakualanuxsiwe and Hamats!a." *Working Papers for the 17th International Conference on Salish and Neighboring Languages.* (Portland: Portland State University)

Hoebel, Edward Adamson. (1966, 1972) *Anthropology: The Study of Man.* New York: McGraw-Hill

———. (1941) "The Asiatic Origin of a Myth of the Northwest Coast." *Journal of American Folklore.* 54:1-12

Hogg, Gary. (1980) *Cannibalism and Human Sacrifice.* London: Robert Hale

Hoskins, John. "Narrative of the Second Voyage of the *Columbia.*" [See Howay's (1941)]

Howay, Frederick William, (ed.). (1941) *Voyages of the Columbia, to the Northwest Coast, 1787-1790 and 1790-1793.* Boston: Massachusetts Historical Society

———. (1940) *The Journals of Captain James Colnett Aboard the* Argonaut *from April 26, 1789 to November 3, 1791.* Toronto: Champlain Society. [Includes "A translation of the Diary of Estevan José Martínez from July 2 till July 14, 1789."]

——— (ed.). (1930) *Zimmerman's Captain Cook, 1781.* Toronto: Ryerson

Hulme, Peter. (1986) *Colonial Encounters: Europe and the Native Caribbean, 1492-1797.* New York: Methuen

Hunter, W. (1940) "Letter from W. Hunter Regarding Voyage of the Vessels *Captain Cook* and *Experiment* to the Northwest Coast in the Fur Trade, 1786." San Francisco, California: White Knight Chapbooks, Pacific Northwest Series 2

Inglis, Robin (ed.). (1992) *Spain and the North Pacific Coast.* Vancouver: Vancouver Maritime Museum

Ingraham, Joseph. "Description of Nootka and Inhabitants, 1789." Archivo General National, Historia, Mexico City, Mexico: Vol. 65

Jacobsen, Johan Adrian. (1884, c.1977) *Alaskan Voyage 1881-1883.* [Translation from the German of *Reise an der Nordwestküste Amerikas, 1881-1883,* by Erna Gunther.] Chicago: University of Chicago Press

Jewitt, John R. (1967) *Narrative of the Adventures and Sufferings of John R. Jewitt.* Fairfield, Washington: Ye Galleon. [Reprint of same title written by Richard Alsop after personal interviews with Jewitt; published in 1815]

———. *The Adventures and Sufferings of John R. Jewitt, Captive of Maquinna.* [See Stewart's (1987)]

Jilek, Wolfgang G. (1974) *Salish Indian Mental Health and Cultural Change: Psychohygienic and Therapeutic Aspects of The Guardian Spirit Ceremonial.* Toronto: Holt, Rinehart and Wilson

Jonaitis, Aldona (ed.). (1991) *Chiefly Feasts: The Enduring Kwakiutl Potlatch.* Vancouver: Douglas & McIntyre

———. (1992) "Chiefly Feasts: The Enduring Kwakiutl Potlatch — From Salvage Anthropology to a Big Apple Button Blanket." *Curator.* 35/4:255-267

Jones, Laurie. (1991) *Nootka Sound Explored: A West Coast History.* Campbell River, British Columbia: Ptarmigan

Kaplanoff, Mark D. Barre (ed.). (1971) [*Joseph Ingraham's*] *Journal of the Brigantine* Hope *on a Voyage to the Northwest Coast of North America, 1790-92.* Barre, Massachusetts: Imprint Society

Karp, Laurence E. (1976) *Genetic Engineering: Threat or Promise?* Chicago: Nelson-Hall

Kendrick, John S. (1986) *The Men with Wooden Feet: The Spanish Exploration of the Pacific Northwest.* Toronto: NC Press

——— (ed.) (1990) *The Voyage of the* Sutil *and* Mexicana: *1792.* Spokane: Arthur H. Clark

Kidd, J.S. (1988) "Scholarly Excess and Journalistic Restraint in the Popular Treatment of Cannibalism." *Social Studies of Science.* 18:749-54

Kilgour, Maggie. (1990) *From Communion to Cannibalism: An Anatomy of Metaphors of Incorporation.* Princeton: Princeton University Press

Kines, Lindsay. (1992) "Listen to the Beat." *Vancouver Sun.* (January 4):D10-13

Knudtson, Peter and Suzuki, David. (1992) *Wisdom of the Elders.* Toronto: Stoddart

Lamb, W. Kaye (ed.). (1984) *George Vancouver, A Voyage of Discovery to the North Pacific Ocean and Round the World, 1791-1795.* London: Hakluyt Society

Las Casas, Bartolomé de. (1971) *History of the Indies.* New York: Harper & Row

Ledyard, John. (1783) *A Journal of Captain Cook's Last Voyage to the Pacific Ocean*. Hartford, Connecticut [See Munford (1963)]

Letts, Malcolm (ed.). (1929) *Hans Staden: The True Story of His Captivity 1557*. New York: Robert M. McBride & Co.

Lewis, Clive Staples. (1947) *The Abolition of Man*. New York: Cambridge University

Lewis, Ioan M. (1971) *Ecstatic Religion: An Anthropological Study of Spirit Possession and Shamanism*. Middlesex, England

———. (1986) *Religion in Context: Cults and Charisma*. New York: Cambridge University

Loeb, Edwin Mayer. (1923) *The Blood Sacrifice Complex*. Menasha, Wisconsin: American Anthropological Association

Lopatin, Ivan. (1945) *Social Life and Religion of the Indians in Kitimat, British Columbia*. University of Southern California Social Science Series, 26. Los Angeles: University of Southern California Press

Lyons, Paul. (1996) "From Man-Eaters to Spam-Eaters: Literary Tourism and the Discourse of Cannibalism from Herman Melville to Paul Theroux." *Multiculturalism and Representation,* Vol. 10 of *Literary Studies East and West*. (Honolulu: University of Hawaii): 67-86

McIlwraith, Thomas W. (1992) [1948] *The Bella Coola Indians*. 2 vol. Toronto: University of Toronto Press

McKelvie, Bruce Alistair. (1946) *Maquinna the Magnificent*. Vancouver, British Columbia: Vancouver Daily Province

MacLaren, Ian S. (1994) "Explorers' and Travellers' Narratives: A Peregrination through Different Editions." *Facsimile*. 12 (Ottawa: Canadian Institute for Historical Micro-reproductions, November):8-16

McNeilly, Kevin. (1997) "His Own Best Narrator: Franz Boas and the Kwakiutl Tales." *Canadian Literature*. (Vancouver, British Columbia): Draft

Mander, Jerry. (1992) *In the Absence of the Sacred: The Failure of Technology and the Survival of Indian Nations*. San Francisco: Sierra Club

Marshall, Yvonne. (1992) "Maquinna, Quadra and Vancouver in Nootka Sound, 1790-95." Draft paper presented at Vancouver Conference, Vancouver, British Columbia, April 1992.

Martínez, Estevan José. (1900) "Diary of the Voyage, in command of the frigate *Princessa* and the packet *San Carlos* in the present year of 1789." William L. Schurz (trans.). Madrid [Located in Special Collections Library, University of British Columbia, Vancouver.]

_____. "A translation of the Diary of Estevan José Martínez from July 2 till July 14, 1789." [See Howay (1940)]

Mead, Margaret (ed.). (1937, 1976) *Cooperation and Competition Among Primitive Peoples*. New York; Gloucester, Mass: Smith. [Includes Irving Goldman's "The Kwakiutl Indians of Vancouver Island."]

Meany, Edmond S. (ed.). (1915) *A New Vancouver Journal on the Discovery of Puget Sound, By [Edward Bell] a Member of the Chatham's Crew*. Seattle: University of Washington

Meares, John. (1967) *Voyages Made in the Years 1788 and 1789 from China to the North-west Coast of America*. Amsterdam: N. Israel; New York: Da Capo

_____. (1790) *Extracts from Voyages Made in the Years 1788-1789, From China to the North West Coast of America*. London: Legographic

Menzies, Archibald. *Menzies' Journal of Vancouver's Voyage, April to October, 1792*. [See Newcombe's (1923)]

Métraux, Alfred. (1928) *La Réligion des Tupinamba*. New York: Oxford University

_____. (1967) *Réligions et magies indiennes d'Amerique du sud*. New York: Oxford University

Mohawk Nation. (1978) "A Basic Call to Consciousness: the Hau de no sau nee [Iroquois] Address to the Western World." *Akwesasne Notes*. (Rooseveltown, New York: Mohawk Nation)

Montaigne, Michel de. "Of Cannibalism." *The Complete Essays of Montaigne*. 1588 [See translation by Frame (1976)]

Mowachaht Band. (1985) *Yuquot*. 3 Vol. Gold River, British Columbia: Mowachaht Band

Moziño Suarez de Figueroa, José Mariano. (1913) *Noticias de Nutka: Diccionario de la lengua de los Nutkeses y descripcion del volcan de Tuxtla*. Mexico City. [See translation by Wilson (1970)]

Munford, James K. (ed.). (1963) *John Ledyard's Journal of Captain Cook's Last Voyage*. Corvalis, Oregon: Oregon State University. [Edited and annotated version of Ledyard's journal, first published in 1783.]

Munro, Margaret. (1993) "In the Footsteps of the Ancients." *Vancouver Sun*. (August 7):1-2

Newcombe, C.F. (ed.). (1923) *[Archibald] Menzies' Journal of Vancouver's Voyage, April to October, 1792*. Victoria, British Columbia: Government of British Columbia

Novo y Colson, Pedro de (ed.). (1934) *Politico-Scientific Voyage Round the World by the Corvettes* Descubierta *and* Atrevida *under the command of the Naval Captains Don Alexandro Malaspina and Don Jose de Bustamente y Guerra from 1789-1794.* 2 vol. Madrid: 1885. [Translation of: Malaspina, Alejandro. *Viaje politico-cientifico alrededor del Mundo por los corbetas Descubierta y Atrevida.* Madrid: 1885. Edited by Carl Robinson, Vancouver, British Columbia.]

Olson, Ronald L. (1940) "The Social Organization of the Haisla of British Columbia." *Anthropological Records.* 2 (5):169-200.

Packard, Vance. (1977) *The People Shapers.* Boston: Little, Brown

Partridge, Eric. (1984) *Dictionary of Slang and Unconventional English.* London: Routledge & Kegan Paul

Patero, Severo. *Fray Severo Patero to Florez, 13 July 1789.* Archivo General de la Nacion, Mexico, Historia, vol. 65. [Portions cited paraphrased in Archer (1980)]

Ramsey, Paul. (1970) *Fabricated Man: The Ethics of Genetic Control.* New Haven: Yale University

Read, Piers Paul. (1974) *Alive: The Story of the Andes Survivors.* Philadelphia: Lippincott

Reid, Susan. (1979) "The Kwakiutl Man Eater." *Anthropologica.* 21:247-75

Rifkin, Jeremy. (1983) *Algeny: Genetic Science and Evolutionist Theories.* New York: Viking

_____. (1985) *Declaration of a Heretic.* Boston: Routledge & Kegan Paul

Robertson, Heather. (1995) "Lust, Murder and 'Long Pig.'" *Canadian Forum.* (April):20-24

Róheim, Géza. (1945) *The Eternal Ones of the Dream.* New York: International Universities Press

_____. (1992) *Fire in the Dragon.* Princeton: Princeton University Press

Rohner, Ronald P. (ed.) (1969) *The Ethnography of Franz Boas.* Chicago: University of Chicago Press

Roquefeuil, Camille de. (1823) *A Voyage Round the World Between the Years 1816-1819.* London: Sir Phillips & Co.

Rosman, Abraham and Rubel, Parla G. (1971) *Feasting with Mine Enemy.* New York: Columbia University

Saavedra, Ramon. Report to Bodega y Quadra aboard *Concepcion,* Nootka Sound, 27 August, 1791. Archivo General de la Nacion, Mexico, stado, leg. 4289. [Cited in Archer's (1992) and Fisher's (1993)]

Sagan, Eli. (1974) *Cannibalism: Human Aggression and Cultural Form.* New York: Harper Row

Sahlins, Marshall and Arens, William. (1979) "Cannibalism: An Exchange." *New York Review of Books.* (March 22):45-47

Sales, Luis. (1794) "Noticias de la provincia de Californias en tres cartas de un sacerdote religiosos hijo del real convento de predicadores de Valencia a un amigo suyo." Valencia

Sanchez, Francisco Miguel. "Historia compuesta de todo lo acaecido en la expedicion hecha al Puerto do Nuca, ano de 1789." Museo Naval, Madrid, vol. 2128. [Portions cited translated in Archer (1992)]

Sanday, Peggy Reeves. (1986) *Divine Hunger: Cannibalism as a Cultural System.* Cambridge and New York: Cambridge University

Schlesinger, Arthur. (1992) "Was America a Mistake?" *The Atlantic.* (September)

Sendey, John. (1977) *The Nootkan Indian: A Pictorial.* Port Alberni, British Columbia: Alberni Valley Museum

Sewid, James. *Guests Never Leave Hungry: The Autobiography of James Sewid, a Kwakiutl Indian.* [See Spradley (1969)].

Shapiro, Robert. (1991) *The Human Blueprint: The Race to Unlock the Secrets of our Genetic Script.* New York: St. Martin's

Silverstein, Alvin and Virginia. (1982) *FutureLife: The Biotechnology Revolution.* Englewood Cliffs, New Jersey: Prentice-Hall

Simpson, Brian. (1984) *Cannibalism and the Common Law.* Chicago: University of Chicago Press

Slemon, Stephen. (1992) "Bones of Contention: Post-Colonial Writing and the 'Cannibal' Question." *Literature and the Body.* Ed. Anthony Purdy. (Amsterdam and Atlanta: Rodopi) 163-77

Socies, Lorenzo. "Noticas de Nutka." Archivo General de la Nacion, Mexico, Historia, vol. 31 [Portions cited paraphrased in Archer (1992); Archer (1980)]

Spradley, James Philip (ed.). (1969) *Guests Never Leave Hungry: The Autobiography of James Sewid, a Kwakiutl Indian.* New Haven: Yale University

———. (1963) "The Kwakiutl Guardian Spirit Quest: An Historical, Functional and Comparative Analysis." Unpublished MA thesis, Department of Anthropology. (Seattle: University of Washington)

Sproat, Gilbert Malcolm. (1987) *The Nootka: Scenes and Studies of Savage Life.* Victoria, British Columbia: Sono Nis

Staden, Hans. (1557) *Hans Staden: The True History and Description of a Country of Savages, A Naked and Terrible People, eaters of Men's Flesh, who Dwell in the New World called America.* [Translated by Letts (1929)]

Stewart, Hilary (ed.). (1987) *The Adventures and Sufferings of John R. Jewitt, Captive of Maquinna.* Seattle: University of Washington

Strange, James. *James Strange's Journal and Narrative of the Commercial Expedition from Bombay to the North-West Coast of America.* [See Ayyar (1928)]

Suría, Tomás de. *Quaderno que contiene el Ramo de Historia Natural y diario de la Expedicion del circulo de Globo . . . 1791.* New Haven, Connecticut: Yale University, Beinecke Library. [Translated by Cutter (1980), Wagner (1936)]

Suzuki, David. (1988) *Genethics: The Ethics of Engineering Life.* Toronto: Stoddart

———. (1992) "Tampering with Nature Risky Move for Science." *Vancouver Province.* (April 16)

Tannahill, Reay. (1975) *Flesh and Blood: A History of the Cannibal Complex.* London: Hamilton

Taylor, Charles. (1991) *The Malaise of Modernity.* Concord, Ontario: House of Anansi Press

———. (1989) *Sources of the Self: The Making of the Modern Identity.* Cambridge, Massachusetts: Harvard

Theroux, Paul. (1992) *The Happy Isles of Oceania: Paddling the Pacific.* New York: G.P. Putnam's

Tobar y Tamariz, José. *Informe que yo Don Jose Tobar y Tamariz, primer piloto de la Real Armada doy al Exmo. Sr. Virrey de N.E. en obedicimiento de su superior orden, comunicado con fecha de 29 de agosto de 1789.* Archivo General de la Nacion, Mexico, vol. 65

Underhill, Ruth. (1945) *Indians of the Pacific Northwest.* Riverside, California: Sherman Institute

Vancouver, George. (1914) "A Narrative of My Proceedings in His Majesty's Sloop *Discovery* from 18th of August to the 26th September 1792 . . ." In *Papers Relating to Nootka Sound and to Captain Vancouver's Expedition.* British Columbia Provincial Archives Report (1913):11-30

———. (1798) *A Voyage of Discovery to the North Pacific Ocean and Round the World; in which the Coast of North-West America has been Carefully Examined and Accurately Surveyed. . . .* London: G.G. and J. Robinson

Vancouver Sun. "Fearful native women. . . ." March 16, 1992

Viana, Francisco Xavier de. *Diario de Viaje.* Montevideo, 1958, 2:91. [Cited in Archer's (1973)]

Villa, Paola et al. (1986) "Cannibalism in the Neolithic." *Science.* (July 25):431-7

Von Puttkamer, Peter and Davis, Wade. (1992) "The Spirit of the Mask." Documentary film about implications of Northwest Coast Indian mask rituals for contemporary society. (National Film Board of Canada: Gryphon Productions Ltd.)

Wagner, Henry Raup (ed.). (1933, 1971) *Spanish Explorations of the Strait of Juan de Fuca.* New York: AMS. [Contains translations of: Eliza, Francisco. "Extracto de la navegacion" and Pantoja y Arriga, Juan. "Extracto de la navegacion . . . 1791."]

———— (ed.). (1936) *Journal of Tomas de Suria of his Voyage with Malaspina to the Northwest Coast in 1791.* Glendale, California: Arthur Clark Company

Walens, Stanley. (1981) *Feasting With Cannibals: an Essay on Kwakiutl Cosmology.* Princeton, New Jersey: Princeton University

Walker, Alexander. "An Account of a Voyage to the North West Coast of America with Observations on the Manners of the Inhabitants and on the Productions of that Country, 1785 and 1786." National Library of Scotland, MS 13780. [Microfilm copy in British Columbia Provincial Archives, Victoria, British Columbia. Also see Fisher and Bumsted (1982)]

Wallas, Chief James. (1981) *Kwakiutl Legends, as told to Pamela Whitaker.* Vancouver: Hancock House

Webster, Gloria Cranmer. (1992) "Chiefly Feasts." *Curator.* 35/4:248-254

Weidenreich, Franz. (1943) "The Skull of *Sinanthropus Pekinensis.*" *Geological Survey of China.* Pehpei, China

White, T.D. (1986) "Cut Marks on the Rodo Cranium: A Case of Prehistoric Defleshing." *American Journal of Physical Anthropology.* (April):503-09

Wiebe, Rudy. (1994) *A Discovery of Strangers.* Toronto: Knopf

Wike, Joyce. (1952) "The Role of the Dead in Northwest Coast Culture." *Selected Papers of the Twenty-ninth International Congress of Americanists.* Ed. by Sol Tax. 97-103

————. (1984) "A Reevaluation of Northwest Coast Cannibalism." *The Tsimshian and Their Neighbours of the North Pacific Coast.* Ed. by Jay Miller and Carol Eastman. (Seattle: University of Washington Press) 239-54

Wilson, Iris Higbie (ed.). (1970) *Noticias de Nutka: An Account of Nootka Sound in 1792.* Toronto: McClelland and Stewart. [Translation of: Moziño Suarez de Figueroa, José Mariano. *Noticias de Nutka: Diccionario de la lengua de los Nutkeses y descripcion del volcan de Tuxtla.* Mexico City: 1913]

Wright, Ronald. (1992) *Stolen Continents: The 'New World' Through Indian Eyes Since 1492.* Toronto: Viking

Wyatt, Victoria. (1992) "Art and Exploration: Northwest Coast Native Artists' Responses to Maritime Explorers and Fur Traders." Paper presented at Vancouver Conference, Vancouver, British Columbia, April 1992.

Young, Dudley. (1991) *Origins of the Sacred: The Ecstasies of Love and War.* New York: St. Martin's

INDEX

Abolition of Man, The by Clive Staples Lewis 239
Adams, Henry (n) 238
Adorno, Theodor W. (n) 238
aggression 243
Alert Bay 219
Alexander VI, Pope 187
Alive, by Piers Paul Read 167
Alsop, Richard (n) 104
America xi
Amerindian rights 188, 192-93
Amerindians 184-85, 187-88, 191-93, 195
Amos, Charlie 111
Anapi 87
anthropophagy xvi, xxii, 36, 162
Apenas 52
Apollonian 179, 229
Arawaks 185
Archer, Christon xxi, 125
Ardrey, Robert 160, 235
Arens, William xx, 160, 164-65, 168-70, 197-202, 204, 208
Argonaut 77, (n) 77
Arima, Eugene xxii
Aristotle 189

Arteaga, Ignacio de 64
Assu, Harry 212
Athabaskans 160
Attali, Jacques 170
avatar 227
Awati 141-42
Aztecs 165, 174, 198, 200

Balboa, Vasco Nunez (n) 66
Barkley Sound 108
Barkley, Charles 84
Bartroli, Tomas xxiv
Basque (n) xii
Baxbakwalanuxsiwae xxv, 133-34, (n) 134, 136-37, 146, 176, 178, 210, 212, 227, 232
Bayly, William 40
Beaglehole, J.C., *The Journals of Captain James Cook . . .* 37
Bell, Edward 98, 101
Bella Bella 132
Bella Coola (n) 134, 150
Benedict, Ruth 179, 226
Bering, Vitus 63
biotechnology 242
bite marks 111

blood sacrifice complex 160
blood-sucking 115
Boas, Franz xix, 73, 129, (n) 130, 132, (n) 132, 135-36, (n) 136, 137, 139, 147, 158, 163, 170, 225, (n) 226, (n) 260
Bodega, Juan 64, 75-76, 98, 101
body parts 39-40, 46-50, 52-3, 57, 60, 64, 67, 76, 78, 103, 122-23
    "deadly hands" (n) 139
    cooked 141
Boem, Johann 188-89
Boit, John 95, 126
Borah, Woodrow 165
Boston 104
brain-eating 161, 168
Brody, Hugh 73
Brown, Vinson 151-52

Caamaño, Jacinto 77-78, 122-24
Callicum 44, 46-48, 57, 59-60, 69-70, 76, 87, 122-23, 180
cannibal 162, 185
    complex xxvi, 198, 201
    dance xx-xxi, xxiv, 94-95, 105, 135, 178, 225, 230, 233, 246
    masks 134
    society 132, 137, 212, 214, 219, 232
    spirits 246
cannibalism 205
    and sublimated aggression 243
    at Fort Rupert 114
    ceremonial xxiii, xxv, 135
    charisma of 204, 207
    compassionate 167
    dietary xvii, xxi, 125
    endo- 167, 174
    exo- 167
    gustatory xvii-xix, xxi-xxii, xxvi, 32, 37, 41, 43, 48, 52, 54, 61, 63, 76, 80, 87, 103, 105, 114-15, 117-123, 125, 161, 165, 198, 204
    ritual xvi-xxiii, xxvi, 54, 61, 63, 73-74, 76-78, 80, 104, 107, 110, 112-13, 115-18, 121-22, 124-27, 129-30, 133, 137, 148, 150, 152-53, 157, 161, 163, 165, 173-74, 180, 183, 187, 196, 201-02, 204-08, 211, 217, 221-22, 230, 233-35, 245-49, 251-56, 259
    sacramental 159
    survival 36, 159, 166
    symbolic xix-xx
cannibalization 243
cannibalize 244
cannibalizing 242, 244, 247
Caribs 185, (n) 185, 187
Carson, Roy 74
Catholic eucharist 174
Cevallos, Ciriaco 82
Charles IX, King 191
Charles V, King 188
Chatham 98, 99
child abductions 111
child killed 113
children 37, 41-42, 65, 67, 69, 77-8, 89-92, 111, 139
China 167
Chirikov, Aleksei 63
Christianity 174, 176, 187-89, 195, 217
Clayoquot Sound 43, 72, 92, 108
Coast Salish 211, 219
Codere, Helen 211
Colnett, James 77

Colombia 62
colonization 184, 187
Columbia 66, 69, 85, 94-95
Columbus, Christopher xii-xiii, 162, 185, 187
Comekela 56, 59
Congolese 198
Contarini, Gasparo xii
Cook's River (Cook's Inlet) 59
Cook, James xviii, 31-37, 39, 43, 63, 82-83, 86, 122-23
Cook, James, *A Voyage to the Pacific Ocean* . . . 31-32, 37, 67
Cook, Warren xv, xxiii
Cooper, Freda 221
coppers 211
corpse-eating 110, 115, 141-43, 146
Cortes, Hernando 165, 187
cosmology 173-75, 179, 204, 229, 241-42, 245, 248
European 175
Cowichan band 220
Crespi, Juan 64
crests 212
Croatia 161
Crosby, Thomas 110-12, 121
Curtis, Edward S. (n) 104, (n) 132, (n) 139, 140, 144, 146-47, (n)   149, (n) 151
Cutter, Donald xx, 87
cycle of resurrection 253

D'Avity, Pierre 191
Dancing Society 149
Dawson, George 113, 121
de Roquefeuil, Camille 105
Dickason, Olive Patricia 184

Dictionary of Slang, by Eric Partridge 166
Dionysian 179, 226, 229
discovery xiii, 32, 41, 98, 193
Discovery of Strangers, A, by Rudy Wiebe 166
dismemberment 141
Dolores, María 70, 78
Douglas, John 31, (n) 32, 36
Douglas, William 59, 62, 66
Drucker, Philip xx, 149, 151, 212, 217
Duff, Wilson (n) 101
Duncan, William 174
Durieu, Paul 195

ecological vision 255-56, 258
ecology 180, 245-46
Edgar, George 111
Edgar, Magnus 111
Edgar, Thomas 42
Ehrlich, Paul 259
Eliza, Francisco 75-77, 91-92
Eskimos 166
Espi, José (n) 67, 78
Esteban 69
eugenics 239
Eurocentrism 204
exploitation 193
Ezekiel 11: 17-21 183

Fanon, Frantz 263
Felice Adventurer 56, 62
Ferdinand II of Aragon, King 188
Fidalgo, Salvador 76, 103
fire 252, 255
Fisher, Robin xxi, 126
flesh-eating 115

Flood Tide of Empire, by Warren
   Cook xv, xxiii
Flóres, Manuel 65-66, 75
Fore 167, 198, 200
Fort Rupert 114, 137, 141
Franciscan, anonymous 67
Franklin, Sir John 166
Freud, Sigmund (n) 163, 205,
   206
Friendly Cove 34, 46, 48, 59, 62,
   69, 72, 85, 96, 98, 106
Friendly Harbour (see Friendly
   Cove)

Gajdusek, D. Carleton 167
Galiano, Dionisio 96
Geertz, Clifford 157, (n) 158
Gelogudzayae (or Crooked Beak)
   134
genetic 242
   apocalypse 251
   manipulation 242
Ghost Dancer 215
Gigedo, Revilla 75-76, 100
Gimi 168
Glass, Aaron 210-11
Goddard, Pliny 212, 217
Goldman, Irving (n) 217, (n)
   226, 232
Goldman, Marlene (n) 32
Gomara, Francisco Lopez de 187
Gray, Robert 62, 66, 69, 85
guardian spirit complex 176, 195-
   96, 212, 214, 219-21, 223, 227,
   229
Gwakiils 141, (n) 141, 142, 143
Gwasilla 133

Haida 85, 132, 146, 149

Haisla 110-12, 139
Hallowell, Alfred I. 184
Hamasaka 143
hamatsa 110-12, 115, 132, 134-37,
   139-42, 144, 149, (n) 149,
   150-51, 153, 178, 209, 211,
   214-17, 221-22, 227, 230,
   232-34, 242, 244, 247, 252,
   256-57
hamatsa dance 132-33, 147,
   209-10
hamatsa poisoned 146
hamshamtses 141
Hanna, James (n) 46, 56
Hannape 44
Haswell, Robert 62
Hawitl 103
headhunting 162
Hearne, Samuel (n) 32
Heiltsuk 132-33, 135, 149, 210
heliga 135
Herodotus 162
Herrera, Antonio de 187
Hezeta, Bruno de 64
Hoebel, E. Adamson 162, 165,
   175
Hood, Sherman 220-21
Hope 85
Horkheimer, Max (n) 238
Hoskins, John 94, 126
Howay, Frederick W. xix
Hoxhogwaxtewae (or *Hoxhok*) 134
Hoxhok 178
human blood drunk 144
human flesh bitten 112
   eaten 141, 144
human rights 193
human sacrifice xxiii, 52, 105,
   109, 137, 160, 165

Hunt, George 73, 114, 130, 137, (n) 139, 140-41, 143-44, 150, 226
Hunter, W. 48

ideal man 179
ideology 199-200, 207
Imperial Eagle 57
Indian xii, 187
Indian Act 148
Ingraham, Joseph 67, 69, 84-86, 124
initiation rites 219
instrumental reason 238
Iphigenia Nubiana 56, 59, 62, 66
Iroquois Indians 239

Jacobsen, Johan Adrian 114-115, 121, 126, 148
James, Clifford (n) 226
Japhet 189
Jesuits 195
Jewitt Lake 73
Jewitt, John 104, (n) 104, 105, 119, 126, (n) 149
John 6: 54-57 173
Jonaitis, Aldona xxiv
Juan de Fuca Strait 43, 76, 92
Jung, Carl 237

Kaiana 56, 59-60, 62
Kendrick, John 62, 66-67, 69, 85
Kendrick, John S. xxiii
Kilgour, Maggie 193
King George's Sound (see Nootka Sound)
King, James 42
kinqalalala 134-35, 151, 215-17
Kitimat 110, 112

Klooh-quahn-nah 109
Koskimo 116
Kuexa 137
kukusiut (n) 134
Kuns, Michael (n) 33
kuru 168
Kwakiutl xxiv-xxv, 70, 91, 124, 132, 134, 147, 149-52, 160, 179, 195-96, 202, 209-12, 217, 219, 221, 226-27, 229-30, 232-34, 244-45, 247, 252-53, 255, 259
Kwakwaka-wakw (see Kwakiutl) 132
Kyemakalus 146

Lady Washington 62, 66, 69, 85
Las Casas, Bartolomé de 185, 188
Le Roy, Löys 189
Ledyard, John 39-40, (n) 40, 43
Lekwiltok 212
Lévi-Strauss, Claude (n) 158
Lewis, Clive Staples 239-240
Lewis, Ioan 204-05, 207-08, 222-23
Loeb, Edwin 160
lokoala 132
long pork 166
Lopatin, Ivan 112
Luera, Nicolas 90

Machoalick 106-07
Mackay, John 52-53, 83-84, (n) 84, 87, 120, 124, 126
Magellan, Ferdinand xii, 187
Malaspina, Alejandro xx, 52, 62, 75, 81-88, 90, 119, 122, 125
Malinowski, Bronislaw K. (n) 158
Mamalilikulla 146

Man-Eater
   (see *Baxbakwalanuxsiwae* 215,
   216
Man-Eating Myth, The, by William
   Arens 197
Maori 163, 198, 201
Maquinna xviii, xxi, 43-44, 46, 50,
   55, 57, 59-60, 62-63, 67, 70, 72,
   76-78, 82-84, 86-87, 89, 91, 95,
   98, 100-01, 104-07, 119, 121,
   123, 126, 140, 180
Maquinna, Anapa (n) 105
Martínez, Esteban 55, 66-67, 69-
   70, 75, 124
mawil 136
McFarlane, A.R. 112
McIlwraith, Thomas F. (n) 134,
   150
McNeilly, Kevin (n) 130
Mead, Margaret 217
Meares, John 55-57, 59, 62, 76,
   78, 83-84, 87-88, 119, 121-23
Menzies, Archibald 99
Metalanuk 261
Métraux, Alfred 202
Mexicana 96
Millar, Mr. 57
Minnesota Indians 162
mission system 64
Moffat, Alexander W. 137, (n)
   137, 141
Montaigne, Michel de 183, 189,
   191
Mouth of Heaven 215
Mowachaht xviii, xxi-xxii, 33-34,
   40, 49, 52, 57, 60, 63-64, 67,
   70, 73, 76, 80, 82-83, 86-87, 98,
   103-05, 117-20, 123-24, 132,
   149, 158, 180

Moziño, José xxiii, 64, 103, 122
Muchalaht 73
Mumford, Lewis (n) 238

Nahwitti 137, 141, 148
Nakwaxdda'xw 133, 221
Nakwoktak 143
Nanaquius 86
Native Brotherhood of B.C. 150
native rights 188
Natsapa 60, 70, 82, 86-88, 123
Naualakum 134
Neanderthal man 161
Nenstalit 134
New Guinea 167, 168
Nimpkish 44, 70, 146
Nishka 149
noble savage 189
nonlem 132
Nootka xviii, xxii, 34, 36-37, 41,
   44, 46, 52, 56, 62, 65-66, 68-70,
   75-76, 82, 85, 87, 89, 91-92, 94,
   98, 101, 104, 115, 122, 124,
   126, (n) 139
Nootka Convention 98, 104
Nootka Sound xxiv, xxvi, 34, 49,
   62-64, 73, 107, 117, 123, 160
North American Indians 165
Northwest Coast Indians xv, xvii-
   xxii, xxiv, xxvi, 33, 37, 43, 64,
   72, 79, 103, 113-14, 117,
   123-25, 127, 153, 161, 163,
   167, 170, 174-76, 179, 181,
   206, 208, 210, 222, 226-27,
   234, 244, 248-49, 251-52, 254,
   256-57, 259-61
Northwest Passage 33, 36, 82
Nuchatlet 82
Nugent Sound 143

nulmal 137
numaym 212
Nunkamais 141
Nuu-chah-nulth (see Northwest
   Coast Indians) 34
Nuxalk 150

Olson, Ronald 139
Omacteachloa 106
Omnium Gentium Mores, by
   Johann Boem 188
On Cannibals, by Michel de
   Montaigne 189
Owikeno 141, 143-44

Paleoindians (n) 33
Pantoja, Juan 91
Papuans (n) 185
Partridge, Eric, *Dictionary of Slang*
   166
Patero, Severo (n) 67, 68
Pekin man 161
Peoples of the Sea Wind, by Vinson
   Brown 151-52
Pérez, Juan 64, (n) 64
Peters, Leonard 221
Pidcock, R.H. 150
Pigafetta, Antonio 187
potlatch 80, 148-49, 180, 248
Primo 91
Princesa 66, 77
Puget, Peter 99

Q!aneqelaku 233
Qoaxqoaxualanuxsiwae (or Raven)
   134
Qomenakula 139, (n) 139
Qominaga, 134
Qua-utz 64

Quatsino 116
Queen Charlotte Islands 69, 85
Quimper, Manuel 76

Raley, George H. 111
Ramsey, Paul 251, 262-63
Raven 178, 245, 260
Read, Piers Paul 167
reproductive intervention 242
Resolution 32, 39, 86
revisionism xiv, xxiii, xxv
Róheim, Géza 163, (n) 163

Saavedra, Ramon 82
sacrifice 105, 251-54, 256-57
   symbolic 171, 173
Sagan, Eli 243
Sahlins, Marshall 204
Salish 132, 221
salmon 253
Samwell, David 41
San Carlos 103
Sanaxet 139-40
Sanchez, Francisco 68
Sanchez, Miguel (n) 67, 69
sanctity 254
Sanday, Peggy Reeves 202, 244,
   247
Sandwich Islands 33, 40
Santa María xii
savage 191, 193-94, 200
savage vs civilized 184
Schlesinger, Arthur xiii
scientism 238
Seaweed, Henry 221-22
Seaweed, Willie 221
secret societies xx, 210, 213
self-purification 219
Sepúlveda, Juan Gines de 188

Sewid, James 212, 219
Seymour Inlet 133
shaman 222-23, 226
Sheshaht 108
Ship Cove (n) 33
Ship's Cove (see Friendly Cove) 39
Skedans 147
skulls 36, 39-41, 48, 50, 57, 59, 73, 87, 123
skulls, carved 115
slave sacrificed 114, 141, 144
slavery 77-78, 89-92, 132, 139, 141, 144, 217
Smith Inlet 133
Smoke 252, 255
socialization 233
Socies, Lorenzo (n) 67, 68
sociology of ecstasy 222
Solo man 162
spirit dance complex 221
Spradley, James 219
Sproat, Gilbert 107, 126
Staden, Hans 164, 202
Starvation Lake 166
stewardship 256-57
Stolen Continents, by Ronald Wright 193
Stone Age Britons 162
Strange, James 46, 48, 52, 83, 122-23
Suría, Tomás de 90, 124
Sutil 96
Suttles, Wayne xxv
Suzuki, David 259

taboo 243
Tamariz, José Tobar y (n) 69
Tannahill, Reay (n) 185, 211

Tao 239-40, 260
Tatooch 43
Taylor, Charles 238, 241
Teyocot 86
Theroux, Paul 166, (n) 166
Thomas, David 220-21
Thompson, David (n) 32
Thompson, John 104-05
Tlawitsis 144, 146
Tlingit 65, 112, 130
Tobar y Tamiriz, José 67
totem 212
Totem and Taboo, by Sigmund Freud 205
totemism xxiii, 196, 205-06
and memorial meal 206
and religion 206
taboos of 206
Tova, Antonio 82
transference 175
transformation 215, 233
transformation and reincarnation 230
transubstantiation 173-74
Trobriand Islanders 168
Tsahahstala 144
tsayeq (tseka) 132
Tsimshian xxii, 132, 149, 174
tsonoqua 209, (n) 209, 215-16
Tupinamba 163, 191, 198, 201
Turner Island 144

Underhill, Ruth 217
United Nations Conference on Indigenous Peoples 239

Valdés, Cayento 96
Vancouver Island Indians xxii

Vancouver, George 96, 98, 101
Vespucci, Amerigo xii, 185
vision quest 217
Vitoria, Francisco de 192
Vizcaino, Juan de la Cosa xii
Voyages of the Columbia, by
    Frederick W. Howay xix

Walens, Stanley 229-30, 232-34,
    253
Walker, Alexander 49, 52-53, (n)
    84, 119-20, 124
Walloonggura ceremony 163
Washing of Tears, The 73
We-Wai-Kai 212
Weidenreich, Franz 162
West Indies 185
Wickaninish 43, 95
Wiebe, Rudy 166

Wike, Joyce xxii, 121, 123, 126,
    (n) 139, 146
Winalagilis 134
wolf dance (n) 104, 104-05, 109,
    132, 149
world view (see cosmology)
Wrangell, Fort 113
Wright, Ronald 193

Xuntem 137

Yahyekulagyilis 143-44
Yi, Zheng 167
Young, Dudley 261
Yumqus 141
Yuquot xviii, 33-34, 96

Zimmerman, Heinrich 40
Zuni 179

ABOUT THE AUTHOR

JIM MCDOWELL is a veteran British Columbia freelance writer, independent reporter and historian. His first career was teaching, which took him into classrooms from California to Seattle, New York City, and Vancouver. He taught elementary school in California and Washington, worked as an inner-city education consultant in Harlem and Brooklyn, and trained teachers at Simon Fraser University. In Vancouver, he also served as the first director of Canada's largest inner-city community centre.

McDowell combines his journalistic skills with a long-standing interest in history that began at Stanford University in the mid-1950s. He has written hundreds of newspaper and magazine articles for Canadian and U.S. publications. He has published *Peace Conspiracy: The Story of Warrior-Businessman Yoshiro Fujimura* (McBo, Irvine, CA 1993), as well as two booklets: one about local history; the other about salmon. *Hamatsa* is the first of two books by McDowell to be published in 1997. *José Narváez: The Forgotten Explorer* (Arthur H. Clark) will profile an overlooked eighteenth century Spanish-Mexican mariner. A third book, describing the early history of the Lake Tahoe region, is in progress.